PARLIAMENTARY PROCEDURE

A TutorText

PARLIAMENTARY

PUBLISHED BY

DOUBLEDAY & COMPANY, INC., GARDEN CITY, N.Y

196

PROCEDURE

by Warren Lehman

PREPARED UNDER THE DIRECTION OF

USI EDUCATIONAL SCIENCE DIVISION

U. S. Industries, Inc.

FOREWORD

". . . It is always in the power of the majority, by their numbers, to stop any improper measures proposed on the part of their opponents," wrote Thomas Jefferson in the first section of his *Manual of Parliamentary Practice* entitled "Adhering to Rules." Jefferson's *Manual,* of course, was primarily based on the long-time established parliamentary practices and decisions utilized by the British Parliament. Continuing, he declared that "the only weapons by which the minority can defend themselves against similar attempts from those in power are the forms and rules of proceeding which have been adopted . . . and become the law of the House."

The above statement is just as applicable to every organized group which utilizes assemblies to determine its policies and programs as it was to legislative bodies in Jefferson's day.

Jefferson included another significant statement in the introduction to his *Manual* which I quote: "It is much more material that there should be a rule to go by than what that rule is; that there may be a uniformity of proceeding in business not subject to the caprice of the Speaker or captiousness of the members." Here is found the real and important reason why all discussion groups or assemblies which hold meetings for the purpose of transacting business of any kind — whether acting as an agent, performing in behalf of the membership, or even if a meeting of the total membership — should have a defined procedure as a guide by which to operate. This assures any assembly of an orderly procedure for the transaction of business, and avoids what otherwise might be chaos.

All organizations of any significance should have a constitution, a set of by-laws, and an accepted standard procedure upon which it can depend if the manner in which it is proceeding should be challenged. This gives the entire membership something definite for its guides and avoids any dependence on the whims and caprices of the presiding officer or any bloc which otherwise might control.

The scope of this work includes the usual subjects covered by texts on general parliamentary procedure. It is uniquely organized, and divided under six general headings, with the first and last devoted to "Speaking Up," and "Practical Politics," respectively. Some practical aspects of procedure for an organized group are also discussed. The work is designed as a course in "Parliamentary Procedure"; arranged not to be read from page to page as one would read a novel, but to be studied after a fashion placing emphasis on subject matter.

The part of the volume entitled "Parliamentary Dictionary" sets forth a series of charts on various motions or questions, arranged alphabetically, showing in each instance the relation of the said motion, or its precedence, to other motions or questions which might be called into play while that question is pending.

This method of presentation is indeed helpful to any user thereof since needed exact data are given in each instance; likewise, the arrangement makes it possible for that information to be readily available to the Chair for use during any meeting of an organized group.

Thus the purpose of this book, as stated in the introduction by its author, Mr. Walter Lehman, is to acquaint the readers with the rules most commonly used in private organizations in America.

CHARLES L. WATKINS
Parliamentarian, United States Senate

CONTENTS

INTRODUCTION

The purpose of parliamentary laws is to help a group of people come to decisions that are agreeable to the majority. Every club, corporation, and democratic country obeys a set of rules when it goes about making up its collective mind. The rules are designed to make it possible for members, stockholders, and citizens (through their representatives) to express themselves fully, to try to sway each other, and to vote as equals when the time for decision is reached.

The purpose of this book is to acquaint you with the rules most commonly used in private organizations in America. If you are an active citizen, you will undoubtedly participate in one or more organizations, for Americans have traditionally banded together as private citizens to get things done: to get better schools, to aid the sick and the poor, to advance their hobby interests — any of a thousand things. If you are active in organizations, you will be a more effective member, and you will enjoy yourself more, if you know the rules for making up the organizational mind.

This book is a self-teaching course following the intrinsic programing method developed by Norman A. Crowder. You will find that the TutorText* method makes learning parliamentary law interesting work. In the first half of the book, you will learn by example how parliamentary rules are applied in practical situations. The second half of the book is a Parliamentary Dictionary, which you will find a valuable permanent reference. In the dictionary, the rules of order are arranged in alphabetical form to enable you to find the answers to your parliamentary questions at a glance.

I would like to thank the many members of the Training Systems staff at the Educational Science Division of the U. S. Industries, with whose help this book was prepared. Special thanks are due Robert Hughes, editorial director, Peter Pipe, and Leighton Steele, each of whom has contributed significantly to the usefulness and readability of this book.

WARREN LEHMAN

---

*TM

A NOTE TO THE READER

This book consists of two separate parts. The first half of the book is a course in parliamentary law. The latter half is a dictionary in which the rules of procedure are presented in a format convenient for ready reference.

The course in parliamentary law is not like an ordinary book. The pages are numbered in the usual way, but they are not read consecutively. You must follow the directions which you find at the bottom of each page.

You will find that reading this book is very much like having an individual tutor. The book will continually ask you questions and correct errors as well as give you information.

Your progress through this course will depend entirely on your ability to choose right answers instead of wrong ones — and on your endurance. It is not recommended, however, that you try to go through this course in one sitting, or even in two or three. The course is divided into lessons, and a number of short learning sessions produces better results than a few long ones.

If you follow the instructions, you will find that it is impossible to get through the course without understanding parliamentary law. And, you will be able to make full use of the parliamentary dictionary when, in your organizational work, a technical problem arises.

CHAPTER I

Speaking Up

Though there is strength in unity, there is also confusion in a crowd. For people to work together effectively they must have methods for making and carrying out their decisions. The methods almost universally accepted are those of parliamentary procedure.

The rules of parliamentary procedure are associated historically with the growth of democratic, representative government. Private organizations today conduct their business with rules directly descended from those used by the Parliament of Great Britain and the United States House of Representatives.

There is hardly an adult in the United States who doesn't belong to some club, society, or association. The variety of these organizations is boundless: parent-teacher organizations, service clubs, neighborhood improvement groups, professional societies, fraternities, labor unions, garden clubs, charitable organizations and political parties.

In this chapter, you will discover the way in which a democratic organization makes up its mind. Later chapters will make you familiar with parliamentary rules in more detail. When you have finished the first half of this book, you should feel comfortable about making yourself heard in any meeting; you should be able to use parliamentary rules to achieve your purposes democratically; in sum, you should be an effective and useful organization member.

The latter half of the book is a Parliamentary Dictionary containing answers to hundreds of parliamentary questions. Chapter III tells you how to make effective use of this dictionary, and from there on you will use it as a reference while you study.

Now, from the two statements below, choose the one that is more accurate and turn to the page indicated.

Almost every organization follows essentially the same set of parliamentary rules.   page 6

Almost every organization follows its own set of parliamentary rules. page 10

You did not follow instructions.

This course in Parliamentary Procedure is not put together like an ordinary book. You do not turn directly from page 1 to page 2 to page 3, and so on. This TutorText course will make no sense if you try to follow that procedure.

Each page that you read will tell you what page to turn to next. Now there was no way you could have arrived at this page if you had followed instructions.

Please return to page 1 and select the correct page to read next.

YOUR ANSWER: He had asked for permission to speak.

That is not the correct way to describe what must have happened. If the old-timer said he had addressed the chair, it is obvious that he meant he had been talking to the chairman. It is also obvious that he was talking to the chairman during a meeting, otherwise he would just have said, "I was talking to the chairman." Since the old-timer was speaking during a meeting, he must have been assigned the right to speak. In parliamentary jargon, the old-timer had been recognized.

That is not the same as being given permission to speak. The chairman is not empowered to give or deny permission to speak, except as he is directed by parliamentary rules of order. As long as the rules for speaking are being obeyed, speaking is a right of every member.

There are times when the chairman may refuse to recognize a speaker who has demonstrated his intent to flaunt the rules by using them for harassment. A chairman should use this power only with great discretion so that he does not arbitrarily violate the rights of any member.

The fact that speaking is a right, not a privilege dispensed by the chairman, is demonstrated by the fact — about which you will read more later — that the chairman cannot cut off the debate on an issue as long as there are members who have a right to speak. If the chairman should attempt to do so, by calling for a vote before everyone who wants to speak has had a chance, the members still to be heard from can insist on the right to speak.

The chairman's job is to keep order, to see that only one person is speaking at a time, and to see that the speaking is done according to the rules. His power to recognize a speaker and assign him the right to speak is his tool for keeping order, not for imposing his will.

Return to page 16 and choose the other answer.

4

[*from page 11*]

YOUR ANSWER: After the chairman asked for items of new business.

Perhaps you did not read the order of business closely enough. Here it is again:

1. Call to order.
2. Reading of the minutes.
3. Reports of officers and permanent committees.
4. Reports of special or temporary committees.
5. Special orders.
6. Unfinished (or old) business and general orders.
7. New business.

Remember, you are the chairman of a *committee* set up to organize a Christmas party. You wouldn't expect to make your report after the chairman asked for items of new business, because:

1. your business is not new, for the committee already exists, and
2. you head a committee and should, therefore, make your report at the appropriate time for your kind of committee.

After you have studied the order of business more carefully, return to page 11 and choose the right answer.

YOUR ANSWER: True.

No, the statement was false, because the order of business is concerned only with general categories. Specific questions may be brought up by members speaking from the floor. The order of consideration is determined by the order in which the matters are brought up, as well as by their parliamentary priority. As long as you violate no rules, you can bring up a proposal and thereby determine the order of its consideration.

The sequence in which specific questions are considered may also be determined by the *orders of the day*. The orders of the day are simply an agenda including those items of business that the chairman knows in advance must be considered.

The order of business, remember, sets only general categories. The orders of the day, to be discussed in more detail in Chapter IV, do determine specific business, but even the orders of the day do not prevent still other specific business from being considered if it is appropriately introduced from the floor.

Now return to page 21 and select the correct answer.

6

[from page 1]

YOUR ANSWER: Almost every organization follows essentially the same set of parliamentary rules.

This is true. Although many groups change the standard rules in one small way or another, the basic rules are used in almost all groups, from the local fraternal organization to the United Nations, and from the Parent-Teacher Association to the United States House of Representatives. Some vary the names for officers, some the order in which meetings are conducted, some the number of votes necessary to pass certain types of measures, but the differences are small compared to the similarities. Once learned, the rules of procedure should guide you in whatever organizational work you do.

One of the names that varies from organization to organization is that of the person who has the job of running the meeting. Generally, such a person may be called the presiding officer. The presiding officer of the Senate is the Vice-President of the United States. The presiding officer of the House of Representatives is called the Speaker of the House. Sometimes a presiding officer is called a chairman, moderator, or president. Whatever the name, though, the duties are much the same. The presiding officer, sometimes referred to impersonally as *the chair,* has the job of supervising the meetings of the organization. In one sense, the job of the chair is to see that the rules of procedure are followed.

But what is the purpose of these rules?

To keep order in the meeting.   page 9

To ensure that meetings are conducted as quickly as possible.   page 13

To ensure that organizations can achieve their purposes democratically.
page 16

YOUR ANSWER: As the first item of business.

Certainly. The secretary's report of the previous meeting, called the *minutes,* is commonly the first item in the order of business.

The principal task of any business meeting is to make decisions. Any member may propose that some action be taken. Such a proposal, formally stated, is called a *motion.* The principal business of a meeting is to make decisions on motions. There are several types of motion. Some are procedural, such as the proposal that the meeting end, or that the subject under discussion be voted on. (Standard ways for stating procedural motions are discussed in Chapter II and listed in the Summary of Rules at the back of the book.) Main motions are matters that you meet to decide — should you throw a party, castigate the city council, or raise dues?

Main motions are expressed according to a formal pattern. The person making the suggestion begins, "I move that. . . ." followed by a concise statement. If no other business is under consideration a person seeks recognition from the chair and speaks as follows:

SPEAKER: "Wouldn't it be a good idea if we threw a Christmas party for the kids at the orphanage?"

CHAIR: "Would you care to state that proposal as a motion?"

SPEAKER: "I *move* that the Springfield Kiwanis Club organize a Christmas party for the benefit of the children at the —— Orphanage."

CHAIR: "Wouldn't it be better if the motion set a date for this party and if you assigned the responsibility to somebody?"

SPEAKER: "We can't set a date unless we make arrangements with the orphanage, so I move that the Springfield Kiwanis Club establish a committee to organize a Christmas party for the benefit of the children at the —— Orphanage, and that the committee assume the responsibility for setting a date convenient to the orphanage and the Kiwanis."

This discussion took place during which section of the order of business?

Unfinished business. **page 15**   New business. **page 29**
Special committee reports. **page 23**

8

[*from page 16*]

YOUR ANSWER: He had been recognized by the chair.

Of course. Presumably, he would not have begun to speak until he had been recognized.

Until you get used to the terminology, it may sound a little odd. If the chair recognizes a speaker, that means the chair gives the speaker *the floor*. Only the person who *has the floor* has the right to speak unless the chair allows an interruption. The interrupter then has the floor. The purpose of placing this control in the hands of the chairman is to assure that only one person is speaking at any time, and that only one subject is being discussed. One of the commonest failings of those who run and participate in meetings is to ignore the restriction to one subject at a time. Rambling and unrelated discussion causes confusion and leads to inaction.

To obtain recognition, a person desiring to speak must get the chair's attention. The way this is done varies according to the situation. If the group is a large one, in which those present are not likely to know each other, the member should rise and address the chair according to its proper title. This may be President, Chairman, or Moderator. If the chair is occupied by a man, the title is preceded by Mister, thus: "Mister President." By using the term *chair,* you sometimes avoid the problem of deciding whether to address a female occupant of the chair as *chairman, chairwoman,* or *chairlady,* each of which is objectionable to some people (though in America a woman is usually called chairwoman). A female presiding officer is addressed as "Madam ——— ," followed by her title.

As soon as the speaker has caught the eye of the chair, he should state his name. However, if the group is small or if the members are familiar with one another, giving names is unnecessary and it is usually not required that members rise either to obtain recognition or to speak. Even in some larger groups, attention is first obtained by raising the hand, though the speaker will rise after he has caught the chairman's eye. It is only polite that in a large group the speaker should stand so that he may be better seen and heard.

Attending an organization meeting for the first time, you attract the attention of the chair:

By raising your hand. **page 12**   By standing. **page 18**

By following what seems to be the custom. **page 21**

9

YOUR ANSWER: To keep order in the meeting.

Keeping order in the meeting is not the whole story. The rules do prevent members from all talking at once or from dragging in irrelevant business, but there are more effective ways of merely keeping order — if that were all that mattered. You could let the chairman dominate the meeting by his personality or influence, and affairs would run smoothly in accordance with his wishes. Though everyone might be nice and quiet, from fear or despair, the meeting would not truly arrive at decisions as a group.

No, the purpose of parliamentary rules is to help organizations serve their purposes in democratic as well as in an orderly fashion.

A common mistake among people inexperienced in organizations is to introduce a new subject while another is being considered. In a well-run meeting, everyone has a chance to discuss each issue fully, but, so that democracy isn't reduced to chaos, members must speak in proper order. One person speaks at a time, and about the proper subject.

Return to page 6 and choose the statement that best describes the purpose of parliamentary rules.

[*from page 1*]

YOUR ANSWER: Almost every organization has its own set of parliamentary rules.

Your answer is not quite right. Although many organizations make small changes in the standard rules to fit their particular needs, almost all groups are set up in much the same way and carry on business in accordance with traditional rules. The aim of parliamentary procedure is to see that the organization runs efficiently and democratically. The rules developed in Parliament and modified in the United States House of Representatives suit this aim very well. Almost every organization uses these rules, either precisely as you find them in this book or with only minor local changes.

If the differences among the procedures were great, there would be little point in learning rules of order. But a world in which every organization had its own rules would be far more confusing than the present one. Return to page 1 and choose the statement that more accurately describes the world in which (as you will see) all meetings can be orderly.

YOUR ANSWER: False.

That is correct. The order of business determines only the sequence in which general categories of business are considered in a meeting. You can raise a point or proposal from the floor, and as long as you do so at the correct time in the general sequence, you will be determining the order in which a specific question is considered.

The standard order in which categories of business are to be considered at all meetings of an organization is usually defined in the constitution or by-laws of the organization. This may be done specifically, or by the adoption of some standard set of parliamentary rules that will be used as arbiter in all procedural matters not covered in the organization's own rules.

The most commonly used order of business is the following:

1. Opening or *call to order*.
2. A reading of a summary of the events of the last meeting. Such a report is called the *minutes* of the meeting. (An example of minutes will be presented later.)
3. A presentation of *reports* by (a) officers, (b) board or executive committee, and (c) standing committees.
4. *Reports* of special or temporary committees.
5. Handling of high priority business specifically set at an earlier meeting for consideration at the present meeting. Such an item is called a *special order*.
6. Handling of business begun but not completed at earlier meetings, and of questions of secondary priority to special orders. These classes are identified as *unfinished business and general orders*.
7. The handling of business not previously introduced or assigned a priority for consideration. This class is called *new business*.

As chairman of a committee to organize a Christmas party for underprivileged children, you would expect to make your report:

After the chairman asked for items of new business.   **page 4**

Just before the handling of special orders.   **page 14**

Just after the minutes have been read.   **page 20**

[*from page 8*]

YOUR ANSWER: By raising your hand.

You might be able to get recognition in some groups by raising your hand — it's the usual procedure in many small groups — but it might take some time before you were recognized by the chairman at large meetings. At some meetings the only way to get the floor is to stand and call out: "Mr. Chairman."

In fact, standing is the more formal and proper procedure. But whether the usual way in any given group is to raise your hand or to stand can best be determined by watching what others are doing.

Return to page 8 and choose the best way to get recognition from the chair when you attend a meeting of an organization for the first time.

YOUR ANSWER: To ensure that meetings are conducted as quickly as possible.

Getting through the business of the meeting as quickly as possible is only part of the story. A group might be organized to act promptly and efficiently yet violate the individual rights of its members. Unless everyone has a reasonable opportunity to express his views, decisions may be undemocratic.

Parliamentary rules help keep meetings orderly and efficient, but their underlying purpose is to ensure that the decisions of the group fairly express the opinions of the majority without slighting minorities or individual members.

A common mistake among people inexperienced in organizations is to introduce a new subject while another is being considered. In a well-run meeting, everyone has a chance to discuss each issue fully, but so that democracy isn't reduced to chaos, members must speak in proper order. One person speaks at a time, and about the proper subject.

Return to page 6 and choose the right answer.

14

[from page 11]

YOUR ANSWER: Just before the handling of special orders.

Right. It is only reasonable to assume that a committee to run a Christmas party is not a permanent or *standing* committee but a temporary one that will be disbanded when the party is over. That being the case, your report will be made after the reports of officers and standing committees and before the handling of special orders, as you can see if you check the order of business again.

1. Call to order.
2. Reading of the minutes.
3. Reports of officers and permanent committees.
4. Reports of special or temporary committees.
5. Special orders.
6. Unfinished (or old) business and general orders.
7. New business.

We have mentioned two factors that help determine the sequence in which items of business are considered, the order of business and, within that framework, the order in which members make proposals from the floor. There is a third factor — the directions that an organization gives itself for handling business at a specific meeting. An organization may adopt, at the beginning of a meeting, a special program of business for that meeting. Or at one meeting an organization may decide to handle a certain issue at a later meeting. Decisions affecting the agenda of a later meeting are the *general* and *special orders* that have been mentioned. Program, general orders, and special orders combined constitute the *orders of the day*. The method for making orders will be discussed later. The fact that there are orders for a meeting does not prevent issues being raised from the floor, except (1) if an adopted program accounts for all available time, or (2) if an entire meeting is set aside by special order for the consideration of one subject.

If you were secretary of the organization, responsible for reporting the proceedings of the previous meeting, you would expect that your report would be made:

As the first item of business.   **page 7**
After the special orders.   **page 22**
After the reading of the minutes.   **page 28**

YOUR ANSWER: Unfinished business.

Perhaps you do not understand what is meant by unfinished business. Unfinished business consists of matters that were discussed at a previous meeting but were left unsettled. Business that is carried over from a previous meeting is said to be unfinished business.

The discussion of the Christmas party resolution clearly hints the section of the order of business during which it took place. Reread the discussion, paying particular attention to the first remark of the speaker from the floor.

Return to page 7 and choose the right answer.

16

[from page 6]

YOUR ANSWER: To ensure that organizations can achieve their purposes democratically.

This is correct. The rules are not merely designed to keep order. Order is kept according to the rules so that the organization can act promptly and efficiently without violating the democratic rights of the members. The purpose of the rules is neither efficiency nor order for their own sakes.

Every business and profession has its jargon. You might as well get used to the jargon of parliamentary procedure. The name *chair* is given to the presiding officer at a meeting, probably because his right to sit in the chair at the front, facing the membership, is a symbol of his authority. Just as you salute the insignia of his rank, rather than the person of a lieutenant, you speak to the chair, rather than to the person occupying it.

To address the chair means, of course, to speak to the person occupying the chair. To speak to the chair or to the membership in any meeting, it is required that the chair take note of the person desiring to speak and assign him the right to do so. The assigning of the right is called *recognizing* the speaker.

One of the duties of the chair, then, is to control the order in which those desiring to speak may do so. (There are rules to guide the chair in this task.) The purpose is very simple: to assure that only one person is speaking, and that only one issue is being discussed at any given time.

If, the first time you attended a meeting of the Rotary, an old-timer told you he had addressed the chair, you can be reasonably sure that:

He had asked for permission to speak.   **page 3**

He had been recognized by the chair.   **page 8**

YOUR ANSWER: Have the group proceed with the discussion of the proposal.

It would be improper for the chairman to have the group proceed with the discussion of an original main motion without a second. Since no one has seconded the motion, there may be no general interest in discussing it. There are times when a chairman may not bother to ask for a second when none has been offered — if, for instance, it is clear from the expressions on the members' faces that they are ready to adjourn. But a main motion, including a new idea or suggestion, should always be seconded. And where, with other motions, the chairman doesn't bother to request a second, a member may object. The failure of anyone to object would show that the group was in favor of considering the motion. The purpose of a second is to show just that.

But in this case, the question concerns an original motion; the chairman would be wrong to have the group proceed with the discussion without a second. Since the motion has not been seconded, the chairman should take some other course of action.

Return to page 29 and decide what the chairman should do.

[*from page 8*]

YOUR ANSWER: By standing.

Only partly right. You would certainly succeed in attracting the attention of the chair at most meetings by rising to your feet, but in some organizations the traditional way of seeking recognition is to raise your hand. It might be awfully embarrassing to you, as a new member of an organization, to stand when everyone else is at ease in his seat. You would get attention, all right, but they might think you were a trifle odd because you didn't do things their way.

In new organizations that have not yet acquired a customary procedure for seeking recognition, it is a good idea to stand rather than to raise your arm. By standing you express unambiguously your desire to speak, and when the chair gives you the floor you will be in a suitable posture to address the group.

But the first time you attend a meeting of an organization, you don't know beforehand how they go about getting recognition from the chair. Return to page 8 and choose the best answer.

YOUR ANSWER: True.

Sorry, but the motion is not quite ready for discussion. One member has "made the motion" and another has "seconded the motion," but one procedural step remains before the motion formally becomes a question. This step is called stating the question.

To state the question for the Christmas party proposal the chairman might say:

"*It has been moved and seconded* that the Springfield Kiwanis Club establish a committee to organize a Christmas party for the benefit of the children at the —— Orphanage and that the committee assume responsibility for setting a date convenient to the orphanage and the Kiwanis." Or, if he were satisfied that all members had heard the question, he might simply say, "Having been moved and seconded, the question before the assembly is Mr. Murray's motion," or, "The question is on the motion to organize a Christmas party."

When the chairman makes his formal statement, the motion becomes a question. Members may then seek the floor to discuss the motion. On the other hand, even after the second, the chairman may rule the motion out of order.

Now return to page 24 and answer the question correctly.

20

[*from page 11*]

YOUR ANSWER: Just after the minutes have been read.

Your answer is slightly off the mark. Take another look at the order of business:

1. Call to order.
2. Reading the minutes.
3. Reports of officers and permanent committees.
4. Reports of special or temporary committees.
5. Special orders.
6. Unfinished (or old) business and general orders.
7. New business.

What kind of committees give their reports right after the minutes have been read? Permanent committees. Is your Christmas Party Committee a permanent one? Probably not. More likely it is a temporary committee to be disbanded after the party. Consider the order of business again, then return to page 11 and choose the right answer.

YOUR ANSWER: By following what seems to be the custom.

Right. You don't want to stick out like a sore thumb, standing when others sit, nor do you want to wait impatiently with your hand in the air while others are getting the floor because they have risen and called the chairman. If the group were just being organized, so that it had no established custom, it would be appropriate to rise rather than raise your hand. Rising to call the chairman is the more common usage and is generally more effective.

The form in which the chairman recognizes the speaker again depends on the practice of the organization and the size of the meeting. In a small group, the chairman may only nod to you. In a more formal or larger meeting, the chairman will recognize you by announcing your name, or by saying: "The Chair recognizes Mr. ———." Then you may proceed to speak.

Of course, you've got to have something to speak about. Every organization has a standard sequence for bringing up different types of subjects. Such a standard sequence is called an *order of business*. It establishes the order in which different general categories of business are to be handled. If you propose to the group that it buy a new desk just after the treasurer has reported a surplus, you will be ruled out of order, not necessarily because the chairman doesn't like your idea, but because there is a period of the meeting devoted to all new proposals. Don't let being ruled out of order worry you; it happens at some time to everyone who is active in organizations.

As you proceed through the text, you will discover when and how things should be done. No matter how familiar you become with the rules, there will be complicated situations where the chair may rule against you. Keep in mind that you have the right, at almost any time, to ask the appropriateness of raising an issue. If you use your right to get parliamentary information whenever you are in doubt, you will avoid the embarrassment of being ruled out of order, and at the same time leave the impression with others that you know your business very well indeed.

Is the following statement true or false?

The order in which each specific question may be considered at a meeting is determined in advance by the order of business.

True.   **page 5**   False.   **page 11**

YOUR ANSWER: After the special orders.

Apparently, you are confused by the question. It stated that you are secretary of the organization, responsible for reporting the proceedings of the previous meeting. What is the report on the proceedings of the previous meeting called? It is called the *minutes*.

Here is the order of business again:

1. Call to order.
2. Reading the minutes.
3. Reports of officers and permanent committees.
4. Reports of special or temporary committees.
5. Special orders.
6. Unfinished (or old) business and general orders.
7. New business.

You don't have to read far in the order of business to see that the reading of the minutes comes first of all. Perhaps you thought that because the minutes dealt with the proceedings of the previous meeting, your report would fall into the class of old or unfinished business. But you were wrong, weren't you?

Return to page 14 and choose the right answer.

YOUR ANSWER: Special committee reports.

You are on the right track but your answer is not quite accurate. The discussion resulted in a motion to establish a committee to organize a Christmas party, but the committee could not — obviously — come into existence before the group thought of establishing it. Since no committee for arranging a Christmas party existed when the speaker made his suggestion, the discussion could not have properly taken place during the section of the order of business devoted to the reports of special committees.

The discussion between the chair and the speaker contains some broad hints as to the section of the normal order of business during which it occurred.

Return to page 7 and choose the right answer.

24

[from page 29]

YOUR ANSWER: Ask if anyone wants to second the motion.

Correct. A main motion should never be considered without a second. However, the failure of anyone to call "Second!" would not prove the proposal lacked support. The chair should, out of respect for the maker of the motion, ask for a second. Because some interested members may not have heard the motioner, the chair should repeat the motion as part of his request for a second. If the group is small, repetition is unnecessary.

The second is still not enough to establish the motion as a question. Not until the chair has formally stated the question does it come before the membership as a question to be decided. Before formally stating the question, the chair must decide whether it is consistent with the purposes and methods of the organization, and whether it is made according to proper procedure (in the proper form and at the right time). The group may question a chairman's decision.

If a proposal to sponsor a Christmas party were made during the wrong part of the meeting, it would be ruled out of order, and so would a proposal that a tax-exempt civic organization endorse a political candidate. The first ruling would be procedural, the second constitutional. In fact, the endorsement of a political candidate by a tax-exempt organization would jeopardize its tax-exempt status.

The chairman gives notice to the group that a motion has become a question by saying: "It has been moved and seconded that. . . ." followed by repetition of the motion. (If a quite long motion has just been read, if copies are available to the members, or if the chair is reasonably certain that the members all heard the motion, he may simply say, "The question is now on Mr. Murray's motion," or, "The question is now on the motion for a Christmas party.") One of the chairman's principal tasks is to keep the group fully informed of the question before it. It is the duty of the chair to state when a new motion becomes a question. When an item of business has been completed, the chair should clearly report the next item to be considered. This procedure is called *stating the question*.

Is the following statement true or false?

If the proposal of a Christmas party is promptly seconded, members may immediately seek the floor to discuss the motion.

True. page 19   False. page 33

YOUR ANSWER: You may speak twice on that motion, too.

Certainly. The stated limitations apply to the discussion of any one specific motion. On a new question, the rights to discussion begin all over again.

The chairman cannot end debate as long as eligible members want to speak, but any member may attempt to close debate on the Christmas party motion and bring it to a vote. A motion to close debate and call for a vote has priority over the main motion but requires a two-thirds vote. Like any motion, the motion to close debate must be voted upon by the group. If two thirds of those voting vote "aye" on the motion to end debate, the Christmas party motion will be voted on immediately. If more than one third vote against the motion to end debate and bring a vote, the group will return immediately to the discussion of the Christmas party. The motion to end debate and bring a vote on the pending question is called the *previous question*. Don't let the term mislead you. If a member says, "I move the previous question," his intention is to end the discussion and have a vote.

The reason the motions to limit or extend debate and the previous question require a two-thirds vote is that they are actually motions to suspend the regular parliamentary rules. Any motion to suspend rules requires a two-thirds vote for adoption so that rules designed to protect the rights of members cannot be easily abandoned. Some rules cannot be suspended at all. These are rules designed to protect the rights of absent members. The rules require that certain motions cannot be made unless the members have been given advance notice so that, if they are interested, they may make a point of coming to the meeting. The rule requiring notice is one that cannot be suspended.

Does the vote on the previous question decide whether or not the Christmas party motion is adopted?

Yes.   **page 32**

No.   **page 39**

26

YOUR ANSWER: That the question is the one before the meeting.

Correct. Stating the question means informing the meeting of the question now before it. Calling the question is short for calling for a vote on the question. (The phrase *putting* the question, which is short for putting the question to a vote, is also used.)

When a chairman has seen or heard the vote, he decides whether the majority was for or against and announces his decision to the group. He may say, "The ayes (nays) have it," "The motion is passed," "The affirmative (negative) has it," or any similar statement that clearly expresses his estimate of the vote.

The question is not formally decided until the chair makes the announcement. If the chair is unsure of the vote, or if some members question his decision, a standing count may be taken. The chairman may ask for a standing count on his own initiative by calling the question again in this form: "All those in favor please rise and remain standing until counted." He counts those standing and then takes the negative vote in the same manner. If at this point a member doubts the chairman's estimate, he may make a motion that a standing count be taken. If that motion receives a majority, then a standing count is taken on the disputed issue.

Immediately after announcing his decision on the vote, the chairman must inform the group of the question before it. Specialized and procedural motions, such as a motion to adjourn, are given priority over main motions; this means they can interrupt the discussion of a main motion. If the question of adjournment was raised during the debate on the Christmas party motion, the organization would decide immediately whether or not to adjourn. Such adjournment cannot be debated, the vote would be called as soon as the question was stated. If the adjournment motion failed, the chair would state that the Christmas party motion was again before the house. As soon as a question is decided and when no other is pending, the chair asks if anything else is to be considered under the present topic, new business, committee reports, etc.

Is the following statement true or false?

In either voice vote or show of hands an actual count is not usually taken.

True. **page 31**   False. **page 36**

YOUR ANSWER: "The motion to have a Christmas party is passed."

An affirmative vote on the previous question has no effect on the outcome of the Christmas party motion. All the vote means is that the membership agrees to end debate and hold an immediate vote on the pending question. If the chairman made such a statement as, "The motion to have the Christmas party is passed," when, in truth, only the motion on the previous question was passed, he would be out of order.

Return to page 39 and choose the answer that best conforms with what the chairman should say after an affirmative vote on the previous question.

YOUR ANSWER: After the reading of the minutes.

Your answer looks good but it is logically impossible. By definition, the minutes are a report on the proceedings of the previous meeting. According to your answer, you would expect to read the minutes after the minutes had been read, thus requiring the members to listen to the minutes twice.

Perhaps you knew that the minutes didn't come after the minutes, but thought, because you were secretary of the organization, that you should give your report in class two of the normal order of business: reports of officers and permanent committees. But your reasoning was wrong.

In all meetings the person responsible for reporting the proceedings of the previous meeting — usually the secretary of the organization — reads the minutes before any other item of business is taken up.

Return to page 14 and choose the right answer.

YOUR ANSWER: New business.

The proposal made by the speaker is clearly a new one, so it should be brought up in that part of the meeting devoted to new business. The chair is responsible for keeping members informed of the class of business before them. After a discussion of subjects that had been introduced at prior meetings, he might say, "Is there any more old business?" If he gets no response, he says, "If there is no more old business, is there any new business?" Members with new motions then seek recognition. If the orders of the day includes some new business, instead of asking for new business, the chair announces whatever is listed. When the planned new business is completed, he will ask, "Is there any more new business?" as notice to members to make their motions.

Merely proposing a motion does not make it open for consideration and action. At least one additional step, and usually two, must be performed to establish a motion as a *question*. A question is an issue that has been recognized as a proper subject for action.

The first of the two steps, and the one that may occasionally be ignored, is *seconding* the motion. A *second* is simply an indication by another member that he, too, is interested in having the proposal discussed. The requirement of a second for all but a few types of motions assures that subjects will not be brought to the floor that are only the pet topics of individual members. Any person who wants to indicate his support for the consideration of a motion that has been made may do so by stating: "I second the motion," "I second it," or simply, "Second." In large groups, the second (this name is given to the person making the second) should stand; it is never necessary to obtain recognition before seconding.

If a second is not offered immediately, the chairman may ask, "Is there a second to the motion?" If the motion may not have been heard by all present, the chair repeats the motion when calling for a second. (The second is not required for certain motions.)

If the chairman heard no second after the motion to sponsor a Christmas party, he would:

Have the group proceed with the discussion of the proposal.   **page 17**

Ask if anyone wants to second the motion.   **page 24**

Drop the motion because of lack of interest.   **page 38**

YOUR ANSWER: That a vote will follow shortly.

When the chairman *states the question,* telling the organization which question is before it, there may be some discussion before he *calls the question,* that is, asks for a vote. Only if the question is undebatable, as is the motion to adjourn, does the chairman ask for a vote immediately after stating the question. But most questions are debatable — after all, that's why you're having a meeting — so stating the question is normally followed by discussion. As soon as the chair states a debatable question, members are free to seek recognition in order to present their ideas.

You can always be certain that when a question has been stated a vote will eventually follow. Organizations must act upon all motions in some manner, if only by voting for another motion that disposes of the main question without a decision for or against it.

However, once the chair has called (or put) the question, you know that a vote will almost certainly follow immediately. *Putting* or *calling* the question are shortened expressions meaning putting the question to a vote, and calling for a vote on the question.

Return to page 33 and choose the right answer.

YOUR ANSWER: True.

Correct. Certain situations, elections, for example, may require that a vote be taken by secret ballot. Other circumstances may require a vote by roll call of members. In such circumstances the votes will actually be counted. Most business is carried on by voice or standing vote and is not counted unless the chair or the membership doubts his estimate.

When a debatable question has been stated, the chair asks, "Is there any discussion?" Those who want to speak for or against the motion may then seek recognition. The rules most commonly accepted for keeping debate in bounds follow.

On any one question:

1. No one may speak for more than ten minutes at a time.
2. No one may speak more than twice.
3. No one may take a second turn until all who desire to speak have had a first opportunity.

The rules for the debate on any pending question may be loosened or tightened by a two-thirds vote of those present. Each organization has its own attitude toward the rules on debate. Often speakers are allowed the floor more than twice in exchanges in which each speaker talks for only a minute or so.

The chair or a member may end an informal discussion by raising a *point of order,* that is, by asserting that the rules of order are being ignored.

When operating according to the rules, debate may continue as long as there are interested members eligible to speak or until all members have used their time. If debate is lagging or members have begun repeating the same arguments, the chair may call for the question. However, if eligible speakers promptly indicate their desire for recognition, the debate proceeds. The chairman cannot cut off debate.

You have spoken twice, ten minutes each time, on the Christmas party motion; later you desire to comment on the proposal that the Springfield Kiwanis invite a city planning lecture; you may:

Speak twice on that motion, too. **page 25**
Speak only if the rules have been changed. **page 35**
Not speak again that evening. **page 40**

YOUR ANSWER: Yes.

The expression "moving the previous question" is confusing and misleading. When a member says, "I move the previous question," he is really asking — in plain English — for an immediate vote on the question presently under discussion.

The previous question must be voted on immediately. Whether it passes or fails determines whether the question before the group will be voted on. If it passes, the group must immediately vote on the question that has been before it, in this case, the Christmas party motion. The outcome of the vote on the previous question does not affect the outcome of the Christmas party motion; it decides only whether or not the Christmas party motion will be voted on immediately.

So when a member moves the previous question, you know he is only asking for a vote on having a vote.

Now return to page 25 and choose the right answer.

YOUR ANSWER: False.

Right. Since your motion has not yet been put as a question, it cannot be discussed until the chair states the question on it. After the second the chair may still rule the motion out of order.

Before a main motion is decided, the members have a right to discuss it, so they can make up their minds intelligently. Such discussion is called the *debate*. Debate is controlled by rules designed to assure that all viewpoints are freely expressed, without taking too much time.

Some motions are undebatable, meaning that they are voted on as soon as stated. Whether stating the question is followed by debate or by an immediate vote depends upon the type of motion. (Different types of motions are considered in Chapters II through V.) Here we consider first the procedure for voting and then the rules for debate.

All questions put before a deliberative organization must be acted upon in some manner. The action may be a positive or negative vote on the question itself, or a vote on another motion, such as one that postpones action on the main motion. However a question is disposed, the disposition results from a vote. On most matters it is necessary only that a simple majority (half the members who vote plus one) vote for a motion to make that motion the rule for the whole organization. Some matters require approval by two thirds of those voting. Each organization decides which matters require a majority and which a two-thirds vote. This decision may be made by the adoption in the constitution of a standard set of rules.

The chairman asks, "Are you ready for the question?" and if there is no objection he assumes the group is ready to vote. The vote may be taken by voice, by a show of hands, or by rising. Whichever method is adopted, the chairman *calls the questions* (asks for the vote), by saying: "The question before the group is whether to adopt the following motion. . . . All those in favor (signify by saying *aye*) (raise your right hands) (please stand)." If the voting method used requires the members to stand or raise their hands, the chair says, "Thank you," or otherwise indicates that they may resume their normal positions. Then the negative vote is taken. "All those opposed (signify by saying *nay*) (raise your right hands) (please stand)."

When the chair states a question, you know:

That the question is the one before the meeting. **page 26**

That a vote will follow shortly. **page 30**

YOUR ANSWER: "The motion to have a Christmas party is defeated."

A negative vote on the previous question — or an affirmative — has no effect on the outcome of the Christmas party motion. All a negative vote means is that the membership prefers not to hold an immediate vote. The outcome of the Christmas party motion need not be negative. Later, when time for debate has been exhausted, or when someone again moves the previous question and the membership decides it is ready to vote, the motion may be passed.

If the chairman made such a statement as, "The motion to have a Christmas party is defeated," he would be out of order.

Return to page 39 and choose the answer that best conforms with what you should expect the chairman to say after an affirmative vote on the previous question.

YOUR ANSWER: Speak only if the rules have been changed.

You forgot that the rules for debate are confined to debate on any *one* question. Although you have spoken twice on the Christmas party motion, ten minutes each time, there is nothing in the rules to keep you from commenting, later in the evening, on the proposal that the Springfield Kiwanis invite a city planning lecturer.

Sometimes the rules for debate can be changed, either loosened or tightened, by a two-thirds vote of the members present, because the issue is especially controversial or complicated, or because there is a general desire to shorten the debate.

But your desire to comment on a new question does not call for changes in the rules. Go ahead and talk.

Return to page 31 and choose the right answer.

YOUR ANSWER: False.

No, as a rule the chairman decides whether the vote is affirmative or negative by listening to the volume of the ayes and nays or making a rough estimate of the number of hands raised for or against the motion. He shows his decision by saying, "The nays have it," "The motion is passed," or anything that clearly expresses his estimate of the vote.

If the vote looks close, or if some members question the decision of the chairman and request a division of the assembly, a standing count may be taken.

But generally there is enough agreement among the members to make an actual count unnecessary for most questions.

Now return to page 26 and choose the right answer.

YOUR ANSWER: "We will now vote on the motion to have a Christmas party."

Right. An affirmative vote on the previous question means the motion to which it refers will be voted on immediately. The vote on the previous question does not decide how the group stands on the Christmas party, only that it wants to vote on the Christmas party immediately. If the vote on the previous question were negative, then the chair would ask for further discussion of the Christmas party.

A negative vote on the previous question indicates that more than one third of the voting members feel unable to make a decision without more discussion. A positive vote indicates that at least two thirds of those present have decided how they want to vote and are ready for the chairman to call the question.

You can see that it is reasonable to require a two-thirds vote to carry the previous question. It is highly desirable that there should be some way of preventing a debate going on for hours because a few members want to air their opinions fully, yet such a control mechanism is a form of restriction on democratic procedures. It is appropriate that to invoke such a restriction should require more than a bare majority.

Of course, as we see in the United States Senate, the requirement of a two-thirds vote to end debate can be used by a small minority to prevent action being taken at all. With one third refusing to allow a debate to end, business in the Senate, favored by a majority, must often be dropped completely. The means used to protect the democratic right to free and full debate is used there to thwart the equally important right of the majority to make binding decisions. However, this problem should not arise in most private organizations where the rules limiting a speaker to two appearances of ten minutes each, places a maximum on the length of any debate. In the United States Senate there is no such limit.

In Chapter II you will be introduced to some of the specialized motions, and to the order in which specialized motions are handled while a main motion is on the floor. Chapter II begins on page 42.

[*from page 29*]

YOUR ANSWER: Drop the motion because of lack of interest.

What's the hurry? Perhaps some of the members did not hear the motion. Perhaps everyone is waiting for someone else to do the seconding. In many organizations a few members do all the seconding; maybe these members are absent or out of hearing.

Main motions should not be discussed until they have been formally seconded. The second need not obtain recognition from the chair before delivering his second. The purpose of the second is to assure that there is some general interest in the motion.

Failure to get an immediate second does not prove a lack of interest. It is up to the chairman to see that the motion gets as much consideration as it deserves.

Return to page 29 and choose the right answer.

YOUR ANSWER: No.

That's correct.

The previous question is undebatable, as well as privileged. In the midst of the debate on the Christmas party, the chair hears:

SPEAKER A: Mr. Chairman! Mr. Chairman!

CHAIR: The chair recognizes Mr. (Speaker A).

SPEAKER A: I move the previous question.

SPEAKER B: Second!

CHAIR: The previous question has been moved and seconded. All those in favor signify by saying "Aye."

THOSE IN FAVOR: Aye!

CHAIR: Those opposed.

THOSE OPPOSED: Nay!

CHAIR: The ayes have it.

If the chairman decides the ayes have it on the previous question, what would you expect him to say next?

"The motion to have a Christmas party is passed." **page 27**

"The motion to have a Christmas party is defeated." **page 34**

"We will now vote on the motion to have a Christmas party." **page 37**

"Is there any more discussion of the proposal to have a Christmas party?" **page 41**

[*from page 31*]

YOUR ANSWER: Not speak again that evening.

Limiting each member to two ten-minute speeches on any one question in no way prevents him from speaking on other questions. Sometimes a group may change its rules of debate to allow more or less time on each question, but never do the rules prevent a member who has commented on one motion from commenting on another.

It goes against common sense to restrict members to two speeches per meeting. Such a regulation would practically stifle debate, because most members want to save their time in order to use it on issues they think really important.

Return to page 31 and choose the right answer.

YOUR ANSWER: "Is there any more discussion of the proposal to have a Christmas party?"

The reason for moving the previous question is that the speaker thinks the group is ready to vote without further debate. If the previous question is passed, as happened here, then debate on the proposed Christmas party must end.

The chairman would be out of order in asking for further discussion, because he would go against the wishes of the group as expressed by their affirmative vote on the previous question.

No more can be said about the proposal; the membership must now vote to decide whether to form the committee.

Return to page 39 and choose the right answer.

CHAPTER II

Entertaining Motions

So far, most of our discussion has been concerned with main motions — proposals that an organization do a certain thing. We have considered how a group makes a decision about such proposals.

But what happens if the members don't want to make up their minds on a proposal right away? What if they would like to consider another matter first? What if they would like to have a committee study the proposal and report later? What if it is getting late and the members would rather discuss the proposal at a special meeting? What if someone violates the rules during a debate? What if a group likes the general idea but wants to make one or more changes?

All of these problems, and many others, may arise at a meeting. There are specialized motions to deal with each problem.

We have already mentioned a few of these specialized motions, such as the previous question and division of the assembly. Actually, there are some thirty or forty of them (depending on how you want to count them). Each specialized motion has its own set of rules. These rules are listed in the Parliamentary Dictionary in the back section of this book. You need to learn the rules for perhaps a dozen motions; learning the rules is easier than it sounds.

The rules we refer to include whether the motion may be debated, whether it requires a majority or a two-thirds vote for passage, whether it may be amended, and how it stands on the scale of parliamentary priority. This chapter will introduce you to the way in which secondary motions are handled in meetings.

On the basis of what you read so far, which phrase do you think best completes the following sentence?

While a motion is being debated;

No other motion may be made. **page 46**

Some other motions may be made. **page 51**

Any other motion may be made. **page 56**

YOUR ANSWER: True; in addition to the immediately pending question, there can be only one other question pending.

No.

Any motion may be interrupted by at least a few others, so that there is always the possibility of having several pending questions. As a matter of fact, this is quite common.

A main motion might be on the floor as well as an amendment. While the amendment is on the floor, it is in order to move still another motion suggesting a way of disposing of the whole question.

Go back to page 51 and reread it. See if it is not reasonable, on the basis of what is said there, to conclude that there may be more than a single pending question and an immediately pending question on the floor at a time.

44

[from page 48]

YOUR ANSWER: A debate limited to the wisdom of specifying that the committee should consist of five members and that those members should be appointed by the chairman.

Correct. Debate is always limited to as narrow a subject as possible. You debate only the question that is immediately pending, except in a few instances where it is obvious that it would be impossible to carry on a debate at all if the limits were not somewhat broader. This limitation is quite important especially in large organizations, where, if free rein were given, the debate would wander all over the map. It will become clear to you that this limitation is reasonable as you see what is actually happening when an amendment has been proposed.

If no limitations had been set on this debate, and if you had already spoken once for ten minutes on the Christmas party motion proper, how much time yould you have available if you wanted to use it to debate this amendment?

One ten-minute period. **page 49**

Two ten-minute periods. **page 55**

YOUR ANSWER: To appoint a five-man committee.

You are jumping the gun. This vote was on the amendment, not on the main motion. The amendment cannot take effect until the main motion is approved.

When a motion is stated as a question, it becomes the property of the meeting. The man who made it can no longer change it, unless the assembly approves the change.

The process of amendment can be viewed as a process of refining and restating the question before the assembly. Viewed in that light, it can be seen that it is necessary to vote to approve an amendment, but that approval of the amendment doesn't have any immediate effect on whether or not the main motion carries.

In approving an amendment, an organization is merely deciding to change the form of the question it intends later to vote on.

Now return to page 55 and select the correct answer.

YOUR ANSWER: No other motion may be made.

You should know better than that! In Chapter I, you were told why consideration of a main motion may be interrupted to allow a specialized motion to be considered. Since the point apparently eluded you, let's look at another example.

It is virtually impossible to adjourn, for instance, if interruption of a main motion is not permitted. With no interruption permitted, adjournment could be proposed only in the interim between the vote on one main motion and the admission of another motion to the floor. If, during a long debate, the proponents of adjournment slumbered through the vote and failed to waken before someone offered another motion, they would be in for another siege of debate before adjournment could be considered!

Such a situation is inconvenient, but the implications for sound democratic practice are even worse. How could anybody propose to amend a motion if an amendment could not interrupt the debate on the main motion? An amendment, after all, is just a specialized motion. Or again, how could anyone object that business was being unfairly handled? No, it must be possible to make at least some motions while others are on the floor.

Now return to page 42 and select a better answer.

YOUR ANSWER: In order from 1 through 5.

That is correct. The appeal will be decided first. Action will then be taken on the motion to commit. (If that passes, all of the remaining pending questions go to the committee. When the committee reports its recommendations on them, they are voted on in the same order of precedence they had when committed.) If the motion to commit fails, then the filling of blanks is completed, perfecting the amendment. The amendment intended to perfect the main motion is then voted on, and, finally, the main motion itself comes up for a vote. Motions are always acted upon in the order opposite that in which they are introduced. The coined word *Lifo* is used to describe a system of inventory control. The word is composed of the initial letters of Last In, First Out. That rule applies to pending motions.

It should be reasonably clear now how specialized motions are handled in a meeting. You should be familiar with such terms as *pending, immediately pending, precedence,* and *yields* and, in a general way, with the process of amendment. If you are interested in learning more about amending, you might take a few minutes to read the article entitled AMEND in the dictionary in the second half of this book. You will find there that we have discussed three of the seven possible ways of making an amendment. The three discussed were to add words, to strike and insert words, and to fill in blanks. You might also want to read the articles entitled POINT OF ORDER and APPEAL, but don't plunge into COMMIT until you are fairly sure of yourself. The best way to approach that article is to read first the articles on COMMITTEE, STANDING COMMITTEE, and SPECIAL COMMITTEE. And, for the moment, don't pay any attention to the tables you find at the head of some of the articles. You will understand them when you have read the next chapter.

In Chapter III, we shall consider in more detail some of the principal specialized motions. Please go on to page 71 for the beginning of Chapter III.

[*from page 57*]

YOUR ANSWER: Yes.

Right. It is perfectly legitimate to interrupt discussion of a main motion to propose an amendment. The motion to amend is debatable, so upon hearing Mr. Peterson's motion and the second, the chairman would say:

"It has been moved and seconded that the Christmas party motion be amended by deletion and insertion so that it will read as follows: That a committee of five from the Springfield Kiwanis be appointed by the chairman to organize a Christmas party, etc. The balance of the motion is unaffected by the proposed amendment. Is there any discussion?"

The chairman, as is his responsibility, has clearly indicated the effect of the motion to amend.

If you were attending this meeting, what would you expect to hear next?

A debate limited to the wisdom of specifying that the committee should consist of five members and that those members should be appointed by the chairman.   **page 44**

A debate in which the whole question of the Christmas party was considered along with the wisdom of this particular variation.   **page 54**

YOUR ANSWER: One ten-minute period.

No, not unless some special limitation was set on the debate, and we said that none was.

According to the ordinary rules of debate, every member has a right to speak twice, a maximum of ten minutes each time, on almost every debatable motion (there are a few exceptions where, on minor matters, a member can speak only once). The right to speak begins anew with each new debatable motion, even when it is a specialized motion interrupting debate on a main motion.

Thus, you have a right to speak for two ten-minute periods on the amendment. And you still have a right to speak for a second ten-minute period on the main motion.

It is possible to amend an amendment. In that case, there would be three pending questions: the main motion, the amendment, and the amendment to the amendment. You would have the right to speak twice, ten minutes each time, on all three of those motions. Thus, you could, if your voice did not give out, speak for a whole hour before the main motion was voted on.

Now return to page 44 and select the correct answer.

50

[*from page 55*]

YOUR ANSWER: To say that the question is now on the Christmas party motion as amended.

Exactly. Having disposed of the amendment, the organization is now ready to finish the discussion that was interrupted. However, the question before the house is now the motion in its amended form. Assuming you had spoken for one ten-minute period when this motion had been immediately pending before, you would have only one ten-minute period left, now that it is again immediately pending.

The process of amending a motion is often called *perfecting* it. A person who is in favor of an amendment to a motion is not necessarily in favor of the motion. He may simply be attempting to make it as acceptable as possible if it is passed. (He may also be trying to make it unacceptable so that it will not be passed. This is a common trick in Congress, although it is not often used in private organizations.) Others, of course, are in favor of the motion but are trying to improve it.

Perfecting a motion, with the exception noted above, is a process of trying to make the motion as acceptable as possible before it is voted on. When the question of the amendment is decided, the amended motion will be up for discussion once again. Since there is another chance to discuss the main motion as the purpose of amendment is only to improve the main motion, and since the vote on the amendment does not affect the later vote on the main motion, the limitation on debate is not a serious restriction on the rights of members. So when the amendment is the immediately pending question, that is the only subject that need be or should be debated.

Let us assume that after the chairman has said, "The question is now on the motion as amended — is there any discussion?" another member seeks recognition and proposes an amendment limiting the expenditures of the committee to $50. Should that amendment be entertained?

No, it shouldn't be.   **page 65**

I don't see why not.   **page 69**

YOUR ANSWER: Some other motions may be made.

That is correct. You will recall that the debate on a main motion was interrupted by a member moving the previous question. Main motions may be interrupted by any other type of motion. (And any type of motion may be interrupted by at least a few other motions.) There are rules specifying which motions may interrupt others and when. These rules define the relative priority of specialized motions.

When a motion on the floor is interrupted by another legitimate motion, the earlier motion is said to *yield* to the later; the later is said to *take precedence* over the earlier.

When one motion yields to another, the motion of higher priority is debated (if debatable) and decided before returning to the original motion. Once a motion has been stated as a question, it is said to be *pending*. It remains pending, even though interrupted by another, until some action is taken on it. The motion actually under consideration at any moment is called the *immediately pending* question.

Is the following statement true or false?

In addition to the immediately pending question, there can be only one other question pending.

True.   **page 43**

False.   **page 57**

52

[*from page 57*]

YOUR ANSWER: No.

Why not?

This is what you know about the situation:

1. A main motion is on the floor.
2. A member has moved to amend that motion.
3. When a main motion is immediately pending, debate may be interrupted by any other type of motion.
4. The amendment must be relevant to the main motion. (We shall discuss that requirement in detail later.)

The amendment qualifies under points (3) and (4) above — a main motion is pending and the amendment is relevant.

The only other test that might be made concerns the legality of the amendment, both in terms of the organization's own constitution and in terms of the law of the land. There is nothing to suggest that either has been violated.

Now return to page 57 and select the correct answer.

YOUR ANSWER: Yes.

That's right. The recommendation of replacing the figure $50 by the figure $100 is an amendment to an amendment. It is called an amendment of the second degree. Amendments of the second degree are permissible.

What if the chairman then hears someone offer a further motion to amend the amendment by substituting $75 for $100. Does he entertain that?

Yes. page 62

No. page 67

[*from page 48*]

YOUR ANSWER: A debate in which the whole question of the Christmas party was considered along with the wisdom of this particular variation.

No. Usually, debate is limited to discussion of the immediately pending question. (The few exceptions are said to open the main question to debate. These exceptions occur only where it would be practically meaningless to debate the specialized motion without debating the main motion.)

In the case of an amendment, debate is confined to the amendment. It is perfectly possible to discuss whether an amendment will improve a main motion without arguing about whether the main motion is a good idea in the first place.

Such an arbitrary division of subject matter may seem like a psychological trick, but, in fact, you do it every day. While considering whether or not to take the highway to work, you may consider the merits of two different turnoffs. But having thought some more about the traffic at that time of day, you may decide to stay away from the highway and go through town after all. The debate on an amendment is handled in just that hypothetical manner. Those for the main motion are trying to amend in such a way as to make the motion as desirable as possible should it be passed. Those opposed are trying to make it as innocuous as possible in case it is passed.

Now return to page 48 and select the correct answer.

YOUR ANSWER: Two ten-minute periods.

Correct. If there were actually that much controversy about Mr. Peterson's amendment, you could speak for as long as twenty minutes in two ten-minute stretches. The time limits on debate begin over again with each new motion, as you learned in Chapter I. They also begin again if a motion is carried over to a later day, though not in a subsequent meeting on the same day.

When the debate on the amendment is ended, the procedure is:

CHAIRMAN: Are you ready for the question?

If no one objects, the chair calls for the vote.

CHAIRMAN: All those in favor, say "Aye."
MEMBERS: Aye!
CHAIRMAN: All those opposed, say "No."
MEMBERS: No!
CHAIRMAN: The ayes have it. The motion is carried.

How would you expect the chairman to proceed from this point?

To appoint a five-man committee.   **page 45**

To say that the question is now on the Christmas party motion as amended.   **page 50**

56

[*from page 42*]

YOUR ANSWER: Any other motion may be made.

No. Many problems would arise if any motion could interrupt any other motion. For instance, if a main motion could be proposed and admitted as a question while a main motion on an entirely different subject was being debated, the result would be chaotic. Two, three, ten, or a hundred different questions could be put before the membership, without a decision on any.

However, it has to be possible to make some motions while others are on the floor. If that were not the case, it would be possible to move adjournment only when no other business was on the floor. If Congress could not adjourn in the midst of a debate on a controversial issue, a meeting might not break up for days. And your neighborhood meeting might last so long that your employer would wonder just what you were doing the night before.

As the rules stand, discussion of a motion that is on the floor can be interrupted by another that is relevant to it, or by the few motions — adjourn, for instance — that have a very special parliamentary status.

Now return to page 42 and select the correct answer.

YOUR ANSWER: False.

Correct: You have noted that any motion can be interrupted by some other motion. So it is quite possible to have several questions pending at any one time. When several motions are pending, most of them will be related. At the bottom of the heap, there will be a main motion. From the debate on that main motion there may arise a motion to amend, another to refer to a committee, and yet another claiming that in the process of debate some rule was violated. As you can see, these motions spring one from the other.

Do you remember the motion concerning the Christmas party? Assume that it had just been moved and seconded.

CHAIRMAN: It has been moved and seconded that the Springfield Kiwanis establish a committee to organize a Christmas party for the benefit of the children at the County Orphanage, and that the committee assume responsibility for setting a date convenient to the orphanage and the Kiwanis. Is there any discussion?

The floor is now open for debate on the motion, and Mr. Peterson seeks recognition.

CHAIRMAN: Mr. Peterson?

MR. PETERSON: I feel that the motion is not specific enough, and therefore move that the motion be amended by deleting the words "the Springfield Kiwanis establish a committee" and inserting the words "a committee of five from the Springfield Kiwanis be appointed by the chairman."

MEMBER: Second.

Would the chair entertain that motion?

Yes.   **page 48**

No.   **page 52**

58

[*from page 61*]

YOUR ANSWER: In reverse order, from 5 through 1.

Stop and consider your answer for a moment. Here is the list of pending questions at this point:

1. Appeal
2. Commit
3. Filling blanks
4. Amendment to limit expenditures
5. Main motion — whether or not to have a Christmas party.

If your suggestion is followed, the main motion will be voted on before the amendments. That won't work very well! The motions were made in the order 5 through 1. The main motion was made first, then the amendment, and so on up the line. But, you will recall, in all cases discussed so far, the last motion made has been the first one decided.

Thus, the amendment to the amendment is decided before the amendment. The amendment is decided before the main motion. The general rule is that the order for acting on pending questions is the opposite of the order in which they were made.

There are other kinds of motions that may be made while others are pending, but we'll deal with those later. They do not affect the present situation.

Now return to page 61 and select the correct answer.

YOUR ANSWER: $50.

The question comes down to this, which figure is least likely to be acceptable as a limitation on the amount to be spent: $50 or $200. In choosing your answer, you were probably thinking that the cause is good — a children's Christmas party — and that you would prefer to spend more for such a cause, rather than less.

But let's ignore the purpose of the expenditure and concentrate on the principle. Isn't it likely that a group will prefer to keep its expenditures down? It is possible that a majority will agree to spend $200. But an even larger number of members are willing to spend $50. (Everyone willing to spend $200 is willing to spend $50, of course.)

Now suppose you're the chairman. What will happen if you call the vote on $50 first? Of course, the $50 figure will pass and that will be the end of it! Remember, in filling a blank, the first suggestion that gets a majority wins.

The effect of voting on the highest figure first is that the "winning" figure is the highest figure acceptable to a majority.

Now return to page 67 and select the correct answer.

60

[from page 64]

YOUR ANSWER: "The question is now on the amendment, limiting the committee's expenditures to $75."

That is what the chairman should say. Filling in the blanks is, in this case, a second-degree amendment. The purpose is to perfect the amendment before voting on it, just as a first-degree amendment is an attempt to perfect a main motion before voting on it. A person who votes for the $75 figure is not necessarily in favor of the amendment. He may only be trying to get the figure as low as possible in the event that it does pass. Scrooge was not the only person in the world who didn't think much of Christmas!

The motion to amend yields to almost as many motions as does a main motion. Step back for a moment and assume that the discussion of the merits of the various sums suggested for the Christmas party was still in progress. At that point it would be perfectly all right for a member to move that, since there is so much dispute, the whole question of the Christmas party should be referred to a committee. (One purpose for referring a matter to committee is to allow a small group to hammer out the details of a proposal and to try to bring about a compromise.) The committee would meet, sometime between regular organization meetings, to draft a report and recommendations to be presented at a subsequent organization meeting.

The motion to refer to committee, called the motion to commit, is itself both debatable and amendable. The debate is restricted to the propriety and details of committing. The motion may be amended to change the committee, to suggest creation of a special committee, and, if the latter, how the committee should be formed.

It would be perfectly appropriate in the debate on the motion to commit for a member to point out that it would be inappropriate to commit because, by the time the report would be received, it would be too late to do a good job of planning the party.

Let us take up the debate, which is getting hot.

MEMBER: The maker of the motion to commit was very foolish. . . .
MAKER OF THE MOTION: Point of order!
CHAIRMAN: The chair recognizes the maker of the motion.

(Continued on page 61)

MAKER OF THE MOTION: The speaker is out of order in his personal
reference to me.

CHAIRMAN: The speaker will please come to order.

MEMBER: I appeal the decision of the chair. I don't feel that any
other construction can be put on the situation.

CHAIRMAN: I will put the matter to a vote. The question is, will the
assembly sustain the decision of the chair?

At this point, the following motions are pending (that is, they still
await final action):

1. Appeal
2. Commit
3. Filling blanks
4. Amendment to limit expenditures
5. Main motion — whether or not to have a Christmas party.

In which order will they be decided?

In order from 1 through 5.   **page 47.**

In reverse order, from 5 through 1.   **page 58**

Neither of the above.   **page 66**

I don't know.   **page 70**

[*from page 53*]

YOUR ANSWER: Yes.

Sorry, but no.

At this point we have (1) a main motion pending, (2) an amendment limiting the amount the committee might spend to $50, and (3) an amendment to the amendment — the latter proposing to change the limitation from $50 to $100.

It is all right to amend an amendment. So what has happened so far is in order.

But, it is not permissible to amend a second-degree amendment (an amendment to an amendment). If the chairman entertained the motion to insert $75 instead of $100, there would be on the floor an amendment to an amendment to an amendment—a third-degree amendment. That is just too confusing and it isn't allowed.

Now return to page 53 and select the correct answer.

YOUR ANSWER: No.

Apparently you did not grasp the significance of a rather peculiar-sounding statement on page 69. Here it is again:

You many amend an amendment, but you cannot amend an amendment to an amendment.

An amendment to a motion is called a first-degree amendment. You can make a motion modifying the amendment. In so doing, you create a second-degree amendment (an amendment to an amendment), which is permissible. But you can't amend a second-degree amendment. Or, as we said, you can't amend an amendment to an amendment.

The problem at hand is to decide whether the motion to limit expenditures is a first-degree or second-degree amendment. If it is a first-degree amendment, it may be amended by a motion to change the amount. If it is a second-degree amendment, then further amendment is not permissible.

(The reason should be obvious — things are confusing enough when you get to the level of second-degree amendments; they would be impossible if third-degree amendments were allowed.)

In order to decide whether the amendment setting a limit in expenditures is a first- or second-degree amendment, let's review the situation.

— A motion was made to create a committee.
— An amendment stating the size and method of appointment of the committee was accepted.
— When the amendment was decided, the immediately pending question was again the main motion.
— At that point, the amendment limiting expenditures was proposed.
— Since no other amendment to the main motion was on the floor, this amendment must be of the first degree.

Now return to page 69 and select the correct answer.

64

[from page 67]

YOUR ANSWER: $200.

You are correct. That is the recommendation the chairman would call to a vote first. Presumably, the suggestion for spending the most money is the least acceptable. (As a rule of thumb it can be said that when selling, the lowest figure is least acceptable; when buying, the highest figure is least acceptable.) At any rate, it is clear that anybody favoring spending any money at all is willing to spend $50. If the voting begins with the highest figure suggested, the amount that carries will be the highest that a majority is willing to spend. If the votes were counted, we might find that 10% of those voting were willing to spend $200, that 30% were willing to spend $100, and that 60% were willing to spend $75. Since the figure of $75 received a majority, it is the accepted figure and there is no need to vote on the $50. The voting would proceed in the following manner:

CHAIRMAN: Are you ready for the question on filling in the blank?

MEMBERS: (Silence — no objection.)

CHAIRMAN: All those in favor of spending $200, signify by saying "Aye."

MEMBERS: Aye.

CHAIRMAN: All those opposed, say "No."

MEMBERS: No.

CHAIRMAN: The negative has it. The question now is on inserting the figure $100 in the blank. All those in favor, say "Aye."

MEMBERS: Aye.

CHAIRMAN: All those opposed, say "No."

MEMBERS: No.

CHAIRMAN: The negative has it. The question is now on inserting the figure $75. All those in favor, say "Aye."

MEMBERS: Aye.

CHAIRMAN: All those opposed, say "No."

MEMBERS: No.

CHAIRMAN: The ayes have it. The figure to be inserted is $75.

At this point, what would you expect the chairman to say?

"The question is now on the amendment, limiting the committee's expenditures to $75." **page 60**

"The question is now on the amended motion to sponsor a Christmas party." **page 68**

YOUR ANSWER: No, it shouldn't be.

To reach that conclusion you must have decided that no more than one amendment may be applied to a motion. It is true that two amendments to a motion cannot be entertained at the same time, any more than two main motions can be entertained at the same time. But you can consider more than one main motion at a meeting if you consider them one after another. You can also consider more than one amendment to a motion as long as the amendments are considered successively. If the amendments are considered sucessively, any number may be applied to a single amendable motion.

As you will discover in a few moments, there are times when it is possible to have several amendments pending, but they will not be amendments to the same motion. For instance, you might have a main motion, an amendment to the main motion, and an amendment to the amendment.

Now return to page 50 and select the correct answer.

YOUR ANSWER: Neither of the above.

No. Consider the situation. Here are the pending motions:
1. Appeal
2. Commit
3. Filling blanks
4. Amendment to limit expenditures
5. Main motion — whether or not to have a Christmas party.

The appeal arose out of the debate on the motion to commit. In this case the appeal concerns only the decorum of a member, so it is not absolutely essential to decide upon it before deciding on the motion to commit — but what time would be better? On the other hand, the point of order being appealed might have concerned the appropriateness of making a motion to commit. In such a case, it would be foolish to go ahead and vote on that motion before the appeal was decided. So the appeal is better decided before the motion to commit.

Now the motion to commit refers to all the other pending motions. If the organization passes over the motion to commit to decide on another motion, the effect is to avoid the purpose of the motion to commit. So this question must be decided immediately after the appeal. Then comes the filling of blanks. Clearly, a group would not vote to approve the amendment without having decided which figure is to be inserted. Nor would it be reasonable to vote on the main motion before acting on the amendment.

If you review the last paragraph, you will see that the logical order for acting on the pending questions is the opposite of the order in which the motions are made. And that is the general rule. A group of pending questions are voted on in the order opposite that in which they are introduced.

Now return to page 61 and select the correct answer.

YOUR ANSWER: No.

Correct. The proposal of a $75 figure, in the form offered, would be an amendment to an amendment to an amendment — which is confusing. And because it gets confusing, it is not allowable to make an amendment to an amendment to an amendment.

However, there seems to be some disagreement in the group about the amount that should be set aside for the Christmas party. This is a perfectly legitimate disagreement and there is a very simple way of handling it without confusion. An experienced chairman, once he heard the amendment raising the figure to $100, would foresee the likelihood of a variety of figures being proposed. He should say, "If there is no objection, let us handle the original amendment by the method of filling in blanks."

According to the method of filling in blanks, the original amendment becomes: ". . . and that the committee's expenditures be limited to (blank)." Filling in the blank is in this case a second-degree amendment. (An original main motion might be made with a blank, in which case filling in the blank would be an amendment of the first degree.)

Once the motion has been stated as having a blank, the chair will entertain proposals for filling in the blank. Without awaiting recognition, any member may propose an amount. All these amounts are noted by the chairman (no seconds are required). When all suggestions have been received, the relative merits of the proposals may be discussed by the regular rules of debate. Notice that there are, in this case, several questions on the floor at once.

When the debate is ended, the chairman arranges the proposals in such an order that the one least likely to be acceptable will be voted on first, the most obviously acceptable last. Then the suggestions are voted on in turn until one gets a majority. The first one to get a majority is the amount that is inserted in place of the blank, and the rest are dropped. (As an example, if an organization is using this method to decide the minimum figure at which it is willing to sell some used office equipment, presumably it is the lowest figure suggested that is the least acceptable.)

Getting back to the party again, if the proposals include the following figures, $100, $50, $200, and $75, which will the chairman call to a vote first?

$50.   **page 59** $200.   **page 64**

68

[*from page 64*]

YOUR ANSWER: "The question is now on the amended motion to sponsor a Christmas party."

Slow down. The vote just completed filled in the blank in the amendment. That was an operation of perfecting the amendment. The process of perfecting an amendment or any other motion does not pass the question being perfected. All that has happened is that the assembly has decided that the amendment should set the limit at $75. Now it remains to vote on the perfected amendment. Only after a vote is taken on the whole idea of providing and setting a limit on funds will it be possible to get back to the main motion.

Now return to page 64 and select the correct answer.

YOUR ANSWER: I don't see why not.

And neither would any competent chairman. Any number of amendments may be proposed successively. There is, however, a limitation on how many amendments can be applied, one on top of the other.

An amendment may be amended, but an amendment to an amendment may not be amended.

That sounds a little more difficult than it is. If we define a couple of terms, we can state it more simply.

An amendment to a motion that is not an amendment is called an amendment of the first degree. An amendment to another amendment is said to be of the second degree. Now let's get back to that complicated-sounding statement, this time using the new terms:

You can amend a first-degree amendment; you cannot amend a second-degree amendment.

Now, go back to the meeting on the Christmas party. Assume that the new amendment has been seconded.

CHAIRMAN: It has been moved and seconded that the Christmas party motion be amended by adding, and that the committee's expenditures be limited to $50. Is there any discussion?

SPEAKER: I move to amend the amendment by striking "$50" and inserting "$100."

MEMBER: Second.

Would the chairman entertain the latest amendment?

Yes.   **page 53**

No.   **page 63**

YOUR ANSWER: I don't know.

That is an honest answer. Let's take it a step at a time.
Look at the list of pending motions again.
1. Appeal
2. Commit
3. Filling blanks
4. Amendment to limit expenditures
5. Main motion — whether or not to have a Christmas party.

The appeal arose out of the debate on the motion to commit. In this case the appeal concerns only the decorum of a member, so it is not absolutely essential to decide upon it before deciding on the motion to commit — but what time would be better? On the other hand, the point of order being appealed might have concerned the appropriateness of making a motion to commit. In such a case, it would be foolish to go ahead and vote on that motion before the appeal was decided. So the appeal is better decided before the motion to commit.

Now the motion to commit refers to all the other pending motions. If the organization passes over the motion to commit to decide on another motion, the effect is to avoid the purpose of the motion to commit. So this question must be decided immediately after the appeal. Then comes the filling of blanks. Clearly, a group would not vote to approve the amendment without having decided which figure is to be inserted. Nor would it be reasonable to vote on the main motion before acting on the amendment.

If you review the last paragraph, you will see that the logical order for acting on the pending questions is the opposite of the order in which the motions are made. And that is the general rule. A group of pending questions are voted on in the order opposite that in which they are introduced.

Now return to page 61 and select the correct answer.

CHAPTER III

Subsidiary Motions

After attending a few meetings, you will discover that there are things you want to do besides originating main motions and debating them. Some of those other actions have already been discussed in a general way — amending, referring to committee, calling the previous question, and so on. However, it has not yet been made clear when these motions may be made, to which other motions they may be applied, and which other motions may be applied to them.

The motions are listed below according to priority; each motion on the list takes precedence over all those listed beneath it.

Set time for continuation of the present session
    (also called, set time to adjourn to)
Adjourn
Recess
Question of privilege
Orders of the day
Table
Previous question
Limit or extend debate
Postpone to a fixed time
Commit (also called refer to committee)
Amend
Postpone indefinitely
Main motions

Don't worry if some of these are unfamiliar. You will get to know them well as you go through the following chapters. Now consider this situation.

CHAIRMAN: The question before the assembly is on limiting the debate on the pending question. Are you ready for the question?

MR. HOLMAN: Mr. Chairman!

CHAIRMAN: The chair recognizes Mr. Holman.

MR. HOLMAN: I move that the assembly recess for one hour.

Should the chair entertain Mr. Holman's motion?

Yes. **page 77**   No. **page 81**

[from page 77]

YOUR ANSWER: Yes.

Right. When the motion to adjourn is an incidental main motion, it yields to any motion higher on the list. Though we haven't included main motions on this list, it should be obvious that main motions are at the very bottom. Main motions, remember, yield to every other type of motion.

Moving upwards on the list, motions of the next class are called *subsidiary motions,* and to these this chapter is devoted. Here is the list again. The motions bracketed are those classed as subsidiary:

Set time for the continuation of the present session.
Adjourn
Recess
Question of privilege
Orders of the day

Subsidiary Motions
{
Table
Previous question
Limit or extend debate
Postpone to a fixed time
Commit
Amend
Postpone indefinitely
}

MAIN MOTION (original or incidental)

The purpose of all subsidiary motions is to modify the normal course of debating and voting on the motion to which they are applied. "Applied" is a key word. For a subsidiary motion to be entertained, it must apply or have reference to a pending motion. You cannot move to amend or postpone a motion that is not pending.

Now give the next question some thought. Which of the following statements is *false*?

When motion x may be applied to motion y, motion y may be said to yield to motion x.   **page 78**

When motion x yields to motion y, motion y must apply to motion x. **page 82**

Motion x may take precedence of motion y without applying to it. **page 87**

YOUR ANSWER: Yes.

It is true that the motion to recess takes precedence of the motion to amend. But just because recess takes precedence, you should not conclude that recess applies to amend. Actually, it is meaningless to say that recess applies to amend. What directions does the motion to recess give concerning the way in which the motion to amend should be handled — other than that debate should be put off for a few minutes while the members grab a bite to eat. But, it cannot really be said that the motion to recess applies to that to amend even in this limited sense. The motion to recess refers to the whole organization and would refer to any motion that happened to be pending at the time.

Now return to page 82 and select the better answer.

YOUR ANSWER: Yes.

Certainly. In Chapter II, you saw an example in which a motion to amend by setting a cost limit on the Christmas party was amended to change the cost originally proposed. That being true, it should be clear that the list of motions you saw earlier offers only a small piece of information; it shows only some of the motions that will be entertained when a given motion is on the floor. That list would suggest that it would be impossible to apply an amendment to an amendment. And it would more than suggest that an amendment could not be applied to a motion to commit. Neither of these conclusions is correct. Both amend and commit are amendable. Here is the list of subsidiary motions once again:

Table
Previous question
Limit or extend debate
Postpone at a fixed time
Commit
Amend
Postpone indefinitely

In some circumstances, a motion to amend can be entertained when a motion to limit debate is immediately pending. Assume that the motion is to limit the debate on the Christmas party motion. Which statement below describes a situation in which a motion to amend will be entertained while one to limit debate is immediately pending?

The motion to amend will be entertained if its purpose is to modify the proposed time limit on the debate. **page 80**

The motion to amend will be entertained if its purpose is to modify the main motion by setting an amount to be spent on the Christmas party. **page 84**

The motion to amend will be entertained in either case, but not if it actually refers to an intervening motion. **page 89**

YOUR ANSWER: Yes.

No. When a motion to postpone indefinitely is immediately pending, the only amendment that could be entertained is one applicable to the main motion. The motion to postpone indefinitely is not amendable. (Can you think of any germane way in which it could be amended?) Since, with the exception of the main motion, that to postpone indefinitely has the lowest priority, no other specialized motions could be pending when that to postpone indefinitely is on the floor. Because of its low priority, it couldn't be entertained if anything but a main motion was immediately pending.

So when the immediately pending question is a motion to postpone indefinitely, there are only two motions to which an amendment might conceivably apply. Of these two, the motion to postpone indefinitely is not amendable. The only choice left is. . . .

Now return to page 80 and select the correct answer.

76

[from page 85]

YOUR ANSWER: A motion to postpone indefinitely can be applied only to the amendment.

No. The motion to postpone indefinitely can be applied only to main motions. Moreover, it takes precedence only of main motions, so it couldn't even get on the floor once any other specialized motion was pending.

The sole purpose of the motion to postpone indefinitely is to kill a main question — to prevent a whole subject from being voted on. If no exception is taken to the main motion, it would be unreasonable to allow an effort to block amendment by indefinite postponement. If the main motion is allowed, surely the members should have the right to perfect it in any legal manner.

Now return to page 85 and select the correct answer.

YOUR ANSWER: Yes.

That is correct. Debate on a motion to limit debate could be interrupted by a motion to recess. The motion lower on the list yields to the higher one.

If the motion to recess passes, the recess is taken immediately, unless it is specified in the motion that the recess should be taken at a later hour. When the recess is over and the meeting is again called to order, the business is taken up exactly where it was interrupted (in this case, right in the middle of the debate on limiting debate).

If the motion to take a recess fails, the group returns immediately to the earlier question. (The chairman says: "The negative has it; the motion to recess fails. The question is now on limiting debate to five minutes per speaker on all pending questions. Are you now ready for the question?")

Motions are divided into five groups. Of these groups, two can be disposed of right away. These are the two types of main motions, called *original main motions* and *incidental main motions*.

Original main motions are those that propose some new action. The class of incidental main motions includes a group of specialized motions that are treated almost as though they were main motions. For example, there are situations — to be discussed later — in which the motion to adjourn is treated as a main motion.

This chapter and the two following are devoted to the other three classes of motions; these classes are called *subsidiary motions, privileged motions,* and *incidental motions*. The list on the first page of this chapter included subsidiary and privileged motions.

Here are the five classes:

Privileged motions   Incidental main motions
Incidental motions   Original main motions
Subsidiary motions

(There are also one or two motions that are not classified. The most important of these is that called *Reconsider;* this is discussed in the Parliamentary Dictionary in the latter half of the book. Study this motion only after you thoroughly know some of the others, because it won't be clear standing by itself.)

Now, if a motion to adjourn were being considered as an incidental main motion, would it yield to a motion to recess?

Yes. **page 72**   No. **page 86**

78

[*from page 72*]

YOUR ANSWER: When motion *x* may be applied to motion *y*, motion *y* may be said to yield to motion *x*.

In choosing this answer, you are saying that the above statement is false. It is not. If you may apply one motion to another — as you apply an amendment to a main motion — the motion that is applied takes precedence; that which has another applied to it is said to yield. You could not apply an amendment to a main motion if the main motion did not yield to the amendment. You have to be able to interrupt a motion to apply something to it.

Now return to page 72 and select the statement that is false.

YOUR ANSWER: No.

On the face of it, it would seem improbable that a type of motion may be applied to itself — or take precedence over itself. But all that means is that the chart of precedence does not tell the whole story. You have already seen, in Chapter II, that it is possible to apply an amendment to an immediately pending amendment. That is just what happened when the blank in the motion on limiting expenditures was filled in. You weren't being told a lie then. Go to page 88 now, and select the right answer; this apparent contradiction will be given more attention in a moment.

YOUR ANSWER: The motion to amend will be entertained if its purpose is to modify the proposed time limit on the debate.

You are correct.

Here is a list of motions again:

Table

Previous question (a)

Limit or extend debate (a)

Postpone to a fixed time (a)

Commit (a)   } Subsidiary Motions

Amend (a)

Postpone indefinitely

Main motions (a)

The motions marked (a) may have amendments applied to them. The only subsidiary motion listed above which cannot have an amendment applied to it is the motion to postpone indefinitely.

Furthermore, when any of the above subsidiary motions — except the motion to postpone indefinitely — is immediately pending, only an amendment to that immediately pending question will be entertained.

For example, suppose a motion to commit is on the floor. Then an amendment which would change the committee to which a measure would be committed is in order. However an amendment to the main motion would be out of order. An amendment to the main motion will be entertained only when the immediately pending motion is the main motion itself, or the motion to postpone indefinitely.

When the immediately pending question is *to table,* no amendments are in order. The motion to table is unamendable and an amendment to the main motion does not take precedence of the motion to table.

Unlike the motion to amend, the motion to postpone indefinitely can be applied only to main motions. You cannot indefinitely postpone an amendment or any other specialized motion.

When the immediately pending question is indefinite postponement of the main motion, may an amendment be entertained that does not apply to the main motion?

Yes.   **page 75**   No.   **page 85**

YOUR ANSWER: No.

Sorry, apparently you misread the description of the list. The motions in the list are ranked in order of precedence. That which has the highest priority is at the top. That with the least priority is at the bottom. A motion on the list takes precedence of any that are below it and yields to any that are above it.

Take a look at the list:

Set time for continuation of the present session
    (also called, set time to adjourn to)
Adjourn
Recess
Question of privilege
Orders of the day
Table
Previous question
Limit or extend debate
Postpone to a fixed time
Commit (also called refer to committee)
Amend
Postpone indefinitely
Main motions

Consider "the previous question." It takes precedence of:

Limit or extend debate
Postpone to a fixed time
Commit
Amend
Postpone indefinitely

That means, if any of the above motions are immediately pending, the previous question may be moved and debated before the debate and vote on the immediately pending question is completed. In short, we say these motions yield to or may be interrupted by the motion on the previous question.

The previous question, in turn, yields to the following motions:

Adjourn
Recess
Questions of privilege
Orders of the day
Table

Now return to page 71 and select the correct answer.

YOUR ANSWER: When motion *x* yields to motion *y*, motion *y* must apply to motion *x*.

Right. That is a false statement. It is possible that one motion may take precedence of another without applying to it. This is true of the motion to adjourn. A motion to have a Christmas party must yield to a motion to adjourn. But the motion to adjourn does not refer in any way to the Christmas party motion.

On the other hand, some motions make sense only as they apply to other motions. This is true of all subsidiary motions. Motions to postpone, amend, or commit can't stand on their own. You must postpone, amend, or commit something. Subsidiary motions may be applied to some motions and not to others. For instance, many motions cannot be amended — adjourn (except when it is an incidental main motion) is one such.

To have a full knowledge of the parliamentary status of a motion, you must know (a) to which motions it yields, (b) of which it takes precedence and where it is applicable, (c) the motions it can be applied to, and (d) the motions that can be applied to it.

In examining a motion, bear in mind that precedence and applicability are two different things. Just because a motion *x* takes precedence of a motion *y*, it doesn't follow that motion *x* applies to motion *y*. However, if motion *x* may be applied to motion *y*, motion *x* must have precedence. It would be meaningless to say that a motion to amend can be applied to a main motion if it were not also true that the main motion yields to the amendment.

Can the motion to recess be applied to the motion to amend?

Yes. **page 73**

No. **page 88**

YOUR ANSWER: Yes.

Certainly. Although this situation would rarely occur, a motion to postpone to a definite time has a higher priority than one to postpone indefinitely, and so would interrupt the debate on the latter.

The motion to postpone to a fixed time is debatable, but the debate can refer to the main motion only as necessary to discuss the wisdom of postponement. Definite postponement may be applied only to main motions, although if subsidiary motions are pending when the main motion is postponed, they, too, are postponed; all are brought up together when the time comes. The postponement should not be to a time later than the next regular session (but when the question is brought up again, it is possible to postpone again).

An item may be postponed to a date, to a date and hour, or until after an expected event has occurred. In the latter case, the question would be in order at the first meeting after the event.

To postpone a question usually makes it a *general order* for the specified time, that is, an order to the organization to take up that question as soon after the specified time as no business is pending. If an item is set as a general order for a specific session but not a specific hour, it is taken up in that session at the time set aside for general orders.

An item of business can be postponed as a *special order*. In that case, if the order specifies a time, the business is taken up at exactly the specified hour, even though other business is pending. A special order set for a given session is taken up at the point in the order of business set aside for special orders.

To make a special order requires a two-thirds vote. Postponement as a general order, on the other hand, requires only a majority. The two-thirds vote is required because the right to interrupt pending business requires suspension of the rules of order. Any permissible suspension of rules of order requires a two-thirds vote.

Can an amendment be applied to the motion to postpone to a fixed time?

Yes. **page 92**

No. **page 99**

YOUR ANSWER: The motion to amend will be entertained if its purpose is to modify the main motion by setting an amount to be spent on the Christmas party.

This answer is wrong. The principle that should have guided you is that which limits debate to the immediately pending question. With one exception, it may also be said that an amendment may be applied only to the immediately pending question.

If, while debating the motion to commit, it were possible to go back to an amendment on the main motion, the debate would be practically impossible to follow.

Now return to page 74 and select the correct answer.

YOUR ANSWER: No.

Right. When a motion to postpone indefinitely is immediately pending, a motion to amend will be entertained only if it applies to the pending main motion. The motion to postpone indefinitely is itself unamendable.

The purpose of a motion to postpone indefinitely is to kill the main motion to which it is applied. A motion "postponed indefinitely" cannot be reconsidered for a set length of time, depending on how frequently an organization meets. (The difference between a meeting and a session is covered under SESSION in the Parliamentary Dictionary at the back of this book.)

The motion to postpone indefinitely prevents reraising the motion to which it refers:

1. for the balance of the session during which it was postponed, if the organization has sessions less frequently than quarterly.

2. for the balance of the session during which it was postponed and for the following session in organizations that meet regularly more often than four times a year.

"Postpone indefinitely" is used by a member who is opposed to a motion and who feels that though a majority of the members do not actively favor it, they might be embarrassed to vote against it. Because of its financial condition, an organization may not want to donate money to a worthy cause and prefers not to go on record as refusing to contribute. By voting to postpone indefinitely, members kill the proposal without saying "no" to it.

Now consider this situation: It is proposed that your mayor be commended. While that question is pending, an amendment is proposed recommending that the mayor's salary be raised. With the amendment now pending, which of the following is true?

A motion to postpone indefinitely can be applied only to the amendment. **page 76**

A motion to postpone indefinitely can be applied only to the main motion. **page 90**

A motion to postpone indefinitely can be applied only to the main motion and the amendment together. **page 93**

None of the above is true. **page 98**

[*from page 77*]

YOUR ANSWER: No.

Under most circumstances, the motion to adjourn does have a very high privilege and would not yield to the motion to recess. However, there are times when the motion to adjourn is treated almost exactly as a main motion.

When the motion to adjourn is an incidental main motion, it will yield to motions that main motions yield to.

The motion to adjourn is treated as an incidental main motion when (1) it is made when no other business is pending, (2) when it is qualified — for instance, to adjourn at a specific time, and (3) when ending the meeting would have the effect of abolishing the assembly, because no provision has been made for further meeting. In any of these circumstances, a motion to adjourn is an incidental main motion and would yield to the motion to recess.

Now return to page 77 and select the correct answer.

YOUR ANSWER: A motion x may take precedence of another motion y without applying to it.

In choosing this answer, you are saying that the above statement is false. It is not.

Any motion except a main motion may interrupt consideration of some other motions. There are times when the interrupting motion applies to the interrupted motion. A motion to amend may apply to a main motion. But there are motions that may interrupt an immediately pending question though they have little or nothing to do with the immediately pending question. It would be meaningless to say that the motion to adjourn a meeting applies to an amendment to a main motion, yet the motion to adjourn may interrupt consideration of an amendment to a main motion.

Now return to page 72 and select a better answer.

[from page 82]

YOUR ANSWER: No.

That is correct. It is meaningless to say that the motion to recess can be *applied* to the motion to amend. You can't recess the motion to amend! You recess the meeting.

However, the fact that you cannot apply the motion to recess to an amendment does not necessarily mean that amendments will not yield to the motion to recess. In fact, amend does yield to recess. Or, to state it the other way round, recess takes precedence over amend. So, when there is an amendment on the floor, debate on it will be interrupted in favor of a motion to recess.

CHAIRMAN: Is there any more discussion on the pending amendment?

MR. WIRTH: Mr. Chairman!

CHAIRMAN: The chair recognizes Mr. Wirth.

MR. WIRTH: It is getting late, and if the rest of the members are in the position I am in, they had an early breakfast, so I move that we recess for lunch until 2 P.M.

MEMBER: Second.

CHAIRMAN: The question is on the motion to recess. Perhaps I should say, "All that are hungry, indicate by saying 'Aye.'"

As a general rule, it is probably better to complete pending business — if it won't take too long — before adjourning or recessing, but there will be times when it is reasonable to break up a debate for the convenience of the members.

Now, consider the following statement — is it true?

A motion to amend can be applied to a motion to amend.

Yes. **page 74**

No. **page 79**

YOUR ANSWER: The motion to amend will be entertained in either case, but not if it actually refers to an intervening motion.

Well, that was a safe guess. Given the choices you had, you couldn't help but be half right by choosing this one. And half right is exactly what you are.

Consider the stringent rules limiting debate to the immediately pending questions when you pick another answer.

Now return to page 74 and try again.

90

[from page 85]

YOUR ANSWER: A motion to postpone indefinitely can be applied only to the main motion.

That is a true statement in the abstract. It is not true when an amendment is already pending, as is the case here. A motion to postpone indefinitely does not take precedence of the motion to amend. Once a motion to amend, or any motion of higher rank has reached the floor, it is too late to propose to postpone the main motion indefinitely. The only chance to postpone indefinitely will occur at that point in the consideration when all subsidiary and other special motions have been disposed of and the main motion is once again immediately pending. That chance would normally occur just before the vote was to be taken on the main motion; however, the chance may occur several times if amendments or other subsidiary motions are proposed successively. It is possible that the stack of applied amendments might grow and shrink several times before the vote is finally taken on the main motion.

Now return to page 85 and select the correct answer.

YOUR ANSWER: No.

It may seem odd, but it would be perfectly all right to make the motion to postpone to a fixed time when that to postpone indefinitely is immediately pending. Postponement to a fixed time has higher priority, so the other will yield. Moreover, the purposes of the two motions, though their names are similar, are entirely different.

The intent of the motion to postpone indefinitely is to kill the main motion. The postponement to a fixed time means exactly what it says — no tricks about it. You move to postpone an issue to a definite time because you want to discuss it and act on it at that time.

If, when the motion to postpone indefinitely is pending, that to postpone to a fixed time is made, the intent is to offer a completely different suggestion for the disposition of the main motion. There is no duplication.

Now return to page 98 and select the correct answer.

92

[*from page 83*]

YOUR ANSWER: Yes.

Correct. The motion to postpone to a fixed time is amendable.

As a general rule, if there is a possibility of disagreement among those who favor a motion, it is amendable. An example makes this clear: there might be disagreement on the time to which a motion is to be postponed, or on whether the postponement should be as a general or as a special order. It is in these respects only that a motion to postpone may be amended, for an amendment must be germane to the motion being amended.

Here is a list of subsidiary motions once again:

Table

Previous question

Limit or extend debate

Postpone to a fixed time

Commit

Amend

Postpone indefinitely.

CHAIRMAN: The question is on the motion to organize a Christmas party.

MR. JENKINS: Mr. Chairman, Mr. Chairman!

CHAIRMAN: The chair recognizes Mr. Jenkins.

MR. JENKINS: I move that the question be postponed until the next meeting.

MEMBER: Second.

CHAIRMAN: It has been moved and seconded that the question on the Christmas party be postponed until the next meeting. Is there any discussion?

MR. HOLMAN: Mr. Chairman.

CHAIRMAN: The chair recognizes Mr. Holman.

MR. HOLMAN: Mr. Chairman, I feel that it would be a mistake to postpone this question as that would leave little time for making arrangements.

MR. NATHAN: Mr. Chairman.

CHAIRMAN: The chair recognizes Mr. Nathan.

MR. NATHAN: I move that we amend the Christmas party motion by adding the words, "and that the money shall be spent on food and gifts, rather than entertainment."

Should the chairman entertain Mr. Nathan's motion?

Yes.   page 97   No.   page 101

YOUR ANSWER: A motion to postpone indefinitely can be applied only to the main motion and the amendment together.

That's not true, and for two reasons.

First of all, the rule is clear-cut: the motion to postpone indefinitely can be applied only to main motions.

Second, the motion to postpone indefinitely has lower priority than the motion to amend and cannot be entertained when amend, or any higher-ranking motion is pending.

Now return to page 85 and select the correct answer.

94

[*from page 101*]

YOUR ANSWER: Yes.

Right. The motion to commit may be amended in areas in which those who favor the motion might disagree — issues such as these: To which committee should the question be referred? When should it report? Should a special committee be created? If so, how should its members be chosen? How many should there be?

A motion to commit may not only refer a question to committee, but may create the committee to which the referral is made. A motion to refer to a newly created committee would be made in much the same form as the main motion that created a committee to run a Christmas party: "I move to refer to a committee of five to be appointed by the chairman." A motion to commit may be applied only to a main motion, but, if adopted, it automatically sends any pending amendments to committee, too. If the motion to postpone indefinitely is pending, it is killed by a decision to commit. These are the only motions that can be affected by that to commit because commit takes precedence only of these motions.

Now, in which of the following situations would a motion to commit be entertained?

When the pending questions are: a main motion, a motion to postpone indefinitely, an amendment to the main motion, and an amendment to the amendment. **page 102**

When the pending questions are: a main motion, an amendment to the main motion, a motion to postpone to a fixed time, and an amendment to the postponement. **page 110**

YOUR ANSWER: Apply only to debate on the amendment; it would not apply to the main motion.

No. The rule here is a little tricky. The motions to extend debate and to limit debate have slightly different effects when they are not qualified. (To qualify in this sense means to specify the applicability of the motion. If you say, "I move to limit debate to five minutes per speaker," your motion is unqualified. If you say, "I move to limit debate to five minutes per speaker on all pending questions," your motion is qualified.)

Now what we had was an unqualified motion to limit debate. When such a motion is adopted, the limits that are set apply to the immediately pending question, but they also apply to any secondary motions that are made after the limit has been adopted, and that apply to the motion that was immediately pending. In other words, the rules assume that if you want to limit a debate on an issue, you want to limit the debate on all the matters that relate to that issue.

The effect of the motion to extend debate is different. When that motion is made without qualification, it is taken as applying only to the immediately pending question. Apparently it is assumed that no one would mean to make debate any longer than necessary.

Now return to page 105 and select the correct answer.

YOUR ANSWER: The limit, if adopted, would apply to the secondary questions arising from the main motion, as well as those arising from the amendment.

Correct. It is possible to specify the motions to which a limitation or extension apply. (Where there is no specification, these motions apply to no motions made prior to the immediately pending question.) But, unless specified to the contrary, a limitation on debate applies equally to subsequent secondary questions.

The time limits so far discussed have been on the lengths of individual speeches. It is also possible to describe a limitation or extension in such terms as: "I move that debate on this resolution end, and the question on it be put at 11:30 A.M." When the debate time is described in such terms, or as a period ("the debate shall last for forty-five minutes"), the motions to commit or to postpone the time limit pass by a simple majority vote. These motions can be entertained only if the time limit is reconsidered and defeated.

Since either limiting or extending debate suspends the rules, these motions require a two-thirds vote. The motions are amendable but not debatable.

Like the motion to limit or extend debate, the previous question applies only to the immediately pending question unless otherwise specified. It can be applied to any debatable question. It can also be applied to a series of questions, as long as the series is continuous and begins with the immediately pending question. Consider the situation below.

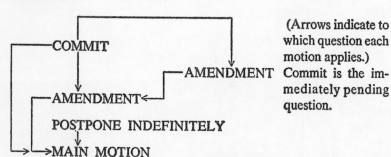

(Arrows indicate to which question each motion applies.) Commit is the immediately pending question.

Could the previous question be called to apply only to the motion to commit and to the first degree amendment?

Yes.   **page 109**   No.   **page 112**

YOUR ANSWER: Yes.

No. An amendment to a main motion may be entertained only when the immediately pending question is either the main motion itself, or a motion to postpone indefinitely. These are the only motions that yield to an amendment applicable to the main motion.

However, the motion to postpone to a fixed time is amendable, so it would be possible at this point to move an amendment to the immediately pending question.

Now return to page 92 and select the correct answer.

98

[from page 85]

YOUR ANSWER: None of the statements is true.

You are correct. Once an amendment is on the floor, the motion to postpone indefinitely cannot be entertained. The motion to postpone indefinitely can be applied only to main motions. And it takes precedence over none but main motions. Next to main motions, that to postpone indefinitely has lowest priority.

The motion to postpone indefinitely is occasionally put to one other use. *Postpone indefinitely* is debatable. And the debate on such a motion can cover the main motion (it is one of the few motions of which this is true). Thus, if the time limit is about to expire on debate of a controversial motion, a member wanting to continue the debate might move to postpone the main motion indefinitely.

He would use this strategy only if certain that the motion to postpone would fail, or if he felt that the main motion would fail without more time to present the arguments in its favor.

The reason for allowing full debate of the main motion while the motion to postpone indefinitely is pending is because of the effect of the postponing motion. Those who support the main motion are given time to convince others that the matter should be acted upon, not killed.

The motion to postpone to a fixed time is much more innocent. It is used when it's not convenient to decide a motion at the time it is made. It may not be convenient because other, more urgent business must be acted upon, or because it would be more satisfactory, in view of the motion itself, to wait until a later time. For instance, it might be moved to recommend to the city council a zoning variation at a time when the council's zoning committee is preparing a comprehensive zoning plan. A member might suggest that the organization wait with its recommendation until the zoning plan is published, so that the motion might be phrased to comment on the committee report.

Would a motion to postpone to a fixed time be entertained if a motion to postpone indefinitely were immediately pending?

Yes.   page 83

No.   page 91

YOUR ANSWER: No.

The question you must ask yourself is whether it would be reasonable to allow an amendment to the motion to postpone indefinitely. To answer that question, you should consider whether there is anything about a motion to postpone to a definite time that would be worth amending, or that members would be likely to want to amend.

It is clear that there is nothing naturally amendable about the motion to postpone indefinitely. A member is either for or against it. There is no qualification that could be made that would make it any more or less attractive.

The above cannot be said of the motion to postpone to a fixed time. Somebody has to say what the time will be. And among those who favor postponement, it is certainly reasonable to expect that there might be disagreement on the time factor.

Now return to page 83 and select the correct answer.

100

[from page 111]

YOUR ANSWER: The limit would apply only to secondary motions arising from the main motion.

You get half a point for that answer, because it is technically correct. Any secondary motion that is on the floor at any time can be said to arise out of the pending main motion. That includes the first-degree amendment and any motions that arise directly from it, as well as those more immediately associated with the main motion. None of those secondary motions would be around if it weren't for the main motion.

You only get half a point for this answer because of the implication that the limit would not apply to the secondary motions arising from the amendment. If the limit is applied to the main motion, it applies equally to all subsequent secondary motions arising from the main motion; that includes the amendment and amendments to the amendment.

Now return to page 111 and select an answer that more adequately describes what you want to say.

YOUR ANSWER: No.

That is correct. An amendment to a main motion is not in order when a postponement to a fixed time is on the floor. Had the amendment applied to the postponement rather than to the main motion, it would have been entertained.

The motion to postpone indefinitely does yield to amendment to the main motion. Passage of the indefinite postponement kills the main motion. There is always a presumption in favor of a motion, to the extent that those in favor of it are given the opportunity to try to get it approved. Allowing amendment — and other subsidiary motions — when the motion to postpone indefinitely is pending, allows proponents to perfect the main motion before the postponement is voted on.

Since the motion to amend was covered in Chapter II, we will not repeat it here. Instead, we'll go on to the motion called commit, which means refer to committee.

Committees may be created for two broad, general purposes. One is to act. (The proposal to create a committee to run a Christmas party is a proposal to create an action committee.) The other purpose is to make recommendations, just as if the committee were an individual member.

Sometimes committees initiate proposals. Other times, a motion made from the floor interests many members, but needs to be polished, changed in detail, or modified to effect a compromise between factions. It is common and sound practice to suggest that a disputed motion — and any pending amendments — be referred to a committee for study and recommendation. The committee also has the power to suggest amendments of its own, or to suggest substitute motions.

The motion to commit is used to send a pending motion and any pending amendments to a committee for the detailed review.

Would you think that the motion to commit is amendable?

Yes. **page 94**

No. **page 106**

YOUR ANSWER: When the pending motions are: a main motion, a motion to postpone indefinitely, an amendment to the main motion, and an amendment to the amendment.

Right. The fact that a second-degree amendment is pending doesn't prevent the motion to commit from being applied. The controlling factor is the motion that is being amended. In this case, the motion being amended is another amendment. An amendment to a main motion yields to the motion to commit. In the other case, the amendment was applied to a motion to postpone to a fixed time. That motion has higher rank than the motion to commit. The motion to commit cannot be entertained as long as the postponement to a fixed time is pending.

By now you should know enough about parliamentary terms to be introduced to the method of notation used in the Parliamentary Dictionary that takes up the latter half of this book.

In the Dictionary, each article describing a type of motion is accompanied by a table and a list of rules. The tables show of which motions each motion takes precedence, and to which motions each yields. Where it will be helpful, the chart is expanded to tell which motions may be applied to the subject motion, and to which the subject motion may be applied. Here, as a sample, is the table that accompanies the article on POSTPONE INDEFINITELY:

1. May be applied when these motions have brought a main question to the floor or when, they are treated as, main motions.	MAIN MOTION	POSTPONE INDEFINITELY	AMEND	COMMIT	POSTPONE TO FIXED TIME	LIMIT OR EXTEND DEBATE	PREVIOUS QUESTION	TABLE	ORDERS OF THE DAY	QUESTIONS OF PRIVILEGE	RECESS	ADJOURN	SET TIME TO ADJOURN TO
SUBJECT MOTION:													
YIELDS TO			●	●	●	●	●	●	●	●	●	●.	●
TAKES PRECEDENCE OF													
MAY BE APPLIED TO	●								1	1	1	1	1
MAY HAVE APPLIED TO IT						●	●						

Across the top are the dozen most common motions, with that of highest priority on the right. If you read across from the heading

"Yields to," you will find a black dot beneath each motion to which postpone indefinitely yields. There are no dots across from "Takes precedence of," because postpone indefinitely takes precedence only to the one motion of which it may be applied. This table is one of those in which a row entitled "May be applied to" is included.

The numbers that you will find sometimes in place of dots refer to brief notes given in the box in the upper left hand corner of the table. The rules mentioned in these brief notes are repeated in detail in the article.

Beneath the table, there is a list of rules and descriptive material about the motion. Here is that list as it is found in the article POST-PONE INDEFINITELY.

Class: Subsidiary Motion
Debatable: YES   *Vote:* MAJORITY
Amendable: NO   *Second needed:* NO
Reconsiderable: See *Notes*   *Can interrupt speaker:* NO

The meaning of these items should be clear, with the possible exception of *Reconsiderable* and *Can interrupt speaker.* A brief digression on these two items would be in order.

There is a motion called *reconsider.* It is used when a member, who voted on the winning side, changes his mind and would like to have the vote taken over again. (You can only ask to have a vote reconsidered on the same day it was taken. If applied to a debatable motion, the motion to reconsider reopens the debate on the contested issue. For more detail, see the article: RECONSIDER.) The motion to reconsider may be applied only to some motions, and to some of those only in certain circumstances. The motion to postpone indefinitely is one of those that can be reconsidered only in certain circumstances. That is the reason it says "See *Notes*" rather than "YES" or "NO" after *"Reconsiderable."* The notes referred to here are not those in the corner of the table but a group of notes found in the text beneath the chart and list. When you find such a notation after any of the items in the list of rules, look down through the text for the word *Notes.* Then look for a note with an appropriate heading on the left. In the article on postpone indefinitely, there is a note headed "Reconsider." There you will discover that the note

(Continued on page 104)

104

[*from page 103*]

on a motion to postpone indefinitely can be reconsidered only if the postponement had passed.

Most motions may be made only when no speaker is on the floor. There are motions of such urgency that you may interrupt a speaker to make them. That is another of the facts that you should be able to find quickly about any motion. As you can see, the motion to postpone indefinitely is not that urgent, for the answer is "NO" to *"Can interrupt a speaker."*

In the Parliamentary Dictionary, words that are all in capital letters are the titles of articles in the dictionary.

As you become adept in the use of the Parliamentary Dictionary, you will find it a valuable, permanent reference work, for it provides a great deal of information in easily accessible form. The generous use of subtitles in almost every article makes it possible for the user to discover at a glance just the information wanted.

To acquaint yourself further with the Parliamentary Dictionary, put your marker here and turn to the article on the page number listed below. Read the article and then return here.

LIMIT OR EXTEND DEBATE   page 281

After you have read the above article, go on to page 105.

NOTE: Before reaching this page, you should have read the article: LIMIT OR EXTEND DEBATE.

Now consider this situation. The principal question before the organization is whether to adopt a motion calling for creation of a committee to study and report upon traffic problems. An amendment is offered that would require the committee to make a supplemental survey of parking facilities in the business district. It soon becomes evident that lengthy debate on the amendment is likely, because of conflicting ideas on the boundaries of the downtown area and because of disputes on the value of the survey. A member moves that, in order to speed the consideration, debate should be limited to five minutes per speaker. If this motion is adopted, it will:

Apply only to the debate on the amendment; it would not apply to the main motion.   **page 95**

Apply to debate on the amendment and on the main motion.   **page 108**

Apply to debate on the amendment and secondary questions arising out of it, but not to the main motion.   **page 111**

[*from page 101*]

YOUR ANSWER: No.

You have overlooked a principle mentioned a few pages back. As a general rule, where there might be disagreement on the details of a motion among those who favor it, amendment is permissible. There are many details associated with the motion to commit that might cause disagreement. For example, two people equally in favor of referring a motion to a committee might disagree completely on which committee should be given the job. Should the arrangements for the annual dinner be referred to the special events committee or to the finance committee? Should a housing code amendment be referred to the housing and planning committee or to the legal committee? Or, whatever committee is chosen, should it report in a week, a month, or six months?

There is plenty of room for honest disagreement among the proponents of the motion to commit. That being the case, it is reasonable to assume that commit is amendable.

Now return to page 101 and select the correct answer.

YOUR ANSW   The motion would be held out of order.

Apparently   u read the article on limit and extend debate as if
it meant that   motion can be applied only to the immediately pending question   at is not true. If the motion is made without being
qualified —   is, without specifying the motions to which it applies
— it cannot   ly to any motion made earlier than the one immediately pendin   owever, there is nothing to stop you from specifying
that the lim   extension is to apply to any group of related questions, wheth   ade earlier or not yet made.

The only   quirement is that the limitation or extension should
apply to a   tions in the series. Once you select the earliest motion and t   atest motion to which the change is to apply, it must
also apply   all motions made in between the two extremes. That
is what is   ant by all the motions in the series.

Now r   n to page 111 and select the correct answer.

YOUR ANSWER: Apply to debate on the amendment and on the main motion.

No, when a motion limiting or extending debate is made without any qualification, it does not apply to anything that came to the floor prior to the immediately pending question. (To qualify in this sense means to specify the applicability of the motion. If you say, "I move to limit debate to five minutes per speaker," your motion is unqualified. If you say, "I move to limit debate to five minutes per speaker on all pending questions," your motion is qualified.)

Now, what we had was an unqualified motion to limit debate. When such a motion is adopted, the limits that are set apply to the immediately pending question, but they also apply to any secondary motions that are made after the limit has been adopted and that apply to the motion that was immediately pending. In other words, the rules assume that if you want to limit a debate on an issue, you want to limit the debate on all the matters that relate to that issue.

The effect of the motion to extend debate is different. When that motion is made without qualification, it is taken as applying only to the immediately pending question. Apparently it is assumed that no one would mean to make debate any longer than necessary.

Now return to page 105 and select the correct answer.

YOUR ANSWER: Yes.

No, the previous question could not be applied in that manner. To apply it only to the motion to commit and to the first-degree amendment would leave out the second-degree amendment, hence leaving a gap in the series.

When the pending motions are voted on, it will be in the reverse order to which they were made. So the first motion will be that to commit. Second will be the second-degree amendment. That must be disposed of before a vote can be taken on the first-degree amendment. Only then will the first-degree amendment be voted on. If the previous question were applied only to commit and to the first-degree amendment, the second-degree amendment would still be open for debate when it came up. That is not permitted.

The previous question must apply to a complete series, each of which will be voted on immediately, in order, and without debate.

Now return to page 96 and select the correct answer.

110

YOUR ANSWER: When the pending questions are: a main motion, an amendment to the main motion, a motion to postpone to a fixed time, and an amendment to the postponement.

You were taken in by the amendment that is immediately pending — the one to the motion to postpone to a fixed time. The motion to commit takes precedence only of an amendment to a main motion. When the amendment applies to a motion of higher precedence than that to commit, the motion to commit cannot be entertained. The motion to postpone to a fixed time is the pending motion of highest precedence. It is controlling.

The motion called *set time for continuation of the present session* (or *to set a time to adjourn to*) is an amendable motion, but it has a higher rank than any other. It would clearly confuse parliamentary proceedings if it were possible to move to commit a main motion while the motion *to set a time to adjourn to* was on the floor. That, however, is what would follow if you conclude that the amendment to a specialized motion, rather than the specialized motion itself, determines the parliamentary situation.

Now return to page 94 and select the correct answer.

YOUR ANSWER: Apply to debate on the amendment and secondary questions arising out of it, but not to the main motion.

Correct. When an unqualified motion is made either to limit or to extend debate, it applies to no motion made earlier than the one immediately pending. However, a motion to limit debate, even when unqualified, applies to all secondary questions that later arise from the immediately pending question. This is not true of a motion to extend debate — when unqualified, this motion applies only to the immediately pending question.

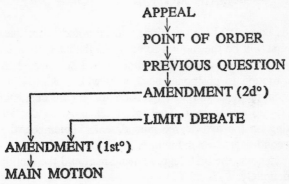

APPEAL
↓
POINT OF ORDER
↓
PREVIOUS QUESTION
↓
——————————————— AMENDMENT (2d°)

————————————— LIMIT DEBATE

AMENDMENT (1st°)
↓
MAIN MOTION

The above illustration shows an amendment of the first degree immediately pending, after which a motion to limit debate was made and adopted. Immediately thereafter, an amendment to the amendment (a second-degree amendment) was proposed during which a member moved the previous question. Assume that someone thought this was incorrectly done and raised a point of order. The chairman disagreed and the member appealed. That is where things stand in the diagram. The time limit set on the amendment applies to debatable questions arising from it.

Had the motion been to extend rather than limit debate, the extension would apply only to debate directly concerned with the first-degree amendment. The second-degree amendment, and all above it, would be debated — where debatable — within the regular limits.

If, while the amendment on parking lots was pending, a member moved to limit debate on the main motion as well as the amendment:

The limit, if adopted, would apply to secondary questions arising from the main motion, as well as those arising from the amendment. **page 96**

The limit, if adopted, would apply only to secondary questions arising from the main motion. **page 100**

The motion would be held out of order. **page 107**

112

[*from page 96*]

YOUR ANSWER: No.

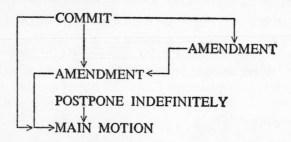

That is correct. These questions will be voted on in the following order. First will be the motion to commit. If that motion is adopted, the first- and second-degree amendments will be referred to committee (the motion to postpone indefinitely will be killed). If the motion to commit fails, the next question to be considered will be the second-degree amendment. That, after all, must be disposed of before voting on the first-degree amendment. Remember, the purpose of the second-degree amendment is to perfect the first-degree amendment. Then come the first-degree amendment and the motion to postpone indefinitely.

The previous question must apply to a continuous series of questions. As soon as one question is voted on, the next is called to a vote. If the previous question were applied only to the motions to commit and the first-degree amendment, the second-degree amendment would be open to debate once the motion to commit was voted. Then the previous question would not apply to a continuous series.

If, in the situation above, the motion for the previous question was unqualified, and if it failed.

The organization would immediately return to debate on the motion to commit. **page 116**

The organization would immediately return to debate on the second-degree amendment. **page 120**

YOUR ANSWER: Yes, the chairman should rule Mr. Jenkins out of order.

You are correct. The motion to table is undebatable. Mr. Jenkins had no business starting to argue against the motion to table.

Here, for review purposes, is the order of precedence of the subsidiary motions:

Table
Previous question
Limit or extend debate
Postpone to a fixed time
Commit
Amend
Postpone indefinitely

When you were first shown the list of basic motions, you will recall that there were five with higher priority than the seven subsidiary motions. This high-priority group is called privileged motions. Chapter IV will cover the privileged motions.

Chapter IV begins on page 114.

CHAPTER IV

Privileged Motions

The motions called privileged have a priority higher than any other class. Unlike subsidiary motions, which may be entertained only when applicable to pending business, privileged motions may be raised at any time. They have nothing to do with the business that is pending.

Because these motions have such high privilege, they are undebatable. The right to debate is incompatible with high privilege. It isn't hard to see why: if a privileged motion was debatable, it would be possible to harass a meeting by continually interrupting pending business to debate, for instance, whether or not to adjourn.

Even with the no-debate restriction, the special privilege of these motions is subject to abuse. Once admitted as questions, they must be voted upon, which takes time and disrupts the continuity of debate. Here is the list of motions again, with the privileged motions indicated.

PRIVILEGED MOTIONS
- Set time for continuation of the present session
- Adjourn
- Recess
- Questions of privilege
- Orders of the day

SUBSIDIARY MOTIONS
- Table
- Previous question
- Limit or extend debate
- Postpone to a fixed time
- Commit
- Amend
- Postpone indefinitely

MAIN MOTIONS

The privileged motion of least priority is:

Set time for continuation of the present session. **page 119**
Orders of the day. **page 122**

YOUR ANSWER: The order referred to is a program.

No. Both the program and special orders are considered sufficiently urgent that to remind the group either has been violated, an interruption is justified. Keep in mind that a program or a special order should be taken up exactly at the designated time, even if it is necessary either to complete pending business abruptly and bring it to a vote, or to abandon pending business until the orders are completed. This is not true of a general order. General orders are taken up as soon after the designated time as no business is pending.

In the case of a program or general orders, the decision whether to interrupt or hastily complete pending business will depend upon the time schedule for the balance of the session. If the time for the entire session is designated to other specific business, there will be no opportunity to return to the business pending when the orders are called for. In that case, the pending business should be brought to a vote immediately after the motion for orders of the day is acted upon. If there is nothing scheduled following the orders, the chair should simply interrupt the pending business and resume its consideration later.

Now return to page 123 and select the correct answer.

116

[*from page 112*]

YOUR ANSWER: The organization would immediately return to debate on the motion to commit.

Right. That would be true if the previous question failed, whether or not it had been qualified.

The last of the subsidiary motions is that to *table*. The motion to table is really a postponement of indefinite duration. However, unlike the motion with name *postpone indefinitely,* the motion to table is not intended to and should not be used to kill the motion to which it is applied. The purpose of the motion to table is to lay aside the pending main motion, reserving the right to bring it back to the floor at a more convenient time. A tabled motion is brought back to the floor by the motion called *take from the table.*

The motion to table can be applied (1) to main motions, (2) to other motions treated as main motions, and (3) to some appeals. (A point of order may refer to individual behavior, to a parliamentary technicality, or to an issue that casts doubt on the propriety of the immediately pending question. An appeal on a point of order that casts a shadow over the pending motion cannot be tabled. If it were possible to table such an appeal, the organization would be in the position of having to go ahead and act on a motion that might later be determined as inappropriate or illegal.)

Now put your marker here and read the articles titled TABLE and TAKE FROM THE TABLE in the Parliamentary Dictionary; then return to the indicated page.

TABLE   page 333
TAKE FROM THE TABLE   page 334

After you have read these articles go on to page 117.

NOTE: Before reaching this page, you should have read the articles:

TABLE
TAKE FROM THE TABLE

Now consider the following exchange.

CHAIRMAN: The question is whether to table the motion on the traffic
   survey. . . .
MR. JENKINS: Mr. Chairman, Mr. Chairman!
CHAIRMAN: The chair recognizes Mr. Jenkins.
MR. JENKINS: I don't think we should consider tabling this important
   issue.
MR. HOLMAN: Call the speaker to order!

Should the chairman rule that Mr. Jenkins is out of order?

Yes.   **page 113**

No.   **page 121**

118

[*from page 123*]

YOUR ANSWER: The order referred to is a general order.

Right. If the orders of the day are general orders, the call for orders of the day may be made only when there is no one on the floor, though it may be made while business is pending.

Consider this situation. The organization is in the midst of a debate at its annual convention. The debate is on whether or not to change the name of the organization. It is 11:05 and a member has just finished speaking. Eleven o'clock was the hour scheduled to begin a detailed program for debate on a constitutional amendment. The chairman apparently has not noticed the hour.

MR. HOLMAN: Mr. Chairman.

CHAIRMAN: The chair recognizes Mr. Holman.

MR. HOLMAN: I move the orders of the day.

CHAIRMAN: The question is on the orders of the day; all those in favor, say "Aye."

MEMBERS: Aye!

CHAIRMAN: Those opposed, "No."

MEMBERS: No!

CHAIRMAN: There not being two thirds for the negative, the motion carries.

On the basis of what you have read, and on your own reasoning, what do you think the chairman should do at this point?

State that the question is now on the amendment scheduled for 11:00.
page 124

Call for a vote on the motion to change the name.   **page 130**

Announce that the organization shall move to the matter scheduled for 11:00 as soon as the pending business is completed.   **page 134**

YOUR ANSWER: Set time for continuation of the present session.

You seem to have the table confused. The highest priority is at the top, the lowest at the bottom. That should be easy to get straight.

The motion you've chosen, set time for continuation of the present session (also called set a time to adjourn to), is generally described as the motion of very highest priority. There are a few motions, to be discussed in Chapter V, that may be applied to this motion, but those to which set a time to adjourn to yields are of a sort that may be applied to any motion.

However, all main, incidental main, subsidiary, and all other privileged motions yield when this motion is properly made.

Now return to page 114 and keep top and bottom straight.

YOUR ANSWER: The organization would immediately return to debate on the second-degree amendment.

Remember, the vote on the previous question has no effect on the motion to which it is applied. Its only purpose is to determine whether the debate on the pending question should end. If the previous question is defeated, the debate on the motion to which it referred is taken up again where it was abandoned when interrupted by the previous-question motion. If the previous question is carried, then a vote is immediately taken on the question or questions to which it was applied.

It is impossible to skip to the second-degree amendment, because the failure of the previous question did not dispose of the motion to commit. Commit is still pending and must be acted upon.

Now return to page 112 and select the correct answer.

YOUR ANSWER: No, the chairman should not rule that Mr. Jenkins is out of order.

Your answer is incorrect.

The motion to table is undebatable. Mr. Jenkins might have been allowed to speak had he intended to do something besides try to debate the motion to table. But it was evident from what he began to say that debate the motion to table was exactly what he wanted to do.

Among the things he could do at this point would be to move any of the motions higher on the list than table, raise a point of order, ask for information, or call for a division of the assembly, etc.

Now return to page 117 and select the correct answer.

122

[from page 114]

YOUR ANSWER: Orders of the day.

Correct. The motion for orders of the day has the lowest priority among the privileged motions. If the motion for orders of the day is pending, any other privileged motion may be entertained. Like subsidiary motions, privileged motions have rank among themselves, the one of highest privilege being the one highest on the list.

The motion entitled orders of the day is more fully described as a call for the orders of the day — a call for the group to return to its proper schedule of business.

The orders of the day consist of up to three parts. The first is the program. (A program specifies the order in which business is to be covered and the time allotted to each item. Programs are usually adopted for large group meetings and for groups which meet infrequently and have a great deal of business to be covered in a short time. When an organization has sessions more often than quarterly, the formality of adopting a program is usually unnecessary.) The second part of the orders of the day is the general orders postponed to that day. The third part is the special orders postponed to that day.

A call for a return to the orders of the day may be made only when the orders have been violated. Since a refusal to follow the orders of the day is a suspension of the rules, it requires a vote of only one third of the members voting plus one in favor of the motion to force a return to the scheduled business. Conversely, two thirds is necessary to continue with business in contradiction to the orders.

Now note down the articles listed below, put your marker here, and read these articles.

ORDERS   page 291

ORDERS OF THE DAY, CALL FOR   page 293

PROGRAM   page 307

After you have read the above articles, go on to page 123.

NOTE: Before reaching this page, you should have read the articles:
ORDERS
ORDERS OF THE DAY, CALL FOR
PROGRAM

There are times when a call for orders of the day cannot interrupt a speaker. This motion cannot interrupt a speaker when:

The order referred to is a program. **page 115**

The order referred to is a general order. **page 118**

The order referred to is a special order. **page 128**

YOUR ANSWER: State that the question is now on the amendment scheduled for 11:00.

If the chairman did that, the organization would most likely run into trouble later on. It is possible to interrupt debate on a pending question in favor of a special order, with the intention of returning to the pending business when the special order is completed. However, this is generally not practical when the order in question is a program. The program was described as "detailed," so it is reasonable to assume that the program accounts for the rest of the time available at the session. Consequently, there is little likelihood that there would be time to return later to the pending question.

For the chairman to state the question on the business scheduled for 11 A.M. without disposing of the pending business in some manner would almost certainly leave that pending business dangling. That kind of situation is to be avoided. Every motion introduced should be disposed of in some appropriate manner.

Now return to page 118 and select the correct answer.

YOUR ANSWER: The debate on the interrupted motion would be taken up immediately after the meeting opened.

You have forgotten the minutes. An adjourned meeting takes up the program or order of business where it was left off at the earlier meeting, with the exception that the minutes should be read.

It is required that the minutes be read as the first item of business at any meeting, in order to determine that the record of the previous meeting is accurate. This requirement may be skipped over by a motion to dispense with the minutes. However, it is then permissible to call up the minutes for reading and approval at any time when no business is pending. At the latest, the minutes should be read at the beginning of the meeting following the one at which they were temporarily put aside (it would be possible, then, to dispense with both sets of minutes to a still later meeting, but this is not good policy (a) because as time passes, corrections will become less accurate, and (b) the point will be reached where the reading of the back minutes becomes a very tedious and time-consuming activity).

In any case, if the minutes are not read, there will at least be a motion to dispense with them intervening between the call to order and the taking up of business left pending at the last meeting.

Now return to page 132 and select the correct answer.

126

[from page 129]

YOUR ANSWER: Yes.

Not unless you make some assumptions.

An adjournment sine die is not privileged when it would abolish an assembly. In saying yes, the motion should be entertained, you are assuming that there is some arrangement for the organization to meet again. That may or may not be true. There are three situations in which an assembly would be abolished by an adjournment sine die. Consider the list below and ask yourself if you know whether any are applicable.

1. A rally, mass meeting, or *ad hoc* (special) meeting. The assembly consists of the people in attendance at such meetings. Whatever the name, these meetings are of temporary organizations, without constitution. Therefore, if such an assembly adjourns sine die, there is no provision for the same group to meet again.

2. A first meeting of an organization, prior to the adoption of a constitution. The constitution, once adopted, would provide for regular future meetings of the members — the assembly. But before a constitution is adopted, an adjournment sine die would have the effect of abolishing the assembly, unless someone were empowered by the assembly to call it together again.

3. A meeting of a body of delegates or representatives when there is no way of bringing the same delegates together again before the next scheduled session. This situation usually occurs where there is a national group whose governing body is an annual convention of delegates. The assembly consists of one set of elected delegates. The delegates elected for the next convention form a different assembly. If there is no provision for calling the same assembly together again, an adjournment sine die is not privileged.

Now return to page 129 and select the correct answer.

YOUR ANSWER: Yes.

Certainly. The pending motion is an amendment. There is no reason why recess should not be proposed during the course of a debate of an amendment.

Now, back to the meeting. The main motion is pending and an amendment to it is immediately pending. The motion to recess has failed and debate is proceeding. You feel that it is desirable to pass over to another question on the agenda leaving debate on the pending question to be finished afterwards.

Which motion would you make?

Postpone to a fixed time.   **page 135**

Postpone indefinitely.   **page 140**

Table.   **page 144**

[*from page 123*]

YOUR ANSWER: The order referred to is a special order.

No. Both the program and special orders are considered sufficiently urgent that to remind the group either has been violated, an interruption is justified. Keep in mind that a program or a special order should be taken up exactly at the designated time, even if it is necessary either to complete pending business abruptly and bring it to a vote, or to abandon pending business until the orders are completed. This is not true of a general order. General orders are taken up as soon after the designated time as no business is pending.

In the case of a program or general orders, the decision whether to interrupt or hastily complete pending business will depend upon the time schedule for the balance of the session. If the time for the entire session is designated to other specific business, there will be no opportunity to return to the business pending when the orders are called for. In that case, the pending business should be brought to a vote immediately after the motion for orders of the day is acted upon. If there is nothing scheduled following the orders, the chair should simply interrupt the pending business and resume its consideration later.

Now return to page 123 and select the correct answer.

YOUR ANSWER: The debate on the interrupted question would be taken up immediately after the reading of the minutes.

That is correct. An adjourned meeting takes up the same order of business as the earlier meeting, at the point at which the business was broken off. The only thing that intervenes is the reading and approval of the minutes, unless they are dispensed with. In that case, the motion to dispense with the minutes intervenes.

You are at the adjourned meeting of the plumbing contractors at which the proposal to supply consultative services on advertising to members is being considered.

CHAIRMAN: Is there any more debate on the motion to direct the executive secretary to provide consultation on members' advertising problems?

MR. CARL: I move that the motion be amended as follows: and that the executive secretary be permitted to spend up to $1,000 in the coming year for the services of an advertising firm and for the publication of such literature as will be approved by the Executive Committee.

MEMBER: Second.

CHAIRMAN: The question is now on Mr. Carl's amendment; is there any discussion?

After some discussion:

MR. JASPERS: This discussion has gone on for some time. I move that we adjourn.

Should the chairman entertain this motion?

Yes.   **page 126**

No.   **page 133**

There is not enough information to tell.   **page 138**

130

[*from page 118*]

YOUR ANSWER: Call for a vote on the motion to change the name.

That's correct. An adopted program has much the same status as a special order and when there is a program, the time of the convention is normally all assigned. It would not be possible to return to the pending question at a later time — that time is assigned, too — so it is necessary to dispose of the pending question immediately.

The chair might also entertain motions to table, commit, or postpone in lieu of the vote, but no debate should be allowed.

When the orders of the day referred to is a special order, it is not usually necessary to take a vote on the pending question, for the debate on the pending question can be taken up again when the special order is disposed of.

When a member calls for the orders of the day, he should not identify the business that would be brought up. He merely says, "I move the orders of the day," or, "Call for the orders of the day."

The motion to adjourn has the second-highest priority. To adjourn means to bring a meeting to an end. There are two ways of adjourning, with and without day. (An adjournment without day is called an adjournment *sine die*.) To adjourn without day means to adjourn without having set a date for a subsequent meeting of the same session. And adjournment sine die, when there is no provision for a subsequent meeting, ends the session. The next meeting of the organization will be the next one regularly called for by the organization's constitution.

Adjournment usually is privileged. There are exceptions, however. Adjourn is not privileged at a rally or at the first meeting of a new organization (where a constitution has not been adopted) because the effect would be to abolish the group. It is also not privileged in the last meeting of a session, because the effect would be to end the session. These are cases — as noted in Chapter III — when the motion to adjourn is treated as an incidental main motion, for example, if it is introduced when no other business is pending.

Now note the articles listed below and the page numbers following. When you have read the articles, turn to the indicated page.

DELEGATE   page 271
ASSEMBLY   page 248
ADJOURN, SET TIME TO, and ADJOURN TO,
                                    Continued on page 131.

After you have read these articles, go on to page 132.

132
[*from page 131*]

NOTE: Before reaching this page, you should have read the articles:
DELEGATE
ASSEMBLY
ADJOURN, SET TIME TO, and ADJOURN TO,
    SET TIME TO
ADJOURN REGULAR MEETING OF A PERMANENT
    ORGANIZATION
ADJOURN IN SPECIAL CIRCUMSTANCES
SET TIME FOR CONTINUATION OF PRESENT
    SESSION
ADJOURNED MEETING
SINE DIE
RECESS
PRIVILEGE, QUESTION OF

At a meeting of plumbing contractors, during the debate on a motion to provide consultative services on advertising to members, a meeting is adjourned to reconvene the next day. At the adjourned meeting, what would you expect to happen?

The debate on the interrupted motion would be taken up immediately after the meeting opened.   **page 125**

The debate on the interrupted motion would take place immediately after the reading of the minutes.   **page 129**

The debate on the interrupted question would be taken up under the heading of old business, after reports and special orders.   **page 136**

YOUR ANSWER: No.

Not unless you make some assumptions.

An adjournment sine die is privileged only when it would not abolish the assembly. In saying it would not be entertained here, you are saying that the adjournment would abolish the assembly. There are three situations in which that would be the result of an adjournment sine die. They are listed below. Consider the list and decide whether you know for sure that any of them are applicable to the situation at hand.

1. A rally, mass meeting, or *ad hoc* (special) meeting. The assembly consists of the people in attendance at such meetings. Whatever the name, these meetings are of temporary organizations, without constitution. Therefore, if such an assembly adjourns sine die, there is no provision for the same group to meet again.

2. A first meeting of an organization, prior to the adoption of a constitution. The constitution, once adopted, would provide for regular future meetings of the members — the assembly. But before a constitution is adopted, an adjournment sine die would have the effect of abolishing the assembly, unless someone were empowered by the assembly to call it together again.

3. A meeting of a body of delegates or representatives when there is no way of bringing the same delegates together again before the next scheduled session. This situation usually occurs where there is a national group whose governing body is an annual convention of delegates. The assembly consists of one set of elected delegates. The delegates elected for the convention form a different assembly. If there is no provision for calling the same assembly together again, an adjournment sine die is not privileged.

Now return to page 129 and select the correct answer.

134

[*from page 118*]

YOUR ANSWER: Announce that the organization shall move to the matter scheduled for 11:00 as soon as the pending business is completed.

No. The chairman could not do that on his own. If the matter scheduled for 11:00 was a general order, that would be the correct procedure, for general orders are taken up as soon after the appointed time as there is no business pending. But special orders and the program must be taken up at the scheduled hour, regardless of other business pending.

To ignore special orders or a program is a violation of rules and to do so requires a suspension of the rules. As you know, a suspension of the rules requires a two-thirds vote. In this case, since the question is stated in reverse order, the two thirds must be on the negative side.

Now return to page 118 and select the correct answer.

YOUR ANSWER: Postpone to a fixed time.

That would be best. You don't want to kill the motion, as would happen with indefinite postponement. (In any case, with an amendment on the floor, indefinite postponement would be out of order.) Neither do you want to gamble on passage of a motion to take from the table to get the motion back before the meeting again. You just want to get the next matter on the agenda settled right away. So you move to postpone the consultative services motion until action is taken on the next matter. Then the question on consultative services is stated automatically by the chairman, immediately after the next item on the agenda is disposed of.

At this point, the following motions are pending:

Postpone to a fixed time

Amendment

Main motion.

At the previous meeting it was decided to postpone as a general order, until 9:30 at this adjourned meeting, a motion to determine in which cities the executive board would meet during the next year. While a member is speaking about the postponement, you notice that it is past 9:30. Should you call for the orders of the day immediately or wait until the speaker has completed his remarks?

Rise immediately. **page 139**

Wait. **page 142**

136

[*from page 132*]

YOUR ANSWER: The debate on the interrupted motion would be taken up under the heading of old business, after reports and special orders.

Apparently you don't have the meeting, session, and adjourned meeting straight in your mind yet.

A meeting is an assembly of members of an organization that lasts from an opening by a call to order to a closing by adjournment, without any interruption, except, possibly, for a recess. The word meeting gives no clear indication of how much business was carried on — whether or not a complete order of business, from minutes to new business, was covered.

A session covers a complete order of business, from the reading of the minutes to the consideration of new business. When an organization meets infrequently — yearly — there may be more business than can be covered in a single meeting. In that case, the annual session may last several meetings. Each meeting covers only a portion of one complete order of business, taking up where the previous one left off and stopping when time is expired or the meeting is adjourned.

An adjourned meeting is a later meeting of a session consisting of more than one meeting. Consequently, an adjourned meeting will not follow a complete order of business. With the exception of certain necessary preliminaries, an adjourned meeting begins its business where the previous meeting left off.

Now return to page 132 and select the correct answer.

YOUR ANSWER: No, the orders of the day are privileged.

It is true that the motion for the orders of the day is privileged. However, the conclusion is not correct. Once the motion has passed bringing the ordered question to the floor, the question has only its normal parliamentary status. The privilege applies to getting the question to the floor, not to keeping it there.

Once on the floor, the scheduled business may have applied to it any motion that would be applicable had the business been introduced as a main motion when no other business was pending.

Now return to page 142 and select the correct answer.

YOUR ANSWER: There is not enough information to tell.

You are correct. You don't know whether a motion sine die would abolish the assembly. That is the test that would determine whether the motion should be entertained. If the adjournment would abolish the session, it can be considered only as a debatable motion — an incidental main motion — and can be entertained only when no business is pending.

CHAIRMAN: I cannot entertain that motion. There is no provision for reconvening this assembly, as this is the last scheduled meeting of this convention and there is no way to call a special meeting.

MR. JASPERS: Mr. Chairman!

CHAIRMAN: Unless it is urgent, Mr. Jaspers, I would like to finish what I was saying. Since an adjournment sine die would abolish this assembly, I can entertain that motion when no other business is pending. The chair will now recognize Mr. Jaspers.

MR. JASPERS: Thank you. I certainly did not intend to abolish the assembly. I just think we need a rest from the discussion. To that end, I would like to move, instead, that we recess for 45 minutes.

Should the chairman entertain that motion?

Yes.   **page 127**

No.   **page 149**

YOUR ANSWER: Rise immediately.

No. If you know that the business scheduled for 9:30 is a general order, you should wait until the speaker is finished. Only when the orders of the day are a program or a special order can you interrupt a speaker to call for the orders of the day.

However, if you should forget the nature of the order and proceed with the interruption, the chair would simply tell you that your motion is out of order and that you should wait until the speaker is finished.

A call to return to a general order is not allowed to interrupt a speaker because the assembly cannot turn to the general order until the pending business is disposed of, anyway. A special order or a program must be taken up at the scheduled time, even if a speaker is interrupted to do so, unless there is a two-thirds vote to the contrary.

Now return to page 135 and select the correct answer.

[*from page 127*]

YOUR ANSWER: Postpone indefinitely.

You would not choose that motion if your intent was to get back to the pending motion. Postpone indefinitely is an innocent-sounding title, but the intent of that motion is to kill the motion to which it is applied. Once the motion to postpone another indefinitely has passed, it is very difficult to bring the pending question back.

There is another reason, too. The motion to postpone indefinitely is not in order when an amendment is pending. The motion to postpone indefinitely has very low priority. It can be entertained only while the main motion alone is pending. It takes precedence of no other motion.

Now return to page 127 and select the correct answer.

YOUR ANSWER: Agree with Mr. Jaspers and allow Mr. Jacobs to resume the floor.

No, Mr. Jaspers seems always to say the wrong thing. The request to have non-members removed from the hall is a question of privilege. And a question of privilege is a privileged motion. (The terms are a little confusing, so try to keep them straight. Privileged motions are the class of motions with highest parliamentary priority. One of the privileged motions is called question of privilege. A question of privilege is a motion concerning the rights of members or of the assembly. The right to hold a meeting in secret is a right of the assembly.)

A question of privilege can alway interrupt a speaker on a question of lower priority. However, it is not always permissible to take action on the question of privilege right away. The goal is to interrupt the speaker as little as necessary. If the matter may be simply decided by the chairman — by his directing that a window be closed — or if the matter is quite urgent, even though requiring a vote, the decision should be made before the speaker resumes.

Since the subject motion is privileged, it could be brought up while a motion to commit is pending. The only point at issue can be whether action should be taken on the question of privilege before the speaker completes his presentation. That decision can be made only on the facts of the individual case. A question of privilege can interrupt a speaker when the matter is sufficiently urgent, otherwise a decision on the question of privilege waits until the interrupted speaker has finished.

In this situation, it is clear that the question raised is urgent. Mr. Peterson is concerned to have a matter debated privately. Mr. Jacobs has already begun to debate the matter that Mr. Peterson is worried about. Surely then, it would be appropriate to have the decision on the question of privilege made before Mr. Jacobs resumes his speech.

Now return to page 147 and select the correct answer.

142

[*from page 135*]

YOUR ANSWER: Wait.

You're right. You may interrupt the speaker only if the orders of the day are special orders or an adopted program. The call for orders of the day is undebatable, so the chairman must put the question as soon as the orders are called for. No second is required.

CHAIRMAN: The orders of the day have been called for. I noticed that it was past 9:30, but the group seemed interested in completing deliberation on this motion we've been at for so long. If we adopt the call, we will have to interrupt this discussion again. But it takes a two-thirds vote to continue the present debate. Are you ready for the question?

MR. CARL: Mr. Chairman.

CHAIRMAN: Yes, Mr. Carl.

MR. CARL: I move the vote be taken by a standing count.

CHAIRMAN: If there is no objection, the vote will be taken by a standing count. (Pause) There being no objection, we shall proceed with the vote. All those in favor of proceeding to the orders of the day, please stand and remain standing until counted. (The chairman counts.) You may be seated. All those opposed, please stand and remain standing until counted. (The chairman counts.) Be seated. The vote is 27 affirmative, 42 opposed. That means 69 were voting. 24 votes would have been sufficient to carry the motion, so the affirmative has it. The question is now on this motion, "That the executive committee shall hold its quarterly meetings during the coming year, one each in New York, Chicago, and San Francisco, and the last meeting at the site of the next annual convention."

Is there any way the members can return immediately to the question that was interrupted by the orders of the day?

No, the orders of the day are privileged. **page 137**

Yes, motions to table or postpone might be made. **page 147**

YOUR ANSWER: He calls the vote on the motion to postpone.

Apparently you forgot that the previous question requires a two-thirds vote. The effect this motion has of cutting off debate is a suspension of the rules. A vote of 35 for, and 31 against, is considerably less than the required two thirds, even though more than a majority favor the previous question.

There were 66 votes cast. To pass the previous question would require at least 44 affirmative votes. Of 66 votes, only 23 are required to defeat the motion.

Now that you realize the previous question was defeated, return to page 158 and select a better answer.

144

[*from page 127*]

YOUR ANSWER: Table.

You could use that motion to achieve your purpose, but there is a better one if you genuinely want to return to the pending question.

If you succeed in tabling the pending questions, they will be held in abeyance, ready to be brought up again at some later time. But in order to take the question from the table, it will be necessary to move and get passed a motion to take from the table. That only makes things more difficult than they need to be.

Presumably, the motion that would most satisfactorily achieve your purpose would have the effect of automatically returning the pending question to the floor at some later time.

Now return to page 127 and select a better answer.

YOUR ANSWER: He returns to the interrupted debate.

Of course. It requires a two-thirds vote to carry the call for the previous question. Thus, the previous question failed. And that being the case, the membership must return to the interrupted debate — that is, the motion to postpone to a fixed time.

Therefore, the chairman says, "The vote is 35 for, 31 against. The negative has it, because with 66 people voting, 44 votes are needed to carry. The question is now on the motion to postpone to a fixed time. Is there any discussion?"

The plumbing contractors will have to be left where they are, their minds still not made up. In the next chapter, we shall find them coming to a conclusion, as we discuss the fifth class of motion.

Now go on to Chapter V, which begins on page 146.

CHAPTER V

Incidental Motions

The fifth and last classification of motions is called incidental motions. The name, incidental, is accurate. Like subsidiary motions, incidental motions arise from pending business. But where subsidiary motions propose alternative ways of disposing of pending business, incidental motions are concerned primarily with the fairness, form, and legality with which pending business is handled. They are incidental to pending business.

One of the incidental motions is *point of order,* with which you are already familiar. This may not seem like a motion, but it is. When a member raises a point of order, he is asserting that there has been some violation of the rules of procedure. Normally, the chairman will decide whether the point of order is correct. When the chairman makes such a decision, he is speaking for the organization. And for an organization to decide that an act — or failure to act — constitutes a violation of its own rules is not essentially different than for an organization to decide to run a Christmas party.

Moreover, the decision of the chair may be questioned by the members through an appeal (another subsidiary motion), in which case the point of order is voted on by the organization, just as if it were a motion.

Now put your marker here and read the article titled INCIDENTAL MOTION on page 278. Then return.

When you have read the article, go on to page 151.

YOUR ANSWER: Yes, motions to table or postpone might be applied.

That might work. If one of these motions carried, the next order of business would be the interrupted debate. These motions can be applied because the call for the orders of the day is privileged, but after the item ordered for consideration reaches the floor, it has its normal parliamentary status. Once on the floor, it is treated as any main motion. The motion to refer to committee might also be used. Assume the motion to refer has been made.

CHAIRMAN: The question is on the motion to refer to committee the question of executive committee sites. Is there any discussion?

MR. JACOBS: Mr. Chairman.

CHAIRMAN: The chair recognizes Mr. Jacobs.

MR. JACOBS: I feel that it would be unwise to refer this question to committee. Action should be taken immediately. The members have some strong feelings about the situation in some of these. . . .

MR. PETERSON: Question of privilege.

CHAIRMAN: You have the floor, Mr. Peterson. Please be seated, Mr. Jacobs.

MR. PETERSON: The discussion of where the board is to meet is likely to raise some very private questions about our status in the various cities. I feel that as a point of organizational privilege, all non-members should be requested to leave the hall.

MR. JASPERS: Point of order! Point of order!

CHAIRMAN: Yes, Mr. Jaspers.

MR. JASPERS: The speaker is out of order. The chair should not allow the interruption of Mr. Jacobs' speech.

What should the chairman do?

Agree with Mr. Jaspers and allow Mr. Jacobs to resume the floor. **page 141**

Disagree with Mr. Jaspers, but allow Mr. Jacobs to resume the floor, withholding action on Mr. Peterson's proposal until Mr. Jacobs has finished. **page 150**

Disagree with Mr. Jaspers and state the question on Mr. Peterson's proposal immediately. **page 158**

148
[*from page 158*]

YOUR ANSWER: He announces that the amendment has been adopted.

No. You're still a little confused on the purpose of the previous question.

When an assembly votes on the previous question, it is deciding whether or not to bring to an immediate vote the question pending when the previous question was moved. Translated into ordinary language, a man who says, "I move the previous question," is saying, "I move that we immediately stop this debate and vote on the question before us." That proposal is itself a motion. It must be voted on to see if the other members agree to stopping the debate. When the members vote on the previous question, they are voting only on whether or not to stop the debate. Their decision on stopping debate has nothing to do with the decision they will make on the pending question. They can vote for ending debate and against adopting the motion; they can vote against ending debate and, when they finally get to the question, vote for it.

Now return to page 158 and select a better answer.

YOUR ANSWER: No.

Why not? The motion immediately pending is an amendment. An amendment is lower down on the scale of priority than the motion to recess. A motion to recess will not be entertained only when the immediately pending question is a privileged motion to adjourn, or a privileged motion to set the time for the next meeting of the same session.

When these two motions are not privileged, as when they are made when no business is pending, they are classed as incidental main motions. When they appear as incidental main motions, they would yield to the motion to recess.

There are no special problems about the motion to recess as there are about that to adjourn. The effect of a recess is never permanent. So there is no reason of priority, nor any special situation that would prevent the motion to recess from being entertained.

A motion to recess may also be an incidental main motion. Just like the two discussed above, it is treated in this manner when no business is pending.

Now return to page 138 and select the correct answer.

150

[*from page 147*]

YOUR ANSWER: Disagree with Mr. Jaspers, but allow Mr. Jacobs to resume the floor, withholding action on Mr. Peterson's proposal until Mr. Jacobs has finished.

As an absolute minimum, the chairman would have to disagree with Mr. Jaspers, but the rest of your statement is questionable. The request to have non-members removed from the hall is a question of privilege. And a question of privilege is a privileged motion. (The terms are a little confusing, so try to keep them straight. Privileged motions are the class of motions with highest parliamentary priority. One of the privileged motions is called question of privilege. A question of privilege is a motion concerning the rights of members or of the assembly. The right to hold a meeting in secret is a right of the assembly.)

A question of privilege can always interrupt a speaker on a question of lower priority. However, it is not always permissible to take action on the question of privilege right away. The goal is to interrupt the speaker as little as is necessary. If the matter may be simply decided by the chairman — by his directing that a window be closed — or if the matter is quite urgent, even though requiring a vote, decision should be made before the speaker resumes.

Since the subject motion is privileged, it could be brought up while a motion to commit is pending. The only point at issue can be whether action should be taken on the question of privilege before the speaker completes his presentation. That decision can be made only on the facts of the individual case. A question of privilege can interrupt a speaker when the matter is sufficiently urgent, otherwise a decision on the question of privilege waits until the interrupted speaker has finished.

In this situation, it is clear that the question raised is urgent. Mr. Peterson is concerned to have a matter debated privately. Mr. Jacobs has already begun to debate the matter that Mr. Peterson is worried about. Surely then, it would be appropriate to have the decision on the question of privilege made before Mr. Jacobs resumes his speech.

Now return to page 147 and select the correct answer.

NOTE: Before reaching this page, you should have read the article: INCIDENTAL MOTION.

You will recall that, when last heard from, the plumbing contractors had just defeated a motion on the previous question by a vote of 35 for and 31 against — two thirds being needed to carry.

Assume for the moment that the chairman had forgotten that the previous question requires a two-thirds vote:

CHAIRMAN: The vote is 35 for and 31 against. The ayes have it and the question is now on postponement.

MR. JOHNSON: Point of order!

CHAIRMAN: Mr. Johnson will state his point.

MR. JOHNSON: Mr. Chairman, the previous question requires a two-thirds vote for passage.

MR. CARL: Mr. Chairman! I rise to a point of privilege.

MR. JOHNSON: Call the speaker to order!

Does Mr. Johnson have legitimate grounds for opposing Mr. Carl's interruption?

Yes. **page 156**

No. **page 159**

152

[*from page 155*]

YOUR ANSWER: Raise a point of order.

Raising a point of order is making an assertion that some irregularity has occurred. The maker of a point of order is not in doubt, at least he probably isn't. You want to find out. You aren't trying to tell the chairman something.

There are situations, as you will discover in a moment, in which a person may raise a point of order just to find out how the chair will decide. This might well be done with the intention of appealing the decision of the chair, if the decision doesn't make the member happy.

But, at the moment, you haven't in mind such a parliamentary trick.

Now return to page 155 and select a better answer.

YOUR ANSWER: I would go ahead and introduce the motion.

That would be the proper procedure. You cannot appeal a chairman's decision on parliamentary inquiry. In making the inquiry, you asked for advice and it was given to you. But advice isn't a ruling. A binding rule, just as in the law, is not made on a hypothetical case. You couldn't take a judge's hypothetical opinion to a court of appeals, and you can't appeal a chairman's opinion expressed in the abstract.

If you dispute the chairman's opinion, the only thing you can do is present him an actual situation on which to rule. Then, if he still disagrees with you, you may appeal his decision.

The question, remember, was whether an amendment was germane. You are appealing the chairman's decision. What is the status of your appeal?

This appeal is debatable and can be tabled.   **page 161**

This appeal can be neither debated nor tabled.   **page 165**

This appeal can be debated but not tabled.   **page 168**

This appeal can be tabled but not debated.   **page 174**

154

[*from page 159*]

YOUR ANSWER: He applied an incidental motion to a privileged motion.

That is correct. A privileged motion was pending. It had been stated by the chair. But Mr. Jaspers noted it was out of order and used an incidental motion to bring that fact to the attention of the chairman.

It is standard practice, on the priority list we have been using, to place incidental motions above the subsidiary and beneath the privileged. This clearly indicates that the incidental yield to the privileged. However, this arrangement demonstrates again the inadequacies of the list, for no indication is given of the fact that an incidental motion may arise from and take precedence of a privileged motion.

The incidental motions, unlike the subsidiary and privileged motions, have no rank among themselves. Subsidiary and privileged motions yield or supersede automatically according to rank. With one or two small exceptions, incidental motions are assigned priority on the basis of relevance. An appeal may arise from a point of order, but another point of order might conceivably arise from an appeal. The test is always whether the content of the incidental motion is relevant to the pending business, and whether it is urgent enough to interrupt pending business.

As a general rule, the mover of an incidental motion may interrupt a speaker. It is up to the chairman to decide whether or not the motion or question is so important that it must be decided before the speaker continues. If it is important, he asks the speaker to take his seat while the question is decided. If it is not important, the chairman allows the speaker to resume and takes up the incidental question when the speaker is finished. In some cases, he may take up the incidental motion after the pending question has been decided.

Now put your marker here, note the articles below, and read them.

When you have read these articles, go on to page 155.

NOTE: Before reaching this page, you should have read the articles:

APPEAL
POINT OF ORDER
PARLIAMENTARY QUESTION
OBJECTION TO THE CONSIDERATION OF A QUESTION
REQUEST FOR INFORMATION

This group of motions and questions is closely related. (Notice that the two types of request for information have very little similarity to motions, since under no circumstances would they be voted on. These requests are called motions apparently only to give them parliamentary status.) Because of the similarity, it is useful to keep their differences clearly in mind.

If you wanted to know whether or not an amendment you had in mind would be entertained, you would:

Raise a point of order.   **page 152**

Request information.   **page 164**

Make parliamentary inquiry.   **page 170**

156

[from page 151]

YOUR ANSWER: Yes.

No. The point of order is an incidental motion. The question of privilege is a privileged motion. One characteristic of any privileged motion is that it has precedence over any motion of any other class that is pending. A privileged motion cannot be entertained when another privileged motion of higher rank is pending, or during a vote.

That being the case, the chairman should not support Mr. Johnson's question of privilege.

When the chairman hears what Mr. Carl's question of privilege is, he may defer action on it until the earlier point of order is disposed. But the raising of the question of privilege is certainly in order.

Now return to page 151 and select the correct answer.

YOUR ANSWER: I would appeal the decision of the chairman.

That wouldn't be courteous and it wouldn't be allowed, either. The chairman is not required to give you lessons in parliamentary procedure, but he will generally give you his best advice on a parliamentary question that is relevant to the situation. That is, you may ask if, in present circumstances, something could be done.

The chairman's advice on a hypothetical question is not binding, either on you or him. Since the advice is given to be helpful and since it is not binding, it is inappropriate to appeal. You only appeal when a decision has been made on a real question. If you had actually moved the amendment and the chairman had rejected it, then you might appeal.

Now return to page 170 and select the correct answer.

158

[from page 147]

YOUR ANSWER: Disagree with Mr. Jaspers and state the question on Mr. Peterson's proposal immediately.

That would probably be the best course. Certainly Mr. Peterson was not out of order in interrupting Mr. Jacobs on a question of privilege. Whether or not the question is significant enough that a decision on it should be allowed to interrupt the speaker must be decided by the chairman (and the decision is appealable). In this case, it was evident that Mr. Jacobs intended to raise the issues on which Mr. Peterson had misgivings. That being the case, it would be reasonable for the chairman to state Mr. Peterson's proposal as a question immediately. A majority vote would carry it. The question would be debatable, amendable, and otherwise treated as a main question.

Let us say that the motion to commit carries. The organization meeting is once more discussing the postponement of the question and the amendment to set a sum to be available for public relations purposes. The debate is in process.

MR. JACOBS: Mr. Chairman.

CHAIRMAN: The chair recognizes Mr. Jacobs.

MR. JACOBS: I move the previous question on the three pending questions.

MEMBER: Second.

CHAIRMAN: It has been moved and seconded that the previous question be called on the motion to postpone, the amendment and the main motion. Are you ready for the vote on the previous question? (Pause) All those in favor, signify by saying "Aye."

MEMBERS: Aye!

CHAIRMAN: All those opposed, "No."

MEMBERS: No!

CHAIRMAN: I am sorry, I am unable to determine which side had it. We will repeat the vote by a standing count. (Proceeds to do so.) The vote is 35 for, 31 against.

Where does the chairman go from here?

He calls the vote on the motion to postpone.   page 143

He returns to the interrupted debate.   page 145

He announces that the amendment has been adopted.   page 148

YOUR ANSWER: No.

That is correct. All incidental motions yield to privileged motions. And remember, a question of privilege is a privileged motion. All Mr. Carl wanted was to get the window shut to close out the noise of an air hammer coming in from the street. He didn't even have a clear idea of what Mr. Johnson and the chairman were talking about.

It is also true that a privileged motion will yield to an incidental motion, when and if the incidental motion arises from the privileged motion.

Assume that the plumbers are back working on the motion to postpone to a fixed time.

MR. FREDRICKS: Mr. Chairman!

CHAIRMAN: The chair recognizes Mr. Fredricks.

MR. FREDRICKS: I move that we adjourn at 10:30.

MEMBER: I second that motion.

CHAIRMAN: The motion is undebatable. All those in. . . .

MR. JASPERS: Point of order!

CHAIRMAN: The member will state his point.

MR. JASPERS: When it is qualified, the motion to adjourn cannot be entertained while another motion is pending.

CHAIRMAN: I beg the assembly's pardon; with all the noise outside, I didn't hear the qualification. The motion to adjourn cannot be entertained. The question is still on the motion to postpone to a fixed time.

Mr. Jaspers was right this time. What did he do?

He applied an incidental motion to a privileged motion. **page 154**

He applied a privileged motion to an incidental motion. **page 169**

[*from page 168*]

YOUR ANSWER: Object to the consideration of the question.

No. An objection to the consideration of a question can be applied only to original main motions. And the motion can be applied only immediately after the main motion has been introduced and before debate has begun or any secondary questions have been applied. You object to other motions by raising a point of order.

This is an important difference because a point of order concerning the admissibility of a motion is handled in an entirely different manner than the motion objecting to the consideration of a question. The point of order is, in this situation, a debatable motion and in any circumstances requires only a majority vote for adoption. The other motion is not debatable and requires a two-thirds vote.

Now return to page 168 and select the correct answer.

YOUR ANSWER: This appeal is debatable and can be tabled.

Well, you're half right.

The appeal is on the chairman's rejection of your amendment on the grounds that it is not germane. There are some appeals that may be tabled and some that may not be. Those motions that can be tabled are those that do not affect the pending business.

If a point of order is raised against a member for debating in an indecorous manner, the member might appeal, contending that he hadn't really said anything out of the way. Whatever the result of this appeal, it will not affect the pending business. An appeal on the decision that an amendment is not germane, on the other hand, might have the effect either of ruling the amendment out of order or admitting it. Obviously, such an appeal must be decided before going back to the pending business. An appeal that affects pending business cannot be tabled, because tabling would leave the decision (on the germaneness of the amendment) up in the air. If the appeal on an indecorum in debate were tabled, there would be no such serious effect.

The rule is that appeals that cannot be tabled can be debated. That is a reasonable rule. It is in keeping with the importance of the questions that it cannot be tabled. It is perfectly reasonable to expect that there might be debate on whether or not a motion is germane, and that the debate would be helpful in bringing the group to a good decision.

Now return to page 153 and select the correct answer.

[from page 173]

YOUR ANSWER: Move to divide the question.

No. If a motion is divided, each of the parts into which it is divided is debated and voted upon as a separate question.

When an assembly agrees to consider a motion or report seriatim, or by paragraphs, they discuss each paragraph or resolution separately, but vote on them as a whole. The chairman, or someone appointed by him reads the first paragraph or resolution. It is open to debate and amendment. When debate and amendment are over, no vote is taken. The chairman reads, or has read, the next paragraph and it is handled in the same manner. When each paragraph has been debated and amended, the chair entertains any amendments to the whole document. Finally, the document is adopted or rejected as a whole on a single vote.

Now return to page 173 and select the correct answer.

YOUR ANSWER: I would raise a point of order.

A point of order is an assertion that something has been done that is wrong. The chairman hasn't actually rejected your amendment. You haven't moved it. If you could charge that the chairman gave you the wrong advice, when he was just trying to be helpful, being a chairman would be an unpleasant job.

No, you can't raise a point of order objecting to advice. You can only raise a point of order when a parliamentary *faux pas* has been committed, or when someone has violated the rules for debating in a polite and decorous manner. If you actually move the amendment, and if it is rejected, your point of order would be in order. (Of course, you might still lose.)

Now return to page 170 and select a better answer.

YOUR ANSWER: Request information.

It is true that you want information. However, the phrase *request information* has a special parliamentary meaning.

When you request information, you want to know some detail about the proposal that is being discussed. What you want could be called factual or substantive information. The question does not concern parliamentary rules. Most often, a request for information is directed to the speaker on the floor rather than to the chairman. It is the chairman who can give you procedural advice. It is the member speaking to a question who can give you substantive information.

Now return to page 155 and select the correct answer.

YOUR ANSWER: This appeal can be neither debated nor tabled.

Well, you're half right.

The appeal is on the chairman's rejection of your amendment on the grounds that it is not germane. There are some appeals that may be tabled and some that may not be. Those motions that can be tabled are those that do not affect the pending business.

If a point of order is raised against a member for debating in an indecorous manner, the member might appeal, contending that he hadn't really said anything out of the way. Whatever the result of this appeal, it will not affect the pending business. An appeal on the decision that an amendment is not germane, on the other hand, might have the effect either of ruling the amendment out of order or admitting it. Obviously, such an appeal must be decided before going back to pending business. An appeal that affects pending business cannot be tabled, because tabling would leave the decision (on the germaneness of the amendment) up in the air. If the appeal on an indecorum in debate were tabled, there would be no such serious effect.

The rule is that appeals that cannot be tabled can be debated. That is a reasonable rule. It is in keeping with the importance of the questions that cannot be tabled. It is perfectly reasonable to expect that there might be debate on whether or not a motion is germane, and that the debate would be helpful in bringing the group to a good decision.

Now return to page 153 and select the correct answer.

YOUR ANSWER: Move to consider it by paragraphs.

Right you are. When a motion or report is considered by paragraphs, each paragraph is debated and amended in turn, but without a final vote being taken. When the document has been completely covered in this manner, the floor is open for amendments to the whole or to any of the parts. When the document is finally perfected, it is adopted or rejected as a whole with a single vote. The division of the question, on the other hand, leads to a separate vote on each part into which the original motion was divided.

Of the principal types of incidental motions, you have now studied all but a few requests and the motion to suspend the rules. Now note down the motions listed below and the page number following. Read the articles and then go ahead to page 167.

REQUEST   page 319
REQUEST TO BE EXCUSED FROM DUTY   page 322
SUSPEND RULES   page 331
REQUEST TO ALLOW A PAPER TO BE READ   page 321
PERMISSION TO WITHDRAW A MOTION   page 296

NOTE: Before reaching this page, you should have read the articles:

REQUEST
REQUEST TO BE EXCUSED FROM DUTY
SUSPEND RULES
REQUEST TO ALLOW A PAPER TO BE READ
PERMISSION TO WITHDRAW A MOTION

The request to allow a paper to be read and that to be excused from duty are reasonably simple and direct motions. The request that is most commonly handled incorrectly is that for permission to withdraw a motion.

Back at the plumbing contractors' meeting, the previous question had just been defeated (that left pending the motion to postpone to a fixed time, the amendment authorizing the expenditure of a $1,000 per year in pursuance of the purpose of the main motion, and the main motion, which would order the executive director to carry on an advertising program to aid local contractors).

CHAIRMAN: The question is now on the main motion.

YOU (for it was you who moved to postpone to a fixed time): Mr. Chairman!

CHAIRMAN: The chair recognizes the reader.

YOU: Mr. Chairman, I request permission to withdraw my motion so that we may get our business completed.

What should the chairman say?

"Permission granted."   **page 171**

"Will the second object to the withdrawal?"   **page 175**

"Is there any objection to the withdrawal?"   **page 178**

168

[*from page 153*]

YOUR ANSWER: This appeal can be debated but not tabled.

That is correct. The rule is that a debatable appeal cannot be tabled. Those appeals are debatable which concern directly the business before the assembly, rather than strictly procedural matters. An appeal following an indecorum in debate is not debatable. An appeal on whether a motion is germane is debatable. The latter will determine whether or not the amendment should be entertained. This question is of more long-range importance than that on an indecorum, which is why debate is allowed. And this appeal cannot be tabled because a decision must be made immediately to determine whether the amendment is to be entertained.

Turn the situation around for a moment. The chairman accepts your amendment, but another member disagrees. To voice his disapproval, he would:

Object to the consideration of the question.   **page 160**

Raise a point of order.   **page 172**

YOUR ANSWER: He applied a privileged motion to an incidental motion.

The classification system is a little confusing until you get used to it. Adjourn is a privileged motion. Point of order is an incidental motion. The point of order arose out of the admission of the privileged motion to the floor. To put the point another way, the point of order (incidental motion) was applied to the motion to adjourn (privileged motion).

This is but one example of how an incidental motion can be applied to the high-priority privileged motions. However, once the incidental motion is on the floor, it can be interrupted by another privileged motion of still higher priority. It would be possible to have some such group of pending motions as this (the most recently made is at the top, the earliest at the bottom):

Adjourn...................................Privileged
Appeal   ⎫
Point of order ⎭ ....Incidental
Orders of the day.....................Privileged
Amendment.............................Subsidiary
Main motion

Two incidental motions arose from — or were applied to — a privileged motion. Then another privileged motion was introduced, to which the incidental motions yielded. Notice that adjourn has higher priority than orders of the day. An arrangement like that below would not work because a higher-priority motion (adjourn) is already pending.

Orders of the day.....................The motion could not be entertained in these circumstances.

Appeal   ⎫
Point of order ⎭ ....Incidental

Adjourn...................................This motion has higher priority than orders of the day.

Now return to page 159 and select the correct answer.

170

[*from page 155*]

YOUR ANSWER: Make parliamentary inquiry.

Certainly. You are not making an assertion, so you would not raise a point of order. Since the information you want is on a parliamentary matter, not on the subject matter that is pending, you would rise to a parliamentary inquiry. If the chairman decided that your amendment was not germane, but you, on further consideration, decided that it was, what would you do?

I would go ahead and introduce the motion.   **page 153**

I would appeal the decision of the chairman.   **page 157**

I would raise a point of order.   **page 163**

YOUR ANSWER: "Permission granted."

If the chairman had not stated your motion as a question, he could give you permission to withdraw it. However, once a motion has been stated as a question, it belongs to the assembly and can only be taken back with their permission. They must approve the withdrawal by vote or by general consent. The chairman does not have the power, now, to grant this request.

Return to page 167 and select the correct answer.

YOUR ANSWER: Raise a point of order.

That's right. An objection to the consideration of a question can be applied only to main motions, only before debate has begun, and before any secondary motions have been introduced. The differences are important. When a point of order directly concerning a question is put in the form of a motion, it is debatable. The objection is not debatable. Because the objection is not debatable, it requires a two-thirds vote.

The purpose of the motion *objection to the consideration of a question* is to allow an assembly to rid itself quickly of main motions that are made frivolously or with obstructive intent. With that purpose in mind, the rule preventing debate and that requiring a two-thirds vote are quite reasonable. Debate is not allowed because time would be consumed — exactly what the motion is intended to prevent. And, if the motion is obviously made for no good purpose, there should be no difficulty in obtaining a two-thirds vote.

There is another group of incidental motions that might cause some confusion. Read the articles listed below before going to the next page indicated.

DIVIDE THE QUESTION   page 272
CONSIDERATION BY PARAGRAPH   page 265
DIVISION OF THE ASSEMBLY   page 273
VOTING   page 339

When you have read these articles, please go on to page 173.

NOTE: Before reaching this page, you should have read the articles:
DIVIDE THE QUESTION
CONSIDERATION BY PARAGRAPH
DIVISION OF THE ASSEMBLY
VOTING

As you could see, divide the question and division of the assembly, despite the similarity of the names, are entirely different motions.

Division of the assembly is one of several related motions concerning voting that have essentially the same parliamentary status. Any request for a different method of voting than that which was employed, or than that which it is expected will be employed, has the same parliamentary status.

Divide the question and consideration by paragraph are concerned with whether a motion or report should be considered as a whole or in parts. If your goal is to debate and amend a report in sections, but to vote on it as a whole, you would:

Move to divide the question.   **page 162**

Move to consider it by paragraphs.   **page 166**

174

[from page 153]

YOUR ANSWER: This appeal can be tabled but not debated.

No, you have things backwards.

The appeal is on the chairman's rejection of your amendment on the grounds that it is not germane. There are some appeals that may be tabled and some that may not be. Those motions that can be tabled are those that do not affect the pending business.

If a point of order is raised against a member for debating in an indecorous manner, the member might appeal, contending that he hadn't really said anything out of the way. Whatever the result of this appeal, it will not affect the pending business. An appeal on the decision that an amendment is not germane, on the other hand, might have the effect either of ruling the amendment out of order or admitting it. Obviously, such an appeal must be decided before going back to pending business. An appeal that affects pending business cannot be tabled, because tabling would leave the decision (on the germaneness of the amendment) up in the air. If the appeal on an indecorum in debate were tabled, there would be no such serious effect.

The rule is that appeals that cannot be tabled can be debated. That is a reasonable rule. It is in keeping with the importance of the questions that cannot be tabled. It is perfectly reasonable to expect that there might be debate on whether or not a motion is germane, and that the debate would be helpful in bringing the group to a good decision.

Now return to page 153 and select the correct answer.

175

[*from page 167*]

YOUR ANSWER: "Will the second object to the withdrawal?"

It is not up to the second to decide whether or not a motion should be withdrawn. He has only indicated his support of it. Further, if it is withdrawn, the second may make it anew on his own. So the chairman has no business asking the second for his feelings.

If a motion has not yet been stated as a question, it is still, so to speak, the property of the mover. The chairman must automatically grant the remover's request for permission to withdraw his motion.

Once a motion is stated as a question, it becomes the property of the assembly and cannot be withdrawn without permission from the assembly. That permission may be given by general consent. Or, if there is an objection, the question is put to a vote.

Now return to page 167 and select the correct answer.

YOUR ANSWER: Yes.

Certainly. It is a second-degree amendment of the type called a substitution.

Which type of motion is an amendment?

A subsidiary motion. **page 180**

A privileged motion. **page 183**

An incidental motion. **page 186**

YOUR ANSWER: Yes.

No, you've probably got divide the question and division of the assembly confused.

Division of the assembly is an incidental motion concerning the method of voting. If passed, it requires that a standing rather than a voice vote be taken. This motion would surely be entertained.

Division of the question is a request that the pending question be voted upon in two or more parts. That motion would not ordinarily be made so late in the debate — though it might be. However, a question can be divided only if it is divisible into parts that will stand alone.

The amendment before the assembly might be said to have two parts — the amount to be spent and the method for approving expenditures, but these parts could hardly be said to be capable of standing alone. If the amount failed to pass, but the method for approving expenditures did pass, the organization would be exactly nowhere.

Now return to page 184 and select the correct answer.

YOUR ANSWER: "Is there any objection to the withdrawal?"

Correct. Asking if there is an objection is a backwards way of voting that is used commonly in acting on incidental motions and, in smaller meetings, even on other issues. This method is called *general consent*. If no one raises an objection, it is assumed that all the members are reasonably willing to go along with the proposal. Should an objection be voiced, the chairman must call for a formal vote. An effective chairman will usually be able to sense when the membership favors a proposal. When he feels this to be the case, he can use the general-consent procedure to speed the process of deliberation.

In asking if there was general consent to the withdrawal, the chairman was asking for a vote on whether or not the organization would relinquish the motion. A vote is necessary to permit withdrawal after the motion has been stated as a question. If the question on the motion had not yet been stated, the chairman would permit the withdrawal without a vote. In neither case would it be necessary to ask the consent of the second. The second is involved only if the request concerned modification of the motion. In that case, the second would be asked if he was willing to apply his second to the motion as modified.

CHAIRMAN: Is there any objection to the withdrawal?

MEMBERS: (Silence)

CHAIRMAN: The motion is withdrawn. The question is now on the amendment that allows the expenditure of $1,000. Is there any more discussion?

MR. JASPERS: Mr. Chairman.

CHAIRMAN: The chair recognizes Mr. Jaspers.

MR. JASPERS: The project we have proposed to us is certainly likely to be beneficial. However, it is a new, experimental idea. We are faced with a twin problem: the need for local advertising — which costs money — and the need to see that we are getting our money's worth. I would like to see more money available to the executive secretary if we can be sure it is used effectively. Therefore, I recommend the following substitute for the amendment before us: that the executive secretary be allowed to spend

(Continue on page 179)

up to $500 per quarter, each quarter's allowance being contingent upon a review by, and approval of, the executive committee of the previous quarter's advertising activity.

Should this motion be entertained now?

Yes.   page 176

No.   page 188

YOUR ANSWER: A subsidiary motion.

True. A subsidiary motion is one directly concerned with the pending motion and its disposition. The incidental motions are concerned with procedural problems affecting pending business. The privileged motions have no connection with pending business.

After considerable debate, the chairman gets no response to his question, "Is there any more discussion of the amendment?" Getting no response, he:

Calls the question.   **page 184**

States the question.   **page 187**

YOUR ANSWER: The question is now on the motion, as amended, to have an advertising campaign.

No. The amendment to substitute one paragraph or resolution for another is treated essentially as any other amendment.

When the substitute is an amendment of the second degree, as is the case here, the first vote taken determines the assembly's choice between the original amendment and the substitute. All the assembly does is decide that it likes one amendment better than the other. So far, that is all that has happened. The second-degree amendment has won out over the first. Just because the substitute is preferred, doesn't mean that it is liked well enough to pass.

What has happened is that the substitute — a secondary amendment — has been approved and made the first-degree amendment. Now it is necessary to see if that substitute amendment will be incorporated into the main motion.

Now return to page 189 and select a better answer.

182

[from page 185]

YOUR ANSWER: Yes.

No. Proposing to adjourn when pending business is completed is a qualified motion to adjourn. It says that the adjournment will take effect later. An unqualified adjournment takes effect immediately if it is adopted.

A qualified adjournment is treated as an incidental main motion. That means it cannot be entertained while there is any pending business. In fact, the motion as made is a parliamentary impossibility. You never make a qualified motion to adjourn when there is pending business, so you can never move to adjourn when pending business is complete.

Now return to page 185 and select the correct answer.

YOUR ANSWER: A privileged motion.

No, a privileged motion has never anything to do with pending business in the way an amendment does.

Privileged motions are those that can be entertained at any time, that are not debatable, and that have more to do with the members or the meeting than with the pending business. They include the motions that affect how long the meeting shall run, what business should be considered next (orders of the day), and when the next meeting should be held.

Now return to page 176 and select a better answer.

184

[from page 180]

YOUR ANSWER: Calls the question.

That is correct. Sometimes the expression *puts the question* is used. In either case, the meaning is that the question is to be voted on. Stating the question is merely informing the assembly of the question before it.

Having announced that he is putting the question to a vote, would the chairman entertain a motion to divide the question?

Yes.   page 177

No.   page 189

YOUR ANSWER: The question is now on the adoption of the substitute amendment.

Right. The first vote was between two amendments: the one originally proposed and the substitute. The substitute was more attractive to the organization than was the original amendment. That still does not mean it is attractive enough to be adopted. An amendment of the second degree by substitution is handled in the same manner as any other second-degree amendment. This means that after action on the second-degree amendment, the first-degree amendment must still be acted upon. A possible source of confusion is that when a substitute becomes the first-degree amendment it gives the appearance of voting on the same question twice.

If the substitute amendment is adopted, the main motion is then the order of business. The amendment passed and the chairman says:

CHAIRMAN: The question is now on the advertising motion as amended. Is there any discussion?

MR. CARL: I move that we adjourn as soon as action is taken on the pending question.

MEMBER: I second the motion.

Should the chairman entertain this motion?

Yes. **page 182**

No. **page 190**

[*from page 176*]

YOUR ANSWER: An incidental motion.

No, incidental motions do not concern the substance or disposition of a pending motion in the way an amendment does.

Incidental motions are concerned with such things as the propriety with which business is being carried on, the method of voting, and requests for certain privileges. They are really incidental to the pending business, for though they arise from pending business, they are not concerned with its substance.

Now return to page 176 and select a better answer.

YOUR ANSWER: States the question.

The difference between stating and calling the question is quite simple, but the expressions are enough alike to be confusing.

To state the question is to announce that it is now immediately pending before the assembly, or that it has been entertained. The chairman should announce at every point where there might be any confusion just what question is immediately pending.

Call the question is short for call for the vote on the question. The phrase put the question means the same thing and is short for put the question to a vote. When the chairman puts or calls the question, he is bringing the question to a vote.

Now return to page 180 and select the correct answer.

188

[from page 179]

YOUR ANSWER: No.

You are being overly cautious. Perhaps the motion fooled you, because it was not discussed in the text before.

Mr. Jaspers' motion is an amendment of the sort called a substitution. The term substitution is used to refer to the deleting of an entire paragraph or resolution and the insertion of another in its place (the expression strike and insert is used to describe the motion to delete and replace words of less than a paragraph).

Prior to Mr. Jaspers' motion is an amendment to an amendment. Amendments to the second degree are permissible.

The amendment called a substitution is treated exactly as any of the other types of amendments of the same degree.

Now return to page 179 and select the correct answer.

YOUR ANSWER: No.

In this case, he certainly would not. The motion to divide the question, you recall, means to separate it into two or more parts to be acted upon independently. The question before the house is the substitute amendment. That amendment was all of a piece; it stated how much was to be spent and under what circumstances. The parts could not stand alone.

The maker of this motion probably had in mind calling for a division of the assembly — that is, a standing vote. That motion would certainly have been in order, as would any similar motion affecting the method of voting.

CHAIRMAN: I cannot entertain the motion to divide the question; the question is really indivisible. We will now proceed to the vote. All those in favor, signify by saying "Aye."

MEMBERS: Aye!

CHAIRMAN: All those opposed, say "No."

MEMBERS: No.

CHAIRMAN: The affirmative has it. The substitute amendment is carried.

At this point the chairman will say:

The question is now on the motion, as amended, to have an advertising campaign. **page 181**

The question is now on the adoption of the substitute amendment. **page 185**

190

[*from page 185*]

YOUR ANSWER: No.

You're right. When the motion to adjourn is qualified in any way, it loses its privilege and becomes an incidental main motion. Adjourn was qualified here by the suggestion that it should take effect later. That being the case, the motion cannot be entertained as long as there is pending business. In fact, this motion — to adjourn upon the completion of pending business — is a parliamentary impossibility.

Since he does not entertain the motion, the chair proceeds to the vote.

CHAIRMAN: The question is on the amended motion. All those in favor say "Aye."

MEMBERS: Aye!

CHAIRMAN: All those opposed, say "No."

MEMBERS: (silence)

CHAIRMAN: The motion is carried unanimously. Mr. Carl, I will now entertain a motion to adjourn.

MR. CARL: So move.

MEMBER: Second.

CHAIRMAN: If there is no objection, the meeting stands adjourned.

Chapter VI begins on page 191.

CHAPTER VI

Practical Politics

Parliamentary law isn't all you need to know to be an effective member of an organization. Parliamentary law is simply a tool in the political process. This final chapter will be concerned with some problems on the border line between parliamentary law and practical politics. The first subject is the main motion.

Almost every organization has both a private and a public face. In any organization certain motions will be proposed purely for the interest or the benefit of members. But almost all organizations also will conduct business intended to have an impact beyond the membership — to tell the world where the organization stands on an issue, or to encourage non-members to do something. The desired activity may be anything from cooperation in an old-clothing drive to co-operation in working for the enactment of legislation. Both the public and private facets of public motions must be considered. It is, after all, necessary to sell an idea to your fellow members before communicating it to the public at large.

Assume that you are a member of a large and effective neighborhood organization in which the full membership meets only quarterly. You want the organization to get behind a proposal you have to get new street lights in the neighborhood. What do you think would be the best way to go about it?

Prepare a speech in favor of the proposal with full documentation of its feasibility, and spring the motion as a surprise at the next meeting. **page 195**

Discuss your idea with your neighbors and make sure they come to the meeting to support you. **page 198**

Select those people in the organization who seem to be listened to in meetings and try to line them up in advance. **page 203**

YOUR ANSWER: Could be divided by a majority vote.

No. There are three classes of multiple resolution motions: *separate, separable,* and *inseparable.* Separate resolutions combined in one motion are two or more essentially unrelated proposals. A motion containing two or more unrelated proposals should be divided into its parts if a single member points out the separateness.

Separable motions include two or more related parts, each of which is able to stand on its own. If any part is adopted, it must make sense without the adoption of the other part. As an example, your organization might consider an educational campaign on zoning laws to consist of a series of lectures and of a pamphlet to be distributed to all who are interested. These proposals are clearly related; the motion proposing them could not be divided at the request of a single member. On the other hand, they stand by themselves. Either one could be adopted alone and it would be complete and sensible.

Inseparable motions are those including two or more proposals that could not stand alone. In the motion at hand, the first resolution, which states a position, could stand alone. The second one, describing how to publicize the motion, could not stand alone. If the first resolution were defeated, the second would be meaningless.

When a motion consists of two or more inseparable resolutions, the only way to pass a part and not the whole is to amend by a motion to strike.

Now return to page 203 and select the correct answer.

193
[*from page 197*]

YOUR ANSWER: Whereas, Every Rotarian should support the battle against creeping urban blight,

There is a special circumstance in which you might want to use such a paragraph, but, as a general rule, you would not. Your purpose in writing a preamble is not to convince your fellow members; you try to do that during the debate on the motion. The purpose of a preamble is to explain to people why your organization takes this position.

A preamble might be addressed exclusively to fellow members if it is passed by a delegate body. In that case, the intention would be to rally the support of fellow members back home in local organizations, who had not participated in the decision. Even in this case, the purpose is not to sell the people who are to vote on the motion, but to explain after the motion is adopted.

Now return to page 197 and select the correct answer.

194

[*from page 207*]

YOUR ANSWER: Line 1.

No, everything in line 1 is all right. All that is necessary here is that the Whereas is capitalized and followed by a comma, and that the word following be capitalized, too. Here is the line. You can see that everything is in order.

"Whereas, The Boy Scouts of America do an admirable . . ."

If you carefully read the rules on the full-page sample, you will find that one of them has been violated in one of the other lines of this resolution.

Return now to page 207 and select a better answer.

YOUR ANSWER: Prepare a speech in favor of the proposal with full documentation of its feasibility, and spring the motion as a surprise at the next meeting.

There are times when surprises are appropriate, and there may even be times when it is useful to spring a parliamentary surprise. But this is not one of them.

Your organization meets only quarterly. When organizations have sessions as often as quarterly, a motion cannot be renewed either during the session in which it was made or in the following session. If your motion is defeated at the upcoming session, you will not be able to re-introduce (renew) it for six months.

If you spring your motion as a total surprise, you won't know what will happen to it. You may miss getting support from people who would be favorably inclined if they had the time to think about the proposal, or if they were flattered by your consulting them in advance, or if small changes were made to satisfy objections or problems that might not have occurred to you. On the last point, two heads are often — not always — better than one.

Of course, it never hurts to have a well-prepared statement and you should always be able to support your proposal with sound arguments. The trouble with your answer is that a good statement is usually not enough.

Now return to page 191 and select the correct answer.

196

[from page 201]

YOUR ANSWER: Members of local groups.

Correct. In a democratic organization, the entire administrative structure is intended to serve the interests of the members. The members of the local organizations elect delegates to represent their interests at the annual convention. The delegates in turn pass their power on to the board of directors they choose. Finally, power is passed to the executive committee. At each level, some measure of power is retained. Things done at one level cannot be done at the level above. For instance, neither the board nor the executive committee can amend the constitution or by-laws.

In large and dispersed organizations, there is the danger that elected officers will run an organization in their own interests. They depend on the parliamentary procedure being a slow and cumbersome tool with which to counteract their grab for power. This is a perennial danger in any democratic society. To resist this threat be watchful and make full and effective use of parliamentary law.

There is a type of organization in which the leadership effectively runs the organization, but where the result is often salutary. These are special-interest organizations that would not exist but for the dedication of a small group, though there may be hundreds or thousands of nominal members who demonstrate their support by paying dues without the intention of actively participating. In a society where worthy causes vie for the citizen's attention, this situation is inevitable. Each of us has a special interest, to which we give time; there are other groups with which we are in sympathy, but to which we cannot devote much time. Organizations that elicit more sympathy than effort can be successful as long as their leaders continue honestly and effectively dedicated to the original purposes. Each has machinery that makes it possible to unseat leaders who have outlived their usefulness, but considerable time may elapse before the need for change is noticed.

Which of the following is an elected officer?

Executive Secretary.   **page 209**   Presiding Officer.   **page 217**

Both of the above.   **page 223**

YOUR ANSWER: Could not be divided.

Right. If this motion were divided, there would be the possibility —
dim, but theoretical — that the first resolution would be defeated and
the second passed. That would leave the secretary mailing out a non-
existent resolution. The fact that the second resolution cannot stand
by itself makes this motion indivisible. When there is an objection to
some part of an inseparable or indivisible motion, that section may
be eliminated only by an amendment to strike it.

When a single member requests division, in effect he raises a point
of order, asking the chair to decide whether, in fact, the motion presented includes separate rather than separable proposals.

You will recall that each paragraph of the sample motion began
either "Whereas" or "Resolved." Those beginning with "Whereas"
form the preamble to the motion. A preamble is an introduction with
a very specific purpose, to explain to the public at large the reason
the motion has been adopted. Its purpose is not to convince the members to vote for the motion. The preamble to the Declaration of Independence is a good example. In a sense, it is the preamble to the
United States. In the first sentence, it is stated that the Declaration
was written because, "A decent respect to the opinions of mankind
requires that they (Americans) should declare the causes which im-
pel them to the separation." The purpose of a preamble has never
been better stated. It is clear, then, that preambles will be included
only in those motions or resolutions that are of great importance and
that are likely to come to public attention. (In a large organization,
a preamble might be included for the benefit of absent members.)

You want to prepare a motion urging the redevelopment of a slum
area. Which of the following would you consider an appropriate paragraph to include in your preamble?

Whereas, Every Rotarian should support the battle against creeping
urban blight,　**page 193**

Whereas, Slums are breeders of crime and disease, and produce tax
income far below the cost of city services,　**page 207**

Whereas, Almost four tax dollars are spent on city services for every
$2.67 collected in slum areas, leaving the city a tax deficit of $367,000
annually,　**page 211**

198

YOUR ANSWER: Discuss your idea with your neighbors and make sure they come to the meeting to support you.

You are on the right track, but why pick on your neighbors? What about the man two blocks away, or the one half a mile away? You can win a point in a meeting by packing the meeting with your friends. However, that is a difficult and uncertain job, and not really in the spirit of parliamentary procedure. And, if you've got a good idea, why not have a little more faith in it, instead of just trying to jam it down people's throats.

When you go back to page 191 to try again, consider what would be the most effective way of *selling* your proposal.

YOUR ANSWER: Line 6.

Right. Line six is the last line of the preamble. As such, it should conclude with a semicolon (;) followed by an uncapitalized "therefore." Basically, a motion consists of one sentence. There is no full stop (period) until the very end. The only exception is when there is more than one proposal. In that case, each of the proposals ends in a period. Each proposal can be looked at as an alternative conclusion to the sentence that begins with the preamble.

If you keep in mind that the whole motion is just one sentence, you will be aided in your drafting job, for you will be conscious of the fact that each paragraph is actually a clause that must grammatically follow the preceding clause and grammatically introduce the next one.

In many organizations, it is the practice to have main motions written out in advance, so that a written copy may be presented to the chair after the motion is made verbally. The maker of the motion, having been recognized, will read his motion, and then immediately bring a written copy to the chair. Putting motions in writing is an especially desirable practice for those motions that are long, important, or carefully worded. The advantages of putting motions in writing ahead of time are obvious: to avoid arguments about the wording of the motion as submitted, to assure that the motion will be recorded properly, to ease the chair's frequent task of repeating the motion, and to avoid the time wasted when, while occupying the floor, a man making a motion fumbles around for the correct words.

Is the following statement true or false?

If an organization meets monthly, it is generally less essential to have a main motion written out in advance than if an organization meets semi-annually.

True.   **page 205**

False.   **page 219**

200

[*from page 205*]

NOTE: Before reaching this page, you should have read the following articles:

COMMITTEE, EXECUTIVE
CONSTITUTION, BY-LAWS AND RULES OF ORDER
EXECUTIVE SECRETARY
PRESIDING OFFICER

Here are charts of two basic types of organizational structure, one simple, the other complex. (Any number of variations and combinations is possible.) The arrows indicate who reports to whom. The source of power in the organization should move in the direction opposite the arrows.

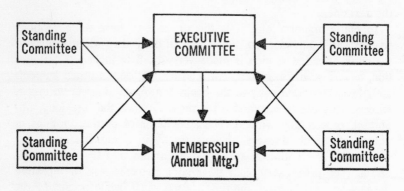

The chart on this page shows an organization with but one set of committees that report to the membership at the annual convention, but to the executive committee during the year. This is an essentially simple arrangement, common in organizations too large to meet frequently, but whose memberships do not run in the thousands.

The chart on the opposite page shows a much more complex national organization composed of local groups. In annual convention, delegates elected by the local organizations choose a board of directors. The executive committee is chosen from among the board members. The executive committee may be composed, automatically, of the officers who are on the board, or the board may have the power to choose the executive committee, either in part or in whole.

(Continued on page 201)

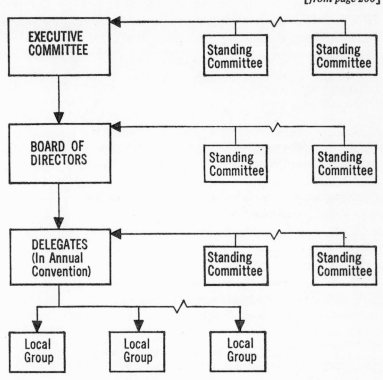

Notice that there are committees reporting exclusively to each organizational level. The functions of these committees should be relevant to the duties of each administrative level, so that there is no duplication. Of course, the local groups may also have fairly complex organizations and their own committees.

In the chart on this page, from where does the executive committee's power to act come?

Members of local groups.   **page 196**
Delegates in convention.   **page 208**
Board of Directors.   **page 214**

SAMPLE TYPED MOTION

1. Whereas, Poorly lighted streets are an
2. encouragement to crime and a threat to
3. the safety of their users, and
4.
5. Whereas, Oak Street, between Locust and May
6. Streets has become a major thoroughfare
7. with a bus line that serves the surrounding
8. residential neighborhood, and
9.
10. Whereas, The lighting in the subject location
11. is entirely inadequate, having been installed
12. before the development of the surrounding
13. area, and
14.
15. Whereas, The government of our city has
16. unallocated funds available for capital
17. improvement during the next fiscal year; therefore
18.
19. Resolved, That the president urge upon the
20. city council at its budget hearing of November
21. 15 our belief that new lighting for the subject
22. area deserves the highest priority.
23.
24. Resolved, That the secretary shall transmit
25. to all other civic organizations a copy of
26. this resolution with a cover letter urging
27. their adoption of similar resolutions.

YOUR ANSWER: Select those people in the organization who seem to be listened to in meetings and try to line them up in advance.

That is undoubtedly the surest way of getting full consideration for your proposal and getting it passed. There are people who are leaders in every group. The support of the leaders is always important, for whether they support or oppose you, others will follow. If the leaders have a chance to think about your idea, and it is sound, they will probably support you.

This approach is not as important in a smaller group but in large and infrequent meetings, parliamentary procedure is usually strictly controlled. That means you will have one chance (a brief one) to make your point. If you haven't spoken in advance with the natural leaders, you will not know whether you are likely to get support or criticism. A small change in your proposal may win over a potential opponent. Consultation with people whose opinions are respected is essentially informal committee work.

Now, let's look at a public motion, but first a word about the terms *motion* and *resolution,* for in parliamentary usage they are often unclear. Sometimes, *resolution* means motion, which, instead of proposing action, commits the group to a position. However, resolution usually means any main motion accepted by the group. When a formal main motion is written out, the word *Resolve* or *Resolved* precedes the statement of the action to be taken (lines 19 and 24). Here, resolved means, "We intend to do it ourselves." An organization with a paid staff says *Ordered* rather than *Resolved,* except in motions of the non-action type.

The motion on the opposite page proposes two actions in a single motion. Under the rules of debate, only one motion may be on the floor at any one time, but the border line between a single motion and several is not always clear. A motion containing unrelated parts should be divided at the request of a single member; one containing related parts may be divided by a majority vote, if the parts can stand by themselves.

The motion in the illustration on the facing page:

Could be divided by a majority vote.   **page 192**

Could not be divided.   **page 197**

204

[*from page 224*]

YOUR ANSWER: Will follow the normal order of business.

No. The normal order of business calls for all kinds of business that would not be possible if there had been no prior meetings. There could be no minutes, no committee or officer reports, no special or general orders, no old business.

Now go to page 224 and select the better answer.

YOUR ANSWER: True.

That is correct, and for several reasons. An organization that meets monthly is likely to operate according to committee debating rules, which make it relatively easy to perfect a motion after it is on the floor. Unpolished motions will be expected, because such frequent meetings do not leave much time for committee work. And, the membership will probably be relatively small; fewer man-hours are consumed in a two-hour discussion among thirty people than in a fifteen-minute discussion in a meeting of 300 people.

The size of an organization and the frequency of its meetings are inversely related. The larger an organization and the more geographically dispersed its members, the less frequent will be its membership meetings. That is simple logistics. It is difficult to bring a large group of people together. A hall must be rented, a schedule worked out, notices sent, speakers invited, living accommodations arranged — a small national convention (200–300 people) can keep a large committee busy for the better part of a year.

Because large organizations tend to have infrequent meetings, they usually delegate their power to an executive committee that acts for the organization in the interim between meetings. The annual membership meetings or conventions are devoted to the choice of officers and executive committee members and to matters of high-level policy. It is impossible for the membership as a whole to approve every single act or expenditure of the organization. The policy and program for the year ahead are determined; then the board or executive committee is directed to carry it out and report next year on the results. (Since the business agenda at an annual meeting is usually quite crowded, it is both polite and wise to have motions written out in advance so that they can be handled with dispatch.)

Now note down the articles listed below and the page number following. Read the articles and then turn to page 200.

206

SAMPLE TYPED MOTION

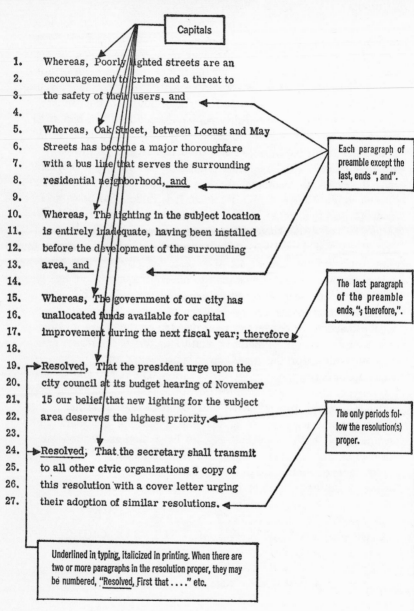

Capitals

1. Whereas, Poorly lighted streets are an
2. encouragement to crime and a threat to
3. the safety of their users, and

5. Whereas, Oak Street, between Locust and May
6. Streets has become a major thoroughfare
7. with a bus line that serves the surrounding
8. residential neighborhood, and

10. Whereas, The lighting in the subject location
11. is entirely inadequate, having been installed
12. before the development of the surrounding
13. area, and

15. Whereas, The government of our city has
16. unallocated funds available for capital
17. improvement during the next fiscal year; therefore

19. Resolved, That the president urge upon the
20. city council at its budget hearing of November
21. 15 our belief that new lighting for the subject
22. area deserves the highest priority.

24. Resolved, That the secretary shall transmit
25. to all other civic organizations a copy of
26. this resolution with a cover letter urging
27. their adoption of similar resolutions.

Each paragraph of preamble except the last, ends ", and".

The last paragraph of the preamble ends, "; therefore,".

The only periods follow the resolution(s) proper.

Underlined in typing, italicized in printing. When there are two or more paragraphs in the resolution proper, they may be numbered, "Resolved, First that . . . ." etc.

YOUR ANSWER: Whereas, Slums are breeders of crime and disease, and produce tax income far below the cost of city services,

That would probably be the most appropriate of the three paragraphs for inclusion in the proposed motion. It states general reasons that will help make clear the intention of your organization, while avoiding argumentativeness and unnecessary detail.

The illustration at left reproduces the motion about the street lights, this time with some notations on proper form. The line numbers on the side are not necessary, and would not be used in the finished motion, as published by your organization. However, it is helpful, if copies of the motion have been distributed to the membership, to include the numbers so that during debate members can indicate immediately the part of the text to which they are speaking. Copies for all members would normally be provided only for the most important matters.

Examine carefully the sample in the illustration on the facing page, noting the points of style, then see if you can pick out the line in the example below in which an error occurs.

1.   Whereas, The Boy Scouts of America do an admirable
2.   job of inculcating the values of citizenship, and
3.
4.   Whereas, The Springfield Boy Scout Troop is an
5.   especially admirable example of the Scouting
6.   movement. Therefore,
7.
8.   Resolved, That the Springfield Kiwanis Club shall
9.   donate one hundred dollars to our troop's fund
10.   raising campaign.

Line 1   **page 194**

Line 6   **page 199**

Line 8   **page 212**

[*from page 201*]

YOUR ANSWER: Delegates in convention.

The power of the executive committee comes through the delegates. In that limited sense, your answer is correct. But ask yourself where the delegates get their power. Do they just have the power to act in the name of the organization?

Now return to page 201 and select a better answer.

YOUR ANSWER: Executive Secretary.

Don't be fooled by the title. Plain secretaries, corresponding secretaries, and recording secretaries are all elected officers. An executive secretary is entirely different. He or she is an employee hired to carry out the tasks assigned by the organization. In a sense, he is equivalent to the American president, to a governor, or to a mayor. Each of these is an executive officer. If you don't read over the word executive too rapidly, you will see that its root is execute, in the sense of *do,* not *kill.* The executive officer is the person who does; what he does is carry out the directions of the legislative or deliberative body.

We elect our president, our governors, and our mayors, but most executive officers are hired employees. In government, we see this trend developing in the city manager plan. The city manager is a hired executive. Businesses hire their executives, too, and the executives carry out the orders of their boards of directors. (In a corporation, the stockholders elect the board of directors. At least theoretically, the power and authority of the executive running the business ultimately comes from the stockholder-owners.)

Now return to page 196 and select a better answer.

210
[from page 215]

YOUR ANSWER: Tell them what you think an organization could do for the neighborhood.

You might mention this in passing, but it is not an approach likely to attract potentially active members. People may join organizations that will do something for them, but they are active in organizations where they are useful and where they can do something.

When you ask a neighbor what he believes to be a problem, you make him think that you are interested in him personally and that you respect his intelligence. Moreover, you are likely to get some good ideas.

Now return to page 215 and select the correct answer.

YOUR ANSWER: Whereas, Almost four tax dollars are spent on city services for every $2.67 collected in slum areas, leaving the city a tax deficit of $367,000 annually,

That is not too bad, but it is not in the tone normally adopted for preambles. Preambles are relatively short — one much larger than that in the sample motion would be unusual, so it is impractical to go into the kind of detail used in the sample above. If every point in a motion concerning slums were supported with that much statistical data, the preamble would be many pages long.

The idea in a preamble is to outline the principle points without arguing them. Assertions are made to justify the resolution (such as "slums are expensive"), but the assertions are not argued. "Slums are costly," does the job, without any argument or explanation.

Now return to page 197 and select a better paragraph.

[*from page 207*]

YOUR ANSWER: Line 8.

No, everything in line 8 is all right. The points to notice were: (a) that Resolved was capitalized; (b) that "it" was italicized (underlined); (c) that "it" was followed by a comma; (d) that the resolution was introduced by "That"; and (e) that "That" was capitalized. Take a look at line 8.

"Resolved, That the Springfield Kiwanis Club shall donate. . . ."
Everything is in order.
If you carefully read the rules on the full page sample, you will find that one of them has been violated in another line of this resolution.

Now return to page 207 and select a better answer.

YOUR ANSWER: The Congress.

The executive committee does act like a congress, insofar as the executive committee makes decisions in a deliberative manner according to parliamentary rules. But who carries out the decisions of the executive committee? Remember, it was said that this organization does not have an executive secretary.

Now return to page 217 and select a better answer.

214

[from page 201]

YOUR ANSWER: Board of Directors.

It is true that if the executive committee is elected by the board of directors, the board of directors gives the executive committee its power. However, you must ask yourself where the board of directors gets the power that it passes on to the executive committee. Do the directors just have the power from nowhere?

Now return to page 201 and select a better answer.

YOUR ANSWER: Get potential members.

That is correct; a constitution can wait. Unless, right in the beginning, your organization is very large or unless there are legal or other special problems, it is possible to go along without a constitution for some time. In fact, an organization can last for years without its organizational structure ever being written down.

An informal organization is possible where the members know one another, know the purposes of the organization, agree to them, and are acquainted with the way in which their fellow members intend to carry out organization affairs. The purpose of writing things down is simply to get them on record, not because the writing performs any magic. Once written down, members not so rigorously selected can enter the organization, discover its purposes, and decide whether or not to accept them. And the document serves as a guide in case there are disagreements on purposes or rules.

The most effective way of enlisting the support of a group of people is to propose to solve a problem that bothers them. (You do not keep people active in organizations by troubling them as little as possible, but, within reason, by keeping them as busy as possible. Everyone likes to be useful.) Your organization, then, will arise from a sense of need on your part, and from your ability to communicate that sense of need to others.

If you had in mind to organize a neighborhood-betterment group, what do you think would be the best way to approach the people you would like to have form the organization's nucleus?

Tell them what you think an organization could do for the neighborhood. **page 210**

Ask them to list what they think are the principal problems in the neighborhood. **page 224**

YOUR ANSWER: Two-thirds.

A two-thirds vote is required to amend a constitution after it has been adopted, but not for the original adoption.

A two-thirds vote is required in places where the interests of members have to be protected. Members who have adopted a set of rules for governing themselves have an interest in maintaining those rules. But before any body of rules has been adopted, you cannot say that anyone has an interest in them. There are no rights that need protection.

Actually, if only a minority supported a proposed constitution, that minority could go off by itself and adopt the constitution it favors. If the minority moved to another room, it would be a majority in its new quarters. A constitution may be adopted by a group of any size. Any group of people can agree to come together and abide by a set of rules.

The reason for specifying a majority vote is that, before an organization is formed, the assembly consists of exactly the number of people present. By virtue of taking the trouble to come to the meeting, a person gets the right to vote. So no matter who comes, the whole organization is present. Thus, a majority vote in this situation is a majority of all the members. A two-thirds vote is usually an alternative to a vote of a majority of the members in organizations where it is unlikely that all the members, or even a majority of them, can be brought together in a single meeting.

Now return to page 221 and select the correct answer.

YOUR ANSWER: The presiding officer.

Correct. The presiding officer may be called president, chairman, or moderator — in some organizations he may be given more esoteric titles. Whatever his title, the presiding officer is the elected leader of the organization. The executive secretary is an employee, not an elected official. Where there is no paid staff, the presiding officer will, in addition to running meetings, carry out many of the tasks that would otherwise be performed by an executive secretary, but the work will be shared among other officers as well.

A paid staff member is a tremendous asset to any organization. Many decisions will be based upon his advice, and he will represent the organization to the world. Consequently, it is important to exercise great care in choosing one. His very value to the organization can give him a great deal of abusable power. An organization can become the tool of its paid staff as well as of its executive committee. With reasonable care, no such threat should ever arise, either from staff or officers, but the possibility always exists. It might appear that these threats could be eliminated by constitutional safeguards. This is only partially true. The more important safeguard is the commitment of the members to the goals of the organization and their active participation.

A threat equally as dangerous, but more likely to occur in the early stages of an organization's life is the choice of officers who are affected by paranoia and delusions of grandeur. Such persons may appear, before they become well known, as especially dedicated and interested workers and no more. Hence, they are likely candidates for office. Once in office, such a person can tear a young organization apart by his refusal to trust his fellow officers and by accusations of usurpation and deceit. When starting a new organization, it is wise to choose as officers only those who are quite well-known to the members.

In an organization without a paid staff, the executive committee is very much like:

The Congress. **page 213**

The President. **page 222**

Both of the above. **page 225**

YOUR ANSWER: Write a constitution.

No, definitely not. A constitution is, in the initial stages of organization, far less important than reaching members. Many organizations — including the government of Great Britain — get along without ever writing a constitution.

When a person has an idea for an organization, he will best begin by talking over his idea with two or three close friends who, he believes, are likely to be interested. From those conversations, his idea is likely to be refined and to be spelled out in greater detail. With the organization idea a little more firmly in mind, he approaches other people whom he knows less well. The circle of interested people spreads in that manner. Close friends are sold on a nebulous idea, less close friends on an idea somewhat better formed, and, finally, complete strangers may be approached, but with the organizational idea fairly well developed.

Only after many people have been spoken with personally will the organizer and his circle of friends reach the point of calling a formal meeting. Only after there has been at least one formal meeting will there be any necessity of writing out a constitution.

If you were to approach your close friends with a draft constitution, they would tend to feel that they were not even needed. Moreover, by depending solely on yourself for the drafting of a constitution, you would be likely to write one defective in some respects. You would certainly write one to which no one else felt in any way morally committed.

Now return to page 225 and select the better answer.

YOUR ANSWER: False.

Admitted, it is a good idea to have your main motions written out in advance — and your amendments as well — wherever it is practicable to do so. However, in some situations the advance preparation is more important than in others. If your organization meets only quarterly, chances are that a great deal of business will have to be disposed of in short order. Then it is (a) impolite to expect people to waste their time while you fumble around for a wording, and (b) likely that the motion will not end up in as good a shape as would have been possible if more thought had been given to it.

Where the organization meets monthly, there is likely to be more time available for amending and perfecting a motion after it reaches the floor than is true in a quarterly meeting.

Now return to page 199 and select the better answer.

220

[from page 224]

YOUR ANSWER: Will not follow the normal order of business.

Of course not. There are no officers to report, no committees to report, no old business, and no general or special orders, and no minutes of any previous meeting. The agenda for a first meeting usually consists of the following:

1. Call to order — usually about ten minutes after the assigned hour.
2. Nomination and election of a temporary chairman — one who will serve until the group is formally organized and regular officers elected. It is usually well to have the person who opened the meeting nominate a temporary chairman who had been previously agreed upon, though nominations may be entertained from the floor.
3. After his election, the temporary chairman takes the chair and proceeds to the election of a temporary secretary. Those are all the officers needed until permanent officers are chosen.
4. The chair introduces the speaker who has been assigned the task of reporting to the group the reason for calling the meeting. Actually, several speakers may be heard.
5. Discussion — after the program, the chairman should open the floor for informal debate, allowing discussion to proceed as long as necessary and allowing individual speeches as long as they don't become tiresome.
6. When the discussion seems to be completed, the chair should indicate willingness to entertain motions, at which time those agreed upon in advance should be made. These might include (a) a motion stating that an organization with the stated purposes should be set up, (b) a motion setting up a committee to draft a constitution, (c) a motion fixing the time to adjourn to — so that a later motion to adjourn will not abolish the group, and (d) any other motions that might be useful in the immediate circumstances — the group may want to go on record immediately on some issue. After the essential business has been disposed of, any motions made from the floor should be entertained.
7. When all business is completed, the chair should entertain a motion to adjourn.

(Continued on page 221)

The committee assigned the task of writing a constitution should be provided with models of constitutions used by other groups with similar purposes. The drafting committee should report back at the next (adjourned) meeting. (It is a good idea to get the names and addresses of all who attend so that they may be sent notices to remind them of subsequent meetings.)

What is the vote normally required for the adoption of a constitution?

Two-thirds.   page 216

Majority.   page 226

222

[*from page 217*]

YOUR ANSWER: The President.

It is true that the term executive suggests the type of responsibilities that the President has, for he is an executive officer. His job is to run the government in accordance with the rules set out originally in the constitution and, in more detail, by the Congress.

The executive committee has such responsibilities. However, it also has legislative responsibilities, within limits set by the constitution. An executive committee is empowered to make many decisions on its own — it cannot, however, change the constitution or reverse a policy decision made at the annual membership meeting. Within those limitations, an executive committee has a great deal of leeway. Moreover, it makes its decisions by the same deliberative process as any other parliamentary organization.

The executive committee, then, is in the position of giving itself orders, in its decision-making capacity, and carrying them out in its executive capacity.

Now return to page 217 and select a better answer.

YOUR ANSWER: Both of the above.

That's a safe-sounding answer. It can't be less than half right. It is also not more than half right.

Don't be fooled by the title executive secretary. Plain secretaries, corresponding secretaries, and recording secretaries are all elected officers. An executive secretary is entirely different. He or she is an employee hired to carry out the tasks assigned by the organization. In a sense, he is equivalent to the American President, to a governor, or to a mayor. Each of these is an executive officer. If you don't read over the word executive too rapidly, you will see that its root is execute, in the sense of *do,* not *kill.* The executive officer is the person who does; what he does is carry out the directions of the legislative or deliberate body.

We elect our President, our governors, and our mayors, but most executive officers are hired employees. In government, we see this trend developing in the city manager plan. The city manager is a hired executive. Businesses hire their executives, too, and the executives carry out the orders of their boards of directors. (In a corporation, the stockholders elect the board of directors. At least theoretically, the power and authority of the executive running the business ultimately comes from the stockholder-owners.)

Now return to page 196 and select a better answer.

224

YOUR ANSWER: Ask them what they think are the principal problems of the neighborhood.

That is usually a very effective way to enlist interest. Many a block club has been started when a person, feeling generally dissatisfied with what was going on in his area, invited a group of neighbors to informally discuss community problems. From a discussion of needs, a sense of purpose can develop and detailed needs and goals can be defined. Besides, this approach has the advantage that your friends immediately feel involved and useful. And, you are gaining ammunition to use in later stages of organization.

When you have two things — a nucleus of interested people and a clear set of purposes — you are ready to start formal organization. Your intention will be to bring together a group of people in a more formal meeting for the purpose of establishing a permanent organization. The group with whom you have discussed neighborhood problems will be the group that plans and calls the larger meeting.

There are certain decisions that must be made in advance of the first meeting: (a) who will open the meeting; (b) who will serve as temporary chairman; (c) who will present to the group the purposes conceived for the organization; (d) any motions to be entertained (they should be drafted and a person assigned to make them at the appropriate time); (e) a time and place for a second meeting, if the group called is so large that finding a place to meet may be difficult.

With these tasks completed, you are ready for your first meeting. The agenda for this meeting:

Will follow the normal order of business. **page 204**

Will not follow the normal order of business. **page 220**

YOUR ANSWER: Both of the above.

Right. Theoretically, the executive committee is purely executive, like the presidency. But within the limits set by the organization's constitution, the executive committee is almost certain to have a broad range of decision-making power. The executive committee, in fact, operates like any other deliberate body, but where there is no staff to direct, the executive committee must carry out its own resolutions.

At some time during your life, there is a good chance that it will occur to you to set up a brand-new organization. Perhaps you will become aware of some problem which no one else seems to be working on effectively. Perhaps you will feel the need for a neighborhood group. Perhaps your intention will be simply to further a personal hobby of joining with others of like mind. The problems you face in trying to get an organization started are probably fewer than you expect. More difficult is the problem of keeping a young organization alive for any length of time. Many people will come to a first meeting or two to see what is happening, but if their interest is not captured, they will not stay.

There are two tasks involved in setting up a brand-new organization: gather a group of people who are interested and willing to join; draft a constitution that reasonably embodies the purposes and functions of the organization.

Which of the two tasks do you think should be done first?

Get potential members.   **page 215**

Write a constitution.   **page 218**

YOUR ANSWER: Majority.

That is correct. As a general rule, a majority vote is sufficient to adopt a constitution. Before a constitution has been adopted, there are not vested interests entitled to the protection of a two-thirds vote. In fact, if a majority were not obtained, there would be no reason why the minority favoring the constitution could not go off to set up its own organization. The splinter group would be smaller, that is all. The point is, before there is a constitution and a membership, it is impossible to define a quorum.

The second meeting will look more like a regular meeting. There will be the call to order, minutes of the previous meeting, and the report of the drafting committee. A drafting committee's report is automatically considered seriatim. As soon as a constitution is adopted, the organization proceeds to the nomination and election of officers. If no method for nomination is described by the constitution, the temporary chairman entertains motions on method. If a nominating committee is proposed, the committee may meet immediately while the organization recesses or handles other business. The committee reports later in the meeting. From that point, elections are handled according to normal procedure. In some instances, it may be better to allow the election of officers to wait for a third meeting to give a nominating committee a chance to do a good job. This is especially important where the organization is large and the members not well-known to each other. After election of officers, the committees designated in the by-laws should be assigned and any other business handled.

The third meeting, then, will be a regular meeting of a permanent organization. You will be rewarded for your efforts with the knowledge that you are a fully participating citizen in a free society. For in a free society, the voluntary organization is the expression of the independence and self-reliance of the citizen.

Parliamentary Dictionary

NOTE

Where you find words printed all in capitals, there is an article of that name containing important related information. Thus, in the article entitled COMMIT, you will find this: "The motion to commit may designate assignment of one or several motions to any committee, including a COMMITTEE OF THE WHOLE. . . ." There is an article entitled COMMITTEE OF THE WHOLE in which you will find more information.

ACCEPT FACTUAL REPORT

	MAIN MOTION	POSTPONE INDEFINITELY	AMEND	COMMIT	POSTPONE TO FIXED TIME	LIMIT OR EXTEND DEBATE	PREVIOUS QUESTION	TABLE	ORDERS OF THE DAY	QUESTIONS OF PRIVILEGE	RECESS	ADJOURN	SET TIME TO ADJOURN TO
SUBJECT MOTION:													
YIELDS TO		●	●	●	●	●	●	●	●	●	●	●	●
TAKES PRECEDENCE OF													

Class: Incidental Main Motion
Debatable: YES   *Vote:* MAJORITY
Amendable: YES   *Second needed:* YES (See *Notes*)
Reconsiderable: YES   *Can interrupt speaker:* NO

Purpose and Effect: When a motion to accept is passed, it means that a report is approved and the committee or person making the report is discharged. Failure of the motion indicates dissatisfaction with the report. This motion should be used only when a report makes no recommendations and does not implicitly commit the organization to a position. This motion is seldom used because it usually is not necessary to discharge the committee or person (See *Notes*) and because reports without recommendations are very infrequent.

Form: "I move the acceptance of the report."
"I move to accept the report of the —— committee."
"I move to accept the report on ——— ."

228

Notes:

<table>
<tr><td>Accept and Adopt</td><td>In allowing this motion, the chairman should make sure that the organization understands its effect. Sometimes an organization will accept a report that makes certain recommendations without realizing that they're actually approving the recommendations. To accept has the same effect as to adopt.</td></tr>
<tr><td>Who Moves</td><td>NOT the maker of a report but a member from the floor moves to accept a report.</td></tr>
<tr><td>Formal and Informal Acceptance</td><td>It is unnecessary for a factual report to be formally accepted by vote. Just reading a report or giving it to the chairman constitutes acceptance. The motion is used only when it seems necessary to indicate that the duties of the committee or official have ended or when there is some doubt that the report will be considered satisfactory.</td></tr>
<tr><td>Call Question and Second</td><td>If no one moves acceptance, the chair may simply call the question. A committee report, since it is already supported by the members of the committee, is equivalent to a motion and second.</td></tr>
<tr><td>Treasurer's Report</td><td>The report of the treasurer is not accepted or adopted, because that would imply approval of the figures. It is simply given to the chairman for referral to an auditor or auditing committee. The report of the auditing committee would be followed by a motion to accept.</td></tr>
</table>

ADJOURN REGULAR MEETING OF A PERMANENT ORGANIZATION

1. If qualified or if made when no business is pending, adjourn is treated as a main motion.	MAIN MOTION	POSTPONE INDEFINITELY	AMEND	COMMIT	POSTPONE TO FIXED TIME	LIMIT OR EXTEND DEBATE	PREVIOUS QUESTION	TABLE	ORDERS OF THE DAY	QUESTIONS OF PRIVILEGE	RECESS	ADJOURN	SET TIME TO ADJOURN TO
SUBJECT MOTION:													
YIELDS TO													●
TAKES PRECEDENCE OF	●	●	●	●	●	●	●	●	●	●	●		

Class: Privileged Motion (See Notes)
Debatable: NO
Amendable: NO
Reconsiderable: NO

Vote: MAJORITY
Second needed: YES
Can interrupt speaker: NO

Purpose and Effect: To close or end a meeting. The motion to ad-journ has different effects in different types of meetings or sessions. [If your organization (a) meets less often than quarterly, (b) is composed of elected delegates, (c) meets in convention or under other circumstances where a session consisting of several meetings takes place, or (d) if your meeting is a mass meeting or other non-permanent group gathering, see ADJOURN IN SPECIAL CIRCUMSTANCES.] The effect of the mo-tion is to make all pending business the old business of the subsequent meeting.

Form: "Mr. Chairman, I move we adjourn."
"Mr. Chairman, I move adjournment."

Notes:

Class	If the motion to adjourn is qualified in any way, it be-comes subject to all the rules for *main motions*.
Privilege	In a permanent organization, the motion to adjourn has the highest privilege next to the motion to SET TIME FOR CONTINUATION OF PRESENT SESSION which can be made after the motion for adjournment but before the vote on adjournment.
When Entertained and Renewed	The motion to adjourn can be entertained by the chair except when a vote is being taken or counted or when no business has intervened since an earlier motion to ad-journ was defeated. The latter limitation assures that the motion to adjourn cannot obstruct the handling of business. If some business has intervened, the motion to adjourn is entertained on the assumption that the group may have finished the business that led it to reject the earlier motion.
Chair Must Announce	The adjournment does not take effect until announced by the chairman.
Chair's Right to Comment	Though the motion is undebatable, the chair may, up to the time of the vote, inform the group that there is busi-ness that should be handled before adjournment.
Announcements from Chair	If there are announcements to be made to the group, the chair should make them before he adjourns the meeting, that is, before announcing the vote.

ADJOURN IN SPECIAL CIRCUMSTANCES

If qualified, made when no business is pending, or if it would have the effect of abolishing the organization, the motion to adjourn is a main motion.	MAIN MOTION	POSTPONE INDEFINITELY	AMEND	COMMIT	POSTPONE TO FIXED TIME	LIMIT OR EXTEND DEBATE	PREVIOUS QUESTION	TABLE	ORDERS OF THE DAY	QUESTIONS OF PRIVILEGE	RECESS	ADJOURN	SET TIME TO ADJOURN TO
SUBJECT MOTION:													
YIELDS TO													●
TAKES PRECEDENCE OF	●	●	●	●	●	●	●	●	●	●	●		

Class: Privileged Motion (See *Notes*)
Debatable: NO (See *Notes*) *Vote:* MAJORITY
Amendable: NO *Second needed:* YES
Reconsiderable: NO *Can interrupt speaker:* NO

Purpose and Effect: To close or end a meeting or session. The effect of the motion to adjourn differs in the special situations below. For the adjournment of a regular meeting of a standing organization and for general comments on adjournment, see ADJOURNMENT REGULAR MEETING OF A PERMANENT ORGANIZATION.

An unqualified motion to adjourn is privileged in convention or continuous session, except for the final motion abolishing the convention when there is no provision for an assembly composed of the same members or delegates to meet again.

Form: "Mr. Chairman, I move we adjourn."
"Mr. Chairman, I move adjournment."

Notes:

Class An unqualified motion to adjourn is privileged in convention or continuous session except for the final adjournment when there is no provision for the same assembly to meet again. If there is a provision for the same body of delegates to be called together again before the next scheduled session (which would be composed of different delegates) the adjournment sine die is still privileged. When there is no provision for subsequent meeting of the same group, the motion to adjourn is a main motion and may be debated.

In Convention In a convention or other session of several meetings, adjournment does not make pending business into old business. That which was pending at one session is taken up immediately after the call to order and the reading of the MINUTES at the next meeting. Reading the minutes of the previous meeting is sometimes dispensed with temporarily.

Meetings
Less than
Quarterly

When an organization meets less often than quarterly, the effect of adjournment is to erase pending business from consideration. The questions erased may be brought up again at the next meeting as new business.

ADJOURN, SET TIME TO, and ADJOURN TO, SET TIME TO

To set the time to adjourn to means to set the time at which the next meeting of the same session will be held. (See: SET TIME FOR CONTINUATION OF PRESENT SESSION.) Do not confuse the above with *set time to adjourn,* which is a variation of the motion to adjourn, differing only in that it is qualified so that it will take effect later. When unqualified, the motion to adjourn takes effect the moment the chair states that it has carried. A qualified motion to adjourn is treated as a main motion. (See: ADJOURN REGULAR MEETING OF PERMANENT ORGANIZATION and ADJOURN IN SPECIAL CIRCUMSTANCES.)

ADJOURNED MEETING

An adjourned meeting is one meeting of a SESSION other than the first one. It is a meeting held as the result of a motion TO SET A TIME FOR THE CONTINUATION OF THE PRESENT SESSION (also called a motion to set a time to adjourn to), or of a convention program that calls for a series of meetings. At an adjourned meeting, the order of business is taken up where it was broken off at the close of the previous meeting. That being the case, an adjourned meeting will not normally hear officers' reports or committee reports — unless the previous meeting broke off before those items of business were considered. The only repetition will be the reading of the minutes, which is in order at the beginning of every meeting, whether regular or adjourned. There can be adjourned regular meetings and adjourned SPECIAL MEETINGS.

ADOPT PROGRAM   See: PROGRAM

ADOPT REPORT CONTAINING RESOLUTIONS OR RECOMMENDA-TIONS (See Notes)

Reports of nomination committees are not adopted.	MAIN MOTION	POSTPONE INDEFINITELY	AMEND	COMMIT	POSTPONE TO FIXED TIME	LIMIT OR EXTEND DEBATE	PREVIOUS QUESTION	TABLE	ORDERS OF THE DAY	QUESTIONS OF PRIVILEGE	RECESS	ADJOURN	SET TIME TO ADJOURN TO
SUBJECT MOTION:													
YIELDS TO		●	●	●	●	●	●	●	●	●	●	●	●
TAKES PRECEDENCE OF													

Class: Incidental Main Motion
Debatable: YES
Amendable: YES   *Vote:* MAJORITY
Reconsiderable: YES   *Second needed:* YES (See *Notes*)
                       Can interrupt speaker: NO

Purpose and Effect: To bring to the floor a committee report containing resolutions or recommendations when these proposals were not previously committed or referred to committee. A program presented as a motion and then referred to the committee is not handled as a resolution made by the committee, even if the committee proposes amending the original motion.

Form: If the recommendations are not in the form of resolutions: "Mr. Chairman, I move the adoption of the recommendations of the —— committee." If the report concludes with resolutions: "Mr. Chairman, I move the adoption of the resolutions of the —— committee."

Notes:

Applicability   This procedure applies only to reports initiated by the committee. (For procedure where the subject of the report was referred to committee, see: ADOPT REPORT ON MATTERS REFERRED TO COMMITTEE.)

Does Not Amend   Adopting the report as amended does not amend the report. The committee's report stands as made and if the report is recorded or published, that which was deleted from the report is shown in brackets; that which was added is shown in italics or is underlined in typed copy.

Who Moves	These motions may be made either by the maker of the report, or by another member. Or the chair may state the question without waiting for a motion.
Minority Report	When a MINORITY REPORT accompanies a committee's report, the chair reads the minority report *after* stating the question on the majority report, thus informing the membership of the minority position. The minority report, however, cannot be acted upon unless there is a motion from the floor to substitute the minority report, in whole or in part, for the majority report. Such substitution is handled as any other (See: AMEND, Substitute a Paragraph).
Call Question and Second	If no one moves acceptance, the chair may simply call the question. The support of two committee members is as good as a motion and a second.
Object	A member may OBJECT TO CONSIDERATION of the motion to adopt a report initiated by a committee (but not to the motion to adopt a committee's report on a matter that had been referred).
Divide	Multiple recommendations may be divided according to the regular procedure for division (See: DIVIDE THE QUESTION).
Nominating Reports	If the report is that of a nominating committee, no motion is made and no vote taken. The report of the nominating committee is a set of nominations to be acted on as such (See: NOMINATIONS).
Membership Reports	The report of a membership committee is acted on immediately. The chair may state the question accepting the proposed members without a motion or second.

ADOPT REPORT ON MATTERS REFERRED TO COMMITTEE OR COMMITTED (See Notes)

Object to consideration of a question cannot be applied. Reports of nominating committees are not adopted.	MAIN MOTION	POSTPONE INDEFINITELY	AMEND	COMMIT	POSTPONE TO FIXED TIME	LIMIT OR EXTEND DEBATE	PREVIOUS QUESTION	TABLE	ORDERS OF THE DAY	QUESTIONS OF PRIVILEGE	RECESS	ADJOURN	SET TIME TO ADJOURN TO
SUBJECT MOTION:													
YIELDS TO.	●	●	●	●	●	●	●	●	●	●	●	●	●
TAKES PRECEDENCE OF													

Class: Incidental Main Motion
Debatable: YES   *Vote:* MAJORITY
Amendable: YES   *Second needed:* YES (See *Notes*)
Reconsiderable: YES   *Can interrupt speaker:* NO

Purpose and Effect: To bring to the floor the resolutions, recommendations, amendments, or substitutes of a committee report on a matter referred to committee. A program made as a motion and then referred to committee is considered according to this procedure.

Form: It is usually most convenient for the chair to state the question; however, the appropriate motion may also be made from the floor.

Notes:

Applicability   If a committee prepares a program, the information here is not necessarily applicable. (For procedure where report initiated by committee, see: ADOPT REPORT CONTAINING RESOLUTIONS.)

No Objections   Consideration of these motions cannot be objected to.

Neutral or Positive Report   If the committee makes no recommendation on the matter referred or if it recommends adoption, the motion as committed becomes the question.

Negative Report   If secondary motions are pending at the time of commitment, the secondary motions are disposed of first in the order in which they were pending at the time of commitment.

Secondary Motions   If the recommendation is against the committed motion, the question is still the motion, but the chairman introduces it by saying, "Notwithstanding the recommendation of the committee," or a similar phrase, to avoid making the group vote on a question stated in the form of a double negative.

Pending Postponement

If a motion is committed with a motion to postpone it pending, the postponement motion is ignored.

Postponement Recommended

If the recommendation of the committee is postponement, the motion referred is not considered unless the organization rejects the motion to postpone.

Amendment Recommended

If the recommendation is for one or more amendments, the amendments are read in context and voted on serially. Then, if no additional amendments are heard from the floor, the question is the motion as amended. By majority vote to suspend the rules, the amendments and the motion may be adopted in one vote.

Substitute Recommended

If the recommendation is a substitute motion, the substitute is voted on first. If it fails, the motion committed becomes the question. If the motion has been committed with amendments, these amendments are considered before the substitute. Then the substitute motion is voted. If it fails, then the question is the original motion as perfected.

If the recommendation of the committee is a substitute for all or part of the motion referred, the substitute is the first question voted on. But amendments to the original motion will be entertained while the substitute is pending. (See: AMEND, Substitute a Paragraph.) If the substitute fails, the motion as committed is the next question. When the motion for which the substitute had been proposed was committed with one or more amendments attached, the amendments to the motion as committed are acted on first. When the motion committed is perfected, the substitute then becomes the question before the house. The substitute may also be amended from the floor. When the substitute is perfected, the group votes on it. If the substitute fails, the organization then votes on the original as perfected.

Call Question and Second

If no one moves the adoption of the report, or whatever motion is appropriate in view of the contents of the report, the chair may state the question without waiting on a motion and second. The report of a committee, since it is supported by a majority of its members, is equivalent to a motion and second.

AGENDA   See: PROGRAM, ORDER OF BUSINESS, and ORDERS

AMEND

1. Amendment to amendment cannot be amended. 2. When it leads to a motion. 3. When not privileged. 4. Takes main motion, too. 5. May apply to amendment alone.	MAIN MOTION	POSTPONE INDEFINITELY	AMEND	COMMIT	POSTPONE TO FIXED TIME	LIMIT OR EXTEND DEBATE	PREVIOUS QUESTION	TABLE	ORDERS OF THE DAY	QUESTIONS OF PRIVILEGE	RECESS	ADJOURN	SET TIME TO ADJOURN TO
SUBJECT MOTION:													
YIELDS TO				●	●	●	●	●	●	●	●	●	●
TAKES PRECEDENCE OF		●											
MAY BE APPLIED TO	●		1	●	●	●				2	●	3	●
MAY HAVE APPLIED TO ·IT			1	4	4	5	5	4					

Class: Subsidiary Motion (See *Notes*)
Debatable: See *Notes*   *Vote:* MAJORITY (See *Notes*)
Amendable: YES (See *Notes*)   *Second needed:* YES
Reconsiderable: YES (See *Notes*)   *Can interrupt speaker:* NO

Purpose and Effect: Amendments are intended to correct or improve reports or motions. (Correction of minutes is a form of amendment but is treated informally. See: MINUTES.) Most often, the purpose of an amendment is to make a motion more acceptable to the organization. The process of amending a motion is called perfecting it. (Not all motions are amendable. Whether a motion is amendable is reported under each specific motion in the Parliamentary Dictionary. A list will be found at UNAMENDABLE MOTIONS.) Before voting on a motion, the membership considers proposed changes or amendments. After these amendments are either accepted or rejected, the motion is considered to be perfected. Then the question before the assembly is the motion as perfected, not the motion in its original form. The vote on amendments can be seen as a process of defining exactly what the question under consideration is.

Types: Motions to amend may be of several types, as considered separately below:

> To Insert or Add Words
> To Strike Out Words
> To Strike Out and Insert Words
> To Insert or Add a Paragraph

To Strike Out a Paragraph
To Substitute a Paragraph
To Fill Blanks

Motions to amend already adopted matters by insertion are main motions; those that strike all or part of a previously enacted motion are rescissions (See: RESCIND). Amendments to a constitution, by-laws, and rules of order are treated under AMEND CONSTITUTION OR BY-LAWS. Corrections of minutes are considered under MINUTES, and amendments to standing rules under STANDING RULES.

Insert or Add Words:

Form	"I move that the word *commendable* be inserted before the word *report*."
	"I move that the words *and shall become effective as of June 30th* be added to the resolution."
	If the motion or report being amended is quite long, it is well to locate the addition or insertion more carefully. For instance, identify the paragraph and line where the change is to be made.
Reconsideration	Once a word has been inserted or added, it cannot be removed except by a subsequent amendment that is an essentially new proposal, e.g., a motion to remove the entire paragraph in which the word or words occur. If a motion to insert is lost, the same words may be inserted by another motion, provided the new motion is essentially a new question, that is, a question to which the subject words are only incidental.

Strike Out Words: The motion to strike can apply only to a single word or to a group of consecutive words. If it is desired to strike out words that are separated, each word or group of consecutive words must be considered as a separate motion. It is usually easier to move to strike out the entire section where the problem arises, and then substitute a new wording (See: *Substitute a Paragraph*).

Form	"Mr. Chairman, I move that the word *cart* be struck out before the word *horse*" (See also: *Insert or Add Words, Form*).
Amendment	A motion to strike may be amended only so that it will remove fewer words from the original motion. If there is a motion to strike the words *bicycles, cars, trucks, and buses,* that motion may be amended by striking from it the word *bicycles,* leaving *bicycles* in the motion, but

not by adding *motorcycles*. Adding *motorcycles* as an amendment to the motion to strike would have the effect of taking *motorcycles* from the original motion.

Reconsideration   If the motion to strike is adopted, the words struck cannot be reinserted except as part of an entirely new amendment. If the motion to strike is not adopted, words to which it referred may still be struck, (a) as part of a motion to strike and insert, (b) by a motion that strikes only a portion of the same words, or (c) by a motion that strikes the same words along with others.

Strike Out and Insert Words: This is one motion in which the two above are combined, but the motion to strike and insert cannot be separated. Consider a motion to strike the word *and* and insert *but* after the word *today*. If the question is divided and the motion to strike passes while the motion to insert does not pass, the motion ends up without a conjunction. If the motion to insert passes, but not that to strike, you end up with *today but and*. This motion can apply only to the striking of consecutive words.

Form   "Mr. Chairman, I move that the word *Street*, after the word *Berkeley*, be struck, and *Avenue* be inserted in its place."

"Mr. Chairman, I move that the words *Since the underpass is poorly lighted* be struck from before the word *we* and the same words inserted after the word *policeman*."

Note that it is not necessary to specify the changes in punctuation and capitalization that will result from a change in wording. The secretary should make such changes where needed. When words are struck and others added in the same place, the inserted words may be completely different from those struck, but when the inserted words are at a different location, they must be essentially the same as those removed. When neither the words nor the location are the same, it is better to strike the whole section and offer a rewritten paragraph.

Amendment   For purposes of amending a motion to strike and insert, the motion is dealt with in two parts. Amendments to the section to be struck are considered first; those to the insertion only after all amendments to the section struck are considered. Then the perfected motion to strike and insert is voted on as a whole.

Reconsideration The fact that a motion to strike and insert fails does not preclude *either* striking or inserting essentially the same words. It is also permissible to strike the same words and insert others, or insert the same words and strike others. Any of these combinations represents an essentially new idea and is, therefore, admissible.

Insert or Add a Paragraph: To insert or add a paragraph is not significantly different from inserting or adding words. Once a paragraph is inserted, it cannot be struck unless it has been significantly amended after insertion, or unless it is struck as part of a motion to strike other material as well. An inserted paragraph can be amended only by additional insertions.

Form "Mr. Chairman, I move that the following paragraph be inserted after the paragraph ending, '*unless the expenditure would produce a deficit.*'" (Read paragraph to be inserted.) The place of the paragraph to be inserted can be identified in any other unambiguous manner.

Strike Out a Paragraph: Amendments are classified for some purposes as of first and second degree. Those of second degree either are or can be amendments to amendments. Those of first degree either are or can be *only* amendments to the question. Thus, to strike or add words may be amendments to other amendments. Those motions that affect whole paragraphs or resolutions can be only of the first degree. You cannot amend the motion to strike and insert words so that the insertion is a whole paragraph. Nor can you amend a motion to insert two paragraphs by moving to strike one of the two. However, the motion to insert a paragraph or paragraphs may be amended by striking or inserting words. The amendment of the wording of the paragraph to be inserted is an admissible motion of the second degree. These comments apply equally to the motion to substitute (discussed below).

Form "Mr. Chairman, I move that the third paragraph be struck."
"Mr. Chairman, I move that the second resolution be struck."

Perfecting *the Paragraph* *to Be Struck* If a main motion is being considered and a first-degree amendment is made, a second-degree amendment may be applied to the first. When a motion to strike a paragraph has been made, amendments are still in order to the main motion. However, such amendments are un-amendable. Thus, there is always a limit of two amendments pending at any time. This rule is a compromise. It allows those who favor retention of the paragraph to attempt to improve it so that it will not be deleted, while not confusing matters completely by allowing three different amendments to be pending at the same time.

Amendment　The motion to strike a paragraph may not be amended, except in the sense noted above (that is, after the motion to strike is made, amending the paragraph to be struck actually operates like a second-degree amendment to the motion to strike).

Reconsideration　If a motion to strike a paragraph is lost, the paragraph may still be struck as part of a subsequent motion to substitute (see below) as part of a motion or to strike the subject paragraph along with others. Similarly, parts of the subject paragraph may be amended by motions to strike or strike and insert, despite the failure to strike the whole paragraph.

Substitute a Paragraph: The motion to substitute one paragraph for another is much like the motion to strike and insert words; however, the term *substitute* always applies to paragraphs or entire resolutions, while *strike and insert* always refers to words.

Form　"Mr. Chairman, I move that the following paragraph be substituted for paragraph one, page two." (Reads paragraph to be inserted.) The paragraph to be removed may be identified in any convenient and clear manner.

Perfecting the Paragraph to Be Struck and the Substitute　In considering the motion to substitute, the friends of the paragraph to be struck are given the opportunity to try to improve the paragraph and save it, just as in the case of the motion to strike a paragraph. As in that case, amendments to the paragraph to be struck are considered, for parliamentary purposes, as second-degree amendments to the motion to substitute. That means the amendments cannot be amended. When all amendments to the paragraph to be struck have been disposed of, the chair will entertain motions (also of the second degree) to amend the paragraph to be substituted. When both have been perfected, the chair will call the question.

Substitutes for an Entire Motion or Report	It is legitimate to move a substitution for an entire motion or report, as long as the substitution is germane, and as long as the whole question is immediately pending. If a report or motion is being considered by paragraphs, it is not appropriate to move a substitute for the whole until the discussion by paragraphs is completed and the chair has announced that the floor is open to amendments to the whole report (See: CONSIDERATION BY PARAGRAPHS).
Reconsideration	After a paragraph has been inserted, it cannot be amended except by additions; the paragraph struck cannot be reinserted except if it has been so modified that reinsertion is a separate question; if the substitute fails, that does not preclude proposing other paragraphs as substitutes for the paragraph to have been struck; and the paragraph to have been substituted may also be inserted if the motion to substitute fails, that is, it may be inserted without striking.

Filling Blanks: This method of amendment is used in circumstances where a motion is made in principle but with certain details left as blanks. The blanks may be, for instance, dates, times, names, or amounts of money. The procedure for filling the blanks is much like that for electing from a group of nominees.

Form	"Mr. Chairman, I move that (blank) amount be set as our annual contribution to the Community Fund." "Mr. Chairman, I move that our surplus income for the year be divided equally among such charitable organizations as will be chosen by the filling in of blanks." It is also permissible for the chairman to suggest creating a blank, if there is general consent. If there are several choices, say for the name to be given the organization or for the streets to be designated as needing new lighting, the chair may suggest that the choices be handled as filling in blanks. The advantage in this procedure is that it allows all choices to be on the floor at once and subjected to debate in which their merits may be compared. Treated as motions to strike and insert, each suggestion would be considered separately and in succession, and the last made would be considered first. The person making a suggestion to fill in the blank

merely says: "John Smith," or "fifty dollars," or "Red Cross."

Suggesting (Nominating)	Making a suggestion for filling in a blank is much like a nomination (See: COMMITTEE, STANDING, *Choosing Officers and Members, Election*) since the acceptable suggestion(s) will be chosen from the list proposed. Except by general consent, no member may make more than one suggestion until all others who want to make a suggestion have done so. In practice, this means that a second proposal can be made if no one objects. No suggestion for filling in a blank need be seconded.
Calling the Question on the Motion Being Amended	It is best to fill in the blanks before the motion is adopted, though it is possible to adopt the motion with blanks to be filled in later. Normally, the question is called on a motion with blanks only if it is assumed that the motion will be defeated. If it is passed with blanks, it becomes necessary to fill the blanks immediately, with only privileged motions intervening.
Voting	The voting order for choices to fill the blanks depends on the subject matter. When the choices are names, the names are voted on in the order suggested, just as are nominations for committee members. If there are no more suggestions than there are blanks, no vote is taken; the blanks are filled and the question called on the main motion. (See: COMMITTEE, STANDING, *Choosing Officers and Election*.) When the choices are between suggestions that clearly differ in acceptability, the choices are brought to a vote in such order that the least acceptable is first, the most obviously acceptable last. As an example, if the blank is an amount of money to be spent, the largest amount is presumably least acceptable and should be first. In this manner, the amount of money spent will be the largest amount acceptable to a majority of the organization, since the first in the series voted that gets a majority is the item accepted. If the blank is a date, depending on the subject the nearest or furthest might be most acceptable. (Where there is a set number of blanks, the voting is ended when enough suggestions have received a majority to satisfy the requirement. Where the number of blanks

is indefinite, all those suggestions are acceptable that receive a majority.)

Notes:

Reconsideration and Negation Any vote on an amendment can be reconsidered under normal procedures (See: RECONSIDER). The chair should not permit amendments which, in effect, negate the vote on a previous amendment. The intention is to relieve the organization from repeated consideration of essentially the same question. However, a proposal negating a previous decision may be permitted if it is ancillary to an otherwise new question. Under types of amendments discussed above, there are paragraphs entitled *Reconsideration*. These paragraphs define actions that would be acceptable because they constitute new questions.

Amend Generally, amendments are amendable, though the motion to strike a paragraph is only amendable in the highly specialized sense noted above, and a proposal to fill a blank is not amendable. Amendments to amendments (called amendments of the second degree) are not amendable.

Debate The motion to amend is debatable only where the motion being amended is debatable.

Unamendable Motions A list of UNAMENDABLE MOTIONS is found under that heading in the glossary.

Previous Question and Debate Limits The previous question and motions affecting limits on debate may be applied to an amendment, or to an amendment to an amendment, without affecting the main question, though the main question may also be included.

Vote All amendments require only a majority vote, even when they apply to motions which themselves require a two-thirds vote.

Improper An amendment is improper and should not be entertained: (1) when it is not germane to the motion to which it is applied; (2) when it, in effect, raises a question that has already been decided (See first Note); (3) when it would simply change the statement of the motion from positive to negative, or vice versa, but not actually change the meaning of the motion. The latter does not preclude a complete reversal of meaning, signifying that the intention of the organization is exactly the opposite of that expressed in the original motion. It does preclude a change that simply reverses the question so that a positive vote is against the motion.

AMEND CONSTITUTION OR BY-LAWS

	MAIN MOTION	POSTPONE INDEFINITELY	AMEND	COMMIT	POSTPONE TO FIXED TIME	LIMIT OR EXTEND DEBATE	PREVIOUS QUESTION	TABLE	ORDERS OF THE DAY	QUESTIONS OF PRIVILEGE	RECESS	ADJOURN	SET TIME TO ADJOURN TO
SUBJECT MOTION:													
YIELDS TO		●	●	●	●	●	●	●	●	●	●	●	●
TAKES PRECEDENCE OF													

Class: Main Motion
Debatable: YES
Amendable: YES (See *Notes*)   *Vote:* See *Voting,* Plurality
Reconsiderable: See *Notes*   *Second needed:* YES
          Can interrupt speaker: NO

Purpose and Effect: To modify, according to any of the forms listed under AMEND, a constitution, by-laws, or rules of order already adopted. (Where the word *constitution* is used below, it should be taken as including by-laws and rules of order.)

Form: The forms used are those discussed under various types of amendments (See: AMEND).

Voting: The principal differences between the procedure for amending a constitution and that for amending a pending motion are two: first, an amendment to a constitution is a main motion (hence subject to amendment in the first and second degrees and indefinite postponement); and second, the plurality required for passage is greater for a constitutional amendment than for an amendment to a pending motion.

The rules for amending a constitution are designed to protect the interests of all members and to protect the constitution from whimsical amendment. Every constitution should define the means by which the organization can amend its basic documents. The method chosen will depend on the needs of the organization. The methods discussed below are those commonly used and they embody the principles that should control amendment procedure.

*Notice
Period*

It is usual to require that the membership be informed well in advance that a constitutional amendment is to be considered at a certain meeting, in order that those interested can have time to consider the proposal and to arrange to attend the meeting. (Sometimes a constitution permits amendments without notice. If so, an extraordinary plurality should be required, as noted below.) The period of the notice will depend on the needs of the organization. A common procedure is to require that notice of intent to propose an amendment be given at *the* (not *a*) previous regular meeting. This works well where an organization meets monthly. When an organization only meets annually, it is usually impractical to require notice at the previous regular meeting; the preferable method is to require one month's notice by mail to all the members. Where an organization meets quarterly, either method may be adopted, or both may be permissible. Sometimes it is desirable to limit constitutional changes to certain meetings; e.g., an organization meeting monthly might allow constitutional amendments only at quarterly or annual meetings.

*Notice, Content
and Form*

A constitution may specify that verbal notice at the previous meeting is sufficient, or that written notice is required. Where verbal notice is sufficient, the fact that a special committee has been appointed to recommend constitutional changes is sufficient notice (except if the constitution requires that the notice include the exact wording of the proposed amendments). A constitution may specify either that notice include the exact wording of the amendment, or that it is sufficient that the general topic of the amendment be reported. If the exact wording is required, notice is not given until the committee makes its report, and then action is taken on the report at the succeeding regular meeting.

*Plurality
Required*

Where a constitution allows amendment without previous notice, a majority of the entire membership should be required for adoption of the amendment. A majority of the entire membership is usually required where an amendment is to be adopted by mail ballot.

Private organizations should not require two thirds of the entire membership to pass a constitutional change because it is unlikely that two thirds of the membership will ever appear at one meeting or return mail ballots. When notice is required, it is the usual procedure to require a two-thirds vote (that is, two thirds of those voting). If it is desired to protect the constitution still further, an organization may require a plurality of two thirds of those present, which is likely to be greater than two thirds of those voting.

Form of Voting

The constitution may specify any normal method of voting — standing or voice, roll call, or secret ballot.

Notes:

Amendment

A constitutional amendment is a main motion. Consequently, it may be amended, and the amendment may be amended. That is, a constitutional amendment is amendable in the first and second degree. Amendments to the pending constitutional amendment require only a majority vote. Because that is the case, certain amendments cannot be permitted. An amendment cannot be so major as to change the intent or the scale of the proposed constitutional amendment, because that method could be used to avoid the requirement that notice be given. For instance, it might be proposed that the constitution be amended to combine the offices of corresponding and recording secretary. It would not be proper to amend that by inserting the phrase, "and hire a person to fill that post."

Effective Date

As with all motions, unless otherwise specified, amendments to constitutions take effect immediately upon adoption. There may be times when this will cause difficulty, in which case the amendment should specify when it is to take effect. The addition of such a clause is a legitimate amendment to a proposed constitutional change.

Reconsider

An affirmative vote cannot be reconsidered. Only if the amendment fails can it be brought up again by this method.

ANNOUNCING VOTE See: VOTING

ANNUL See: RESCIND

APPEAL (DECISIONS OF THE CHAIR)

1. Takes precedence of any motion from which it arises. 2. Only when the appeal is debatable.	MAIN MOTION	POSTPONE INDEFINITELY	AMEND	COMMIT	POSTPONE TO FIXED TIME	LIMIT OR EX-TEND DEBATE	PREVIOUS QUESTION	TABLE	ORDERS OF THE DAY	QUESTIONS OF PRIVILEGE	RECESS	ADJOURN	SET TIME TO ADJOURN TO
SUBJECT MOTION:													
YIELDS TO									●	●	●	●	●
TAKES PRECEDENCE OF	1	1	1	1	1	1	1	1	1	1	1	1	1
MAY HAVE APPLIED TO IT				2	2	2	●						

Class: Incidental Motion
Debatable: (See *Notes*)　　　　*Vote:* MAJORITY
Amendable: NO　　　　　　　　*Second needed:* YES
Reconsiderable: YES　　　　　*Can interrupt speaker:* YES

Purpose and Effect:　To have a procedural decision of the chairman reviewed by the assembly, which has final authority and may overrule the chairman. An appeal can be made only at the time the ruling is made. (An answer to a parliamentary inquiry is not a decision and cannot be appealed, though an appeal might be made when the answer is acted on. Thus, if a member asks whether a motion is in order and the chair assents, the reply cannot be questioned until the motion has been submitted, at which time a member who disagrees could raise a point of order. If the chairman persists in entertaining the motion, his decision is then open to appeal.)

Form:　"Mr. Chairman, I appeal from the decision of the chair."
　The chair puts the question so that an affirmative vote will favor the chair, for example: "Will the (organization, society, club) sustain the decision of the chair?"

Notes:

When Debatable　　An appeal is debatable only when it concerns the merit or appropriateness of the business before the house. For example, an appeal on a decision that an amendment is not germane would be debatable. But if the appeal concerns the order of business, for instance, rather than the business itself, it is undebatable.

Debate Limits　　When the appeal is debatable, no member may speak more than once, except that the chairman may make a closing statement in defense of his decision.

248

Tie Vote	In the event of a tie vote, the chair is sustained.
Chair's Privilege	Even if the motion is undebatable, the chairman may state the reasons for his decision before calling the question.
Secondary Appeals	If, while an appeal is pending, another decision is also appealed, the second appeal is not considered immediately, but must wait until the original appeal has been decided and until no other business is pending.
Tabled Appeals and Motions	If a debatable appeal is tabled, the motions that the appeal affected are tabled, too. (If the business were continued without decision on the appeal, there would hang over the question the possibility that it would be considered out of order.) This does not apply to undebatable appeals because appeals that are undebatable concern purely procedural matters. A later decision that a matter was handled at the wrong time would not invalidate the action taken.

APPOINT COMMITTEE See appropriate committee, but especially COMMITTEE, STANDING

AS IF IN COMMITTEE OF THE WHOLE See: COMMITTEE OF THE WHOLE, QUASI-

ASSEMBLY

Assembly has both an informal and a technical meaning. In the informal sense, assembly means simply the group of people at a meeting.

In a technical sense, an assembly is the organization constituted by the people at a meeting, and those others, present or not, who are qualified to attend. The group of people attending a mass meeting or a rally constitute the assembly, for by virtue of coming to the mass meeting, a person becomes qualified to vote in its deliberations.

In a large organization composed of member or affiliated local groups, it is common to run the central organization through an annual CONVENTION of delegates representing the local groups. The convention is an assembly composed of all those people who have been elected delegates by local organizations, and who have actually appeared at the convention site and had their credentials accepted.

State and national legislatures are assemblies in this sense. The life of this type of assembly runs, at most, from one election to another. (The life of the assembly at a rally or mass meeting lasts until an adjournment SINE DIE.) If, at any point during its potential life span, an assembly adjourns sine die and without any provision for its meeting again — not even at the call of the chairman — the assembly is abolished.

In a permanent organization in which the members run the organization directly through membership meetings, the assembly is a permanent body consisting of the members. Since there is always provision for future meeting prescribed by the constitution, an adjournment sine die is always a privileged motion.

BALLOT

A form or blank slip of paper on which a member indicates his vote (See: VOTING).

BOARD OF DIRECTORS (or MANAGERS) See: COMMITTEE, EXECUTIVE

BY-LAWS See: CONSTITUTION, BY-LAWS, AND RULES OF ORDER

CALL THE QUESTION

Ask for the vote on the question, or ask if the assembly is ready to vote. The chairman calls the question (sometimes referred to as putting the question, but not to be confused with STATE THE QUESTION), and he should stand while doing so to indicate that he has the floor.

Debatable Motion: When the assembly appears to have completed debate, the chair asks, "Are you ready for the question?" If, after he has waited a moment for response, no one seeks recognition, the chair states: "The question is on. . . ." When the question is on a resolution, the chair should have it read, instead of describing it, if: (1) a lengthy debate has intervened since the original reading, (2) amendments have been made since the last full reading, or (3) a member asks to have it reread. When it is clear to the assembly what question is being decided, the chair proceeds with the vote in the appropriate manner. (The rules on *Undebatable Motions* are applicable if debate has been closed by the PREVIOUS QUESTION or by operation of a time limit (See: LIMIT OR EXTEND DEBATE, PROGRAM, and ORDERS).

The Pause: After asking, "Are you ready for the question?" the chair should pause long enough to allow anyone acting with reasonable promptness to seek recognition. If the pause is too short, the chair may be interrupted while carrying on the vote by a person seeking to continue debate. The chair does not have the right to cut off debate.

Undebatable Motions: When a motion is undebatable or where debate has been cut off by the previous question or by a time limit, the chair needn't ask if the assembly is ready for the question. He merely states: "The question is on. . . ." reading the motion if necessary (there are times when a main resolution may be undebatable; see RECONSIDER), and then proceeds with the vote.

Vote: For rules covering different voting procedures, see VOTING.

CALLED MEETING   See: SPECIAL MEETING

CHAIRMAN   See: PRESIDING OFFICER

CLERK   See: SECRETARY

COMMIT, REFER, OR RECOMMIT

1. Killed by passage of motion to commit. 2. Takes main motions, too.	MAIN MOTION	POSTPONE INDEFINITELY	AMEND	COMMIT	POSTPONE TO FIXED TIME	LIMIT OR EXTEND DEBATE	PREVIOUS QUESTION	TABLE	ORDERS OF THE DAY	QUESTIONS OF PRIVILEGE	RECESS	ADJOURN	SET TIME TO ADJOURN TO
SUBJECT MOTION:													
YIELDS TO					●	●	●	●	●	●	●	●	●
TAKES PRECEDENCE OF		1											
MAY BE APPLIED TO	●		2										
MAY HAVE APPLIED TO IT			●		2	●	●	2					

Class: Subsidiary Motion
Debatable: YES (See *Notes*)   *Vote:* MAJORITY
Amendable: YES (See *Notes*)   *Second needed:* YES
Reconsiderable: See *Notes*   *Can interrupt speaker:* NO

Purpose and Effect: To have a proposal discussed informally, usually by a smaller group, because the rules of debate in COMMITTEE are more conducive to detailed study. One effect is postponement of action on the question until the committee has made its report. The motion to commit may designate assignment of one or several motions to any committee, including a COMMITTEE OF THE WHOLE (though it is unusual to refer matters to an executive committee). Referral to committee of the whole avoids the delay otherwise inherent in the motion to commit.

Form: The motion to refer may be stated simply: "Mr. Chairman, I move the question be referred." However, the motion may also specify the committee to which the question is to be referred (either an existing committee or one to be created). If the motion calls for the creation of a SPECIAL COMMITTEE, it may also include:

1. the size of the committee, and
2. the method by which the committee is to be selected.

If these two details are not specified in the motion, and the motion is not amended to include them, the committee's size and method of selection must be considered immediately after the passage of the motion to refer. Consideration of these two matters then has priority over all but privileged motions. (For complete details on creation of committees, see COMMITTEE, SPECIAL, *Creation,* and for detail on methods that may be adopted for selecting committee members, see COMMITTEE, STANDING, *Choosing Officers and Members.* The motion may also include instructions to the committee; see INSTRUCT A COMMITTEE.)

Notes:

Consider Informally	The motion to CONSIDER INFORMALLY is a variety of the motion to refer.
Applicability	The motion to refer can be applied only to main motions, though it affects all the motions that are subsidiary or incidental to the main motion.
Debate	The debate on the motion to refer must be limited to the appropriateness of referring; the main motion cannot be discussed except insofar as the discussion is relevant to the propriety of committing it.
Effect on Secondary Motions	If a motion to postpone debate indefinitely is pending, it is erased by the passage of a motion to commit. All other subsidiary and incidental motions follow the main motion to committee. When the committee makes its report, the subsidiary and incidental motions are taken up in proper order along with any others proposed in the report. (See: ADOPT REPORT.)
Choice of Committees	If the motion to refer does not specify the committee, after the vote the chair asks, "To which committee shall the question be referred?" If more than one committee is suggested, they are voted on in the following order, the first to receive a majority vote winning: committee of the whole, quasi-committee of the whole, consider informally, standing committees in the order suggested,

and special committees. If special committees of different sizes are proposed, the largest is considered first.

Special Committee Created	If the motion is to be referred to a special committee, the next question is the method of appointment. (See: COMMITTEE, STANDING, *Choosing Officers and Members.*)
Selection of Members	After the method of selection is decided, the next matter of business, yielding only to privileged questions, is the selection of members.
Reconsider and Discharge	The motion to commit cannot be reconsidered after the committee has begun to consider the question. Then, a motion to discharge the committee, requiring a two-thirds vote, would be in order.
Amendment	Amendments to the motion to refer must be germane, e.g., affect the choice of committees, the method of appointment, the time at which the committee is to report, and so on.
Instruct Committee	It is appropriate, even after a motion has been committed, to make a separate motion to INSTRUCT A COMMITTEE in some manner, for instance, the time at which to report, the feelings of the organization, and so on. The same effect may be accomplished by an amendment to the motion to refer.

COMMITTEE

A group appointed by an organization to carry out a specific task or a series of related tasks. It is increasingly common for independent organizations to call themselves committees; however, this usage is inaccurate. In parliamentary procedure, a committee is always a subsidiary organization created by a larger organization. A subcommitee is a committee created by a committee.

Types: One broad division lies between *executive committees* (also called board of directors, managers, or trustees) and all others. Executive committees are empowered to perform the business of the organization between meetings and are subject to constitutional limitations and to review by the organization at its membership meetings. All other committees are limited in purpose to specific assignments. Those limited to specific assignments include the following:

Standing Committees	Permanent standing committees are normally established by the constitution or by-laws of the organization. Standing committees perform functions that recur throughout the life of the organization, e.g., membership, promotion, program arrangement, and so on.
Special Committees	Special committees are organized to fulfill one specific task; they disband as soon as this task is completed.
Committees of the Whole	Committees of the whole are general meetings that decide to act as special committees in order to obtain the advantage of less formal rules of debate. Similar advantages can be obtained by deciding to act as a quasi-committee of the whole, or by deciding to consider informally.
Sub-committees	Subcommittees may be permanent in standing committees or executive committees, but are more often special and temporary. When a subcommittee is the creation of an executive committee, it is commonly referred to as a committee. Since committees always report to the organization that created them, subcommittees report to the committee from which they came, never to the membership. The committee itself reports to the membership.

Committees may also be classified as *advisory* or *action* committees. This distinction is used when special committees are organized, although it doesn't affect their parliamentary status. As a rule, committees set up to advise or to make recommendations should represent all points of view. Action committees are generally smaller and should be composed only of those who favor the action being taken.

Rules: The parliamentary rules used in a board or executive committee are often defined in the by-laws. In other cases, the by-laws may empower the executive committee to make its own rules. Other committees, and executive committees unless the by-laws forbid it, follow simpler rules than does the parent organization. The most important rules follow (only those with asterisks apply to a committee of the whole):

Chairman	If a chairman is not appointed by the organization that created the committee, he is normally the first person named to the committee. However, when no one is specifically designated, the committee may be empowered to elect its own chairman.
Secretary	Large committees and all standing committees elect a

secretary. In small committees the chairman may perform the secretary's function. In citizen advisory committees to public agencies, it is common practice to provide a member of the agency staff as secretary.

Records

Any papers, reference material, or records necessary to the committee in conjunction with its assigned task are turned over to the committee chairman by the organization secretary and are returned to the secretary when the assigned task is completed.

Calling Meetings

The committee chairman is responsible for calling committee meetings. If he fails or refuses to do so, a meeting may be called by any two members.

Privacy

Generally, the deliberations of a committee are private, and unless the committee decides otherwise, nothing but the report of the committee, as voted on by its members, is transmitted to the organization.

Debate Procedure

Members of the organization may be requested or may request to appear before committees, but in no case do non-committee members have a right to attend the deliberations of a committee.

*Motions to close or limit debate are not allowed.

*There is no limit on the number of times a person may speak.

*Except in very large committees, speakers do not stand.

*The chairman does not stand to put the question.

*Motions are not seconded.

The chairman does not leave the chair to speak. In fact, in naming the committee chairman it is advisable to select a person who is interested in the subject of the committee and will make a full contribution during debate.

Reconsideration

Regardless of the amount of previous discussion, reconsideration is allowed at any time, so long as reconsideration is requested by a person who did not originally vote on the losing side. The motion to reconsider requires a two-thirds vote if:

1. the reconsideration is requested at a meeting other

than the one at which the original motion was passed, or

2. there was no advance notice of the reconsideration.

Debate *If a report or lengthy set of resolutions is to be initiated by the committee, it is normal for one person to be asked to write a draft. This draft is then considered by the committee seriatim. (See: CONSIDER BY PARAGRAPH.)

Motion to Postpone *If a resolution is referred to committee while a motion to postpone indefinitely is pending, the motion to postpone is ignored.

Quorum A quorum is a majority of the committee.

(See: COMMITTEES by name, and also COMMIT, REFER OR RECOMMIT; COMMITTEE REPORTS; INSTRUCT A COMMITTEE; ADOPT REPORT ON MATTERS REFERRED TO COMMITTEE; ACCEPT FACTUAL REPORT; ADOPT REPORT CONTAINING RESOLUTIONS OR RECOMMENDATIONS; EX OFFICIO MEMBERS OF COMMITTEES.)

COMMITTEE, EXECUTIVE

Function: An organization that meets infrequently (quarterly or annually) usually appoints an executive committee to which is delegated almost all the authority of the organization during the period between meetings. An organization may meet infrequently because its membership is large and unwieldy. It is impractical to expect a mass organization to decide every detail of administration and every policy matter. That is the reason for representative government. An executive committee or board of directors stands in relation to the whole organization much as the President and Congress combined stand to the American people. Just as congressmen and Presidents may fail to be re-elected if they dissatisfy their constituents, the executive committee of an organization may be replaced at the annual meeting. Unlike the American Government, the executive committee is subject also to specific review and the possibility of being overruled by members in annual meeting.

Membership: The size of an executive committee and the method for selecting its members are normally defined in the constitution. In common practice, the executive committee consists of the officers of the organization, the chairmen of standing committees, the paid executive, if there is one, and sometimes additional members chosen by vote. Executive committees and boards of directors are normally fairly large as committees go, seldom including fewer than 10 members and often 50 or more. One reason for a large executive board is to have a pool from which to draw members of board committees. Because these committees are often very active in an organization of broad interests, the burden on any individual can be too great if the committee is small.

Another reason for a large executive committee is to associate prominent people with the organization, even though their active participation is not expected. In such situations, it is common to have three levels of administration: the organization itself in annual meeting, a large board of directors drawn from the membership (that may meet quarterly), and an executive committee of the board which carries on the day-to-day business of the organization. It is common practice to give board members overlapping tenures. Thus, when the term of office is two years, half are elected in each year, and when the term is three years, one third are elected each year.

Officers: The officers of the board or executive committee are normally officers of the organization, though they need not be.

Meetings: Normally there are regular meetings weekly, biweekly, or monthly. The chairman or two members may call special meetings.

Rules of Procedure: The executive committee operates exactly like a small deliberative body, following the standard order of business adopted by the organization, and all the other rules, except that debate is simplified to encourage freer discussion (See: COMMITTEE, *Rules*). The by-laws of the executive committee may be fixed by the organization, or the executive committee may be empowered to form its own by-laws.

Reports: The executive committee is required to report its activities at least annually. Such a report, usually brief, includes such statements as "The Community Welfare Committee sponsored a Health Fair, attended by 3500 people, at which 485 polio shots, 1250 chest X-rays, and 220 dental examinations were administered. Fourteen public and private agencies cooperated. The Membership Committee carried on a drive producing. . . ." and so on. The report of the executive committee, like all reports, is recorded and published as given, amendments being shown as indicated under ADOPT REPORTS.

COMMITTEE OF THE WHOLE

Function: A committee of the whole is a meeting of the entire organization constituted as a committee, acting either in the place of a standing committee to which the issue would normally be referred, or as a special committee. When the group desires the freedom of discussion allowed by committee rules but does not want to refer an issue to committee, the general membership may constitute itself as a committee of the whole.

The committee of the whole can only consider questions referred to it by the entire organization. Its own actions have the same status as those of any other committee. (For simpler methods of obtaining the advantages of a committee of the whole, especially for small groups, see COMMITTEE OF THE WHOLE, QUASI-, and CONSIDER INFORMALLY.)

Officers: The chairman of the organization does not serve as chairman of a committee of the whole; he appoints someone else to the chair and goes to the floor as an ordinary member. Frequently, the chairman of the committee to which the matter might otherwise have been referred acts as chairman of the committee of the whole. This arrangement allows the chair to participate actively in the debate.

Procedure and Rules: The rules of debate are those for all committees (as listed under COMMITTEE, *Rules*). Any time limit on debate must be imposed before the group goes into the committee of the whole.

Creation	A committee of the whole is formed when there is a majority vote on the motion "That we go into committee of the whole to discuss. . . ." As soon as the motion is adopted, the chairman vacates his seat, as noted under *Officers,* above. This motion has the same parliamentary status as the motion to refer.
Admissible Motions	The only motions that a committee of the whole can make are to amend and to adopt the matter referred to the committee, to appeal a decision of the chair, and to rise and report. All other motions — including to table, to postpone, and to limit debate — are forbidden.
Appeals	Members may appeal the decisions of the chair, and the appeals must be voted on immediately. Each member may speak only once on the appeal.
Reconsider	The motion to reconsider is not entertained in the committee of the whole.
Rise and Report	This motion is equivalent in a committee of the whole to adjournment in regular meetings. The same motion is used in special committees when they are ready to report, i.e., at the meeting which the committee expects will be its last. The motion to rise and report is privileged and is acted on exactly as the motion to adjourn.
Afterwards	When the motion to rise and report has been adopted,

the chairman immediately returns to the rostrum. The committee of the whole reports to the organization and the organization acts on the report in the same manner as it would on any other committee report.

COMMITTEE OF THE WHOLE, QUASI-

The quasi-committee of the whole (as if in committee of the whole) is especially useful for small organizations. It differs from the committee of the whole in the following ways:

1. The chairman of the organization retains the chair instead of appointing a substitute.
2. The quasi-committee of the whole automatically ends when the question is voted on. Thus, no formal closing procedure like the motion to rise and report is required.

The motion to act as if in committee of the whole is a special form of the motion to refer. Note that when the quasi-committee of the whole approves a resolution on the question referred to it, that action is not the final decision of the entire organization. Passage merely indicates that the quasi-committee of the whole is satisfied that the motion has been perfected as far as possible. When the committee has approved the resolution, the chair immediately presents it to the organization as if it were the report of any regular committee. The resolution is then considered in the same manner as any committee report.

COMMITTEE REPORTS

Types: Committee reports fall into two general classes, informational reports and reports that make recommendations to the organization. Those reports intended to provide information either describe the activities of an action committee, or offer the organization special information gathered by the committee. Such reports keep the membership aware of what its committees are doing, or provide information to aid the organization in its deliberations. Committee reports offering only information are unusual. They occur when no recommendation was requested or when the committee could not agree on a recommendation.

The other class of committee reports, those which make recommendations, may come from action committees or deliberative committees. These reports should be weighed seriously because the committee has probably given the question more thorough consideration than have any of the organization's individual members.

Activity Report: The purpose of activity reports is obvious. All that need be said of them is that they should be simple and to the point. Where appropriate, the information included should be set in context. For example: "The community health committee reports that this year's TB campaign resulted in 873 free chest X-rays being administered. This was 187 fewer than the previous year, the fall-off being attributed to poor weather during the period of the drive," or "This was 212 more than the previous year, credit for which is due to the active cooperation of the ladies' auxiliary."

Recommendations: The purpose of reports that include recommendations is to give to the organization the benefit of the committee's thinking on the subject referred to it (or on the proposal initiated by it). Normally, most of the work of an organization is done by committees for the obvious reason that it is very difficult, if not impossible, to hammer out a proposal or argue its pro's and con's in detail in a large organization meeting. Since the purpose of a report making recommendations is to aid the organization, the committee should include in its report full substantiation for the conclusions and recommendations arrived at. It is only necessary that care be taken not to include extraneous material and that arguments not be documented and proved at such length as to weary the reader or listener. The requirement of a full presentation carries with it the responsibility for presenting the argument as concisely as possible.

Form: A factual report will be in direct narrative form. A report including recommendations should be divided into either two or three sections. The first will be the committee's argument for its own position. The second part, which may be eliminated, is a preamble, or public statement of the reasons for the committee's action. The third part is made up of the recommendations. The recommendations should be in the form of motions. By supplying a set of motions with or without the preamble, the committee simplifies the task of the organization. It is then not necessary for the proposals to be rewritten as formal motions (See: MOTION).

Presentation: Any report is read to the organization, either by the committee chairman or by some other person assigned the task. The reading takes place at that part of the meeting devoted to hearing committee reports. The reports of standing committees are read in the order provided in the by-laws; those of special committees in the order of their creation. If there is no provision at a meeting for the report of a committee, the chairman of the committee may announce, at a time when no business is on the floor, that a report is ready. The chair may allow the reading by general consent or call the matter to a vote. A majority will permit the report to be read. If it is desired to present a committee report other than at the time provided, it is necessary to suspend the rules (See: SUSPEND RULES).

Amendments: A committee's recommended amendments to a resolution referred to the committee are to be read in context. The document being amended should be read at sufficient length to make the intent of the amendments understandable.

Action on Informational Reports: If the report includes nothing requiring action by the organization, the reading of the report constitutes its receipt by the organization. If the report is final, the committee is automatically discharged from responsibility for the subject as soon as its report is received, i.e., as soon as it is read. The committee's responsibility for the subject can be re-established only by a motion to recommit; this is the usual manner of indicating dissatisfaction with a report. If there is any question as to whether the report is satisfactory, the chairman may ask if the report should be accepted, or a member may move acceptance. Receipt without comment does not imply that the organization adopts the interpretation or recommendation in a report (See: ACCEPT FACTUAL REPORT).

Action on Reports Including Recommendations: See ADOPT REPORT CONTAINING RECOMMENDATIONS and ADOPT REPORT ON MATTERS REFERRED TO COMMITTEE.

When a report includes recommendations, it is adopted by the organization only after an appropriate motion for adoption has been made. This motion should be made by the member reporting (See: ADOPT REPORT CONTAINING RECOMMENDATIONS and MINORITY REPORT).

COMMITTEE, SPECIAL

Function: A special committee makes reports and recommendations on specific issues or subject areas for which the organization has no appropriate standing committee. The committee exists only until its specific assignment has been fulfilled. For example, a service organization may decide that it wants to investigate a bond issue for building a new firehouse. The subject matter is outside the competence of any existing committee, so a special committee is created to study the proposal and present a recommendation to the organization. A special committee may also be created for a specific activity, such as organizing a fund-raising event.

Creation: A special committee is created as a result of a motion from the floor. When there is no appropriate standing committee to handle the question, a special committee may be created as an integral part of the motion to refer. The mover may say, "Mr. Chairman, I move the referral of the question to a committee of five to be appointed by the chairman." Note that this motion specifies the mode of selecting the committee. (Selection may be made in several ways. See: COMMITTEE, STANDING, *Choosing Officers and Members*.)

When the motion to refer includes the creation of a committee, adoption of the motion leaves the appointment of the committee on the floor. Appointment of the committee then has priority over all but privileged motions. If the appointments are to be made by the chairman, he may ask permission to appoint the committee later.

A motion creating a committee may also suggest members to be included on the committee. This procedure is acceptable in small meetings, and it is often used when the mover knows which members are principally concerned with the subject area.

There will also be occasions when a special committee is created as part of a main motion. A member might state, "Since the question of a firehouse bond issue is a topic of broad public concern, I think we ought to take an informed position on the question. To that end, I move the creation of a committee of seven to study and prepare a resolution on the firehouse bond issue." Such a motion is a main motion and therefore may be postponed indefinitely; this is not the case with the motion to refer.

In whatever form the creation of a committee is proposed, the size and method of selecting members may be amended. The motion to create a committee may also be amended to refer the subject matter to an existing committee.

If the motion to refer does not specify the committee to which the question should be referred, specification of committee has the floor immediately upon passage of the motion to refer. If the group decides to refer to a new committee without specifying how it is to be created, creation of the committee and then selection of members have the floor. Each successive step has priority over all but privileged motions.

Members: For advice on selecting, see COMMITTEE, *Types*. For methods of selecting, see COMMITTEE, STANDING, *Choosing Officers and Members*.

Officers: Special committees often have only a chairman, who also performs the function of secretary. (For methods of selection, see COMMITTEE, STANDING, *Choosing Officers and Members*.)

Reports: Special committees are expected to report on the matter referred to them. Since special committees last only until the organization receives the report, they make no annual report (See: COMMITTEE REPORTS).

Discharge or Dissolution: The committee is dissolved when its report has been received. It may be discharged by a majority vote of the organization if it fails to report on time. Otherwise, it may only be discharged from its responsibilities by a two-thirds vote. When a special committee feels its report is completed, the meeting is closed by the motion to rise and report instead of a motion to adjourn. (See: COMMITTEE OF THE WHOLE, *Procedure and Rules*, Rise and Report.) If the committee takes several meetings to complete its task, all meetings but the last are adjourned.

COMMITTEE, STANDING

Function: Permanent committees, called standing committees, are named in the constitution or by-laws. They are intended to fulfill continuous or recurring needs of the organization. Almost every large organization has a standing Membership Committee with responsibility for recruiting members, keeping records of members, and determining whether applicants for membership meet the organization's requirements. Other common standing committees are Finance, Program, Publicity, and Auditing. The purpose of the organization determines what standing committees will be maintained. A neighborhood-betterment organization might have standing committees concerned with schools, zoning, public safety, and city planning. A service organization might have a Hospital Visiting Committee, a Scholarship Committee, and an Entertainment and Fund Raising Committee.

Committees responsible for handling events that recur regularly but infrequently, such as nominations and annual banquets, are on the border line between standing and special committees: they may be treated as either. Members of standing committees are normally selected once a year; members of special committees when the committees are set up. Members of unclassified, borderline committees may be chosen either when their annual functions are performed, or when all standing committees are organized.

A standing committee may initiate resolutions in its area of competence and may be called upon to make proposals or to report on motions referred to it by the organization.

Membership: Unless there is provision for overlapping tenure, all members of standing committees are normally chosen at the time organization officers are elected. Even with overlapping tenure, committee officers are chosen annually if organization officers are elected annually. The membership may be chosen in any of several ways: election, appointment by the chairman of the organization, or appointment by the chairman of the committee. It is often advisable for an action committee to let the committee chairman choose members with whom he knows he can work well. For advisory committees, election or appointment of the membership by the organization chairman is preferable because these methods are more likely to produce a representative group. If so stated in the constitution, the chairman (and occasionally other officers) may be ex officio members of all committees (See: EX OFFICIO MEMBERS OF COMMITTEES).

Officers: Each committee has a chairman; standing committees (always) and special committees (sometimes) have secretaries, too. The chairman and secretary or the chairman alone may be appointed by the organization's chair or elected by the general membership. The secretary is sometimes appointed by the committee chairman. The committee chairman may also be the first person appointed or elected to serve on the committee. If the committee elects its own officers, the first person selected for the committee acts as temporary chairman until regular officers are chosen.

Choosing Officers and Members: The methods of choosing committee members and officers are applicable to special as well as standing committees. An organization's method for choosing members of standing committees is designated in the constitution or by-laws; the method applicable to special committees is designated in the motion to create the committee. The motion to create a committee, in turn, is usually part of OF THE WHOLE, *Procedure and Rules, Rise and Report.*) If the committee REPORTS, and COMMIT, REFER, OR RECOMMIT.)

Election	When a chairman alone is elected, he is chosen in the same manner as any other officer (See: ELECTIONS). When all members are to be elected and no more members are nominated than there are vacancies, the chairman puts the question, "Shall those nominated be accepted as composing the committee?" When there are more nominations than vacancies, the chair puts the question on each candidate in order of nomination. The chair proceeds through the list until enough nominees to fill the vacancies have been elected by majority vote. A member has no right to make a second nomination until all who want to nominate have done so. However, he may make such nominations if no one objects. (The farther down on the list a nominee is, the less likely he is to be chosen).
	Nomination may be by committee or from the floor or by the chairman (see below). Where the membership of the committee is selected by vote of the organization, the usual practice is that the committee chairman either be the first committee member chosen, or that he be elected by the committee.

Appointment by Organization   The chairman of the organization sometimes has the right to appoint the chairman and members of a committee. He must announce his choices, but he need not put them to a vote. If the organization meets frequently, the chairman makes his announcement of standing committee choices at the meeting succeeding his election. Where the organization operates through an executive committee, that committee may be given the right to approve appointments, except when standing committee chairmen automatically become executive committee members. In such situations committee chairmen should be elected.

If the organization chairman does not choose to appoint a special committee during the meeting at which it is created, he must ask permission by majority vote to appoint it later.

Nomination by Organization Chairman   In both special and standing committees, the chair may be given the exclusive right to make nominations. The chair calls the question on his whole slate of nominees, unless there is an objection, in which case nominees are voted on individually. If the chair's list is not accepted completely, he nominates additional members until the vacancies are filled.

Nomination or Appointment by Committee Chairman   An elected or appointed chairman may be empowered to pick his own committee. The permission may be granted as a right to nominate or as a right to appoint. In either case, the procedure is the same as if the chair were performing the function, except that the committee chairman nominates from the floor.

Reports: Standing committees report at least once a year, summarizing all their activities. They may also be called upon to report at regular meetings of the organization or of the executive committee. They must report any committee business that requires action by the organization. They must also report on items referred by the organization. (See: COMMITTEE REPORTS, and COMMIT, REFER, OR RECOMMIT.)

Discharge: A standing committee may be discharged of responsibility for matters referred to it. This requires a two-thirds vote of the organization or a simple majority if there has been previous notice. The motion to discharge is a main motion.

Meetings: Standing committees usually have periodic meetings, but they should not be too frequent. Calling together a committee, or any organization, when there is not sufficient business to justify members taking the trouble to come discourages people from participation. When a large task arises, the committee may decide to meet more frequently until the task is completed. Special meetings may be called either by the chairman or by any two members.

CONSIDERATION BY PARAGRAPH, OR SERIATIM

	MAIN MOTION	POSTPONE INDEFINITELY	AMEND	COMMIT	POSTPONE TO FIXED TIME	LIMIT OR EXTEND DEBATE	PREVIOUS QUESTION	TABLE	ORDERS OF THE DAY	QUESTIONS OF PRIVILEGE	RECESS	ADJOURN	SET TIME TO ADJOURN TO
SUBJECT MOTION:													
YIELDS TO				●	●	●	●	●	●	●	●	●	●
TAKES PRECEDENCE OF		●											
MAY BE APPLIED TO	●		●										

Class: Incidental Motion
Debatable: NO
Amendable: NO
Reconsiderable: NO

Vote: MAJORITY
Second needed: (See *Notes*)
Can interrupt speaker: YES

Purpose and Effect: To have a constitution, by-laws, or a long and complicated motion or report considered one paragraph at a time. It is unnecessary for such consideration that the paragraphs be able to stand alone, because consideration seriatim does not mean that the parts are adopted separately. The paragraphs, divisions, or sections, with their amendments, are read and considered individually and in order. When no more amendments to a paragraph or section are submitted, the group moves to the next paragraph. When the entire motion or report has been read and amended, the chair entertains amendments to the whole (as a result of amendments to later paragraphs, earlier paragraphs may have to be changed, too) and finally the whole is voted upon. After the chair has opened the floor for amendments to the whole it is permissible to move a substitute for the whole report. (See: AMEND, *Substitute a Paragraph*.)

Form: "Mr. Chairman, I move consideration by paragraphs (or 'consideration seriatim')." The chair then reads or has another (the secretary or the maker of the motion) read the first paragraph. When that is read, he calls for amendments. When there are no more, he calls for the reading of the second paragraph, and so on. When all paragraphs have been read, the chairman asks for amendments to the whole. When the document is perfected, the question is called on the whole. It is now necessary to reread the entire report. The preamble is considered after the perfection of all the resolutions but before the vote (See *Preamble* below).

Notes:

Motion	The chairman may at his own initiative put the question to consider by paragraph without a motion from the floor. If the motion is made from the floor, however, a second is normally required.
General Consent	The decision to consider by paragraphs is usually made by general consent without the formality of a vote. If there is any objection, the chairman must bring the question to a vote.
No Subsidiary Motions	No subsidiary motions may be applied to the motion to consider by paragraphs.
Preamble	If the previous question has been moved after the discussion of the text, but before discussion of the preamble, the preamble is excluded from the question unless specified. Thus, the motion could be adopted without the preamble, in which case, the preamble might be considered separately. If the motion fails, the preamble is also dead.

CONSIDER INFORMALLY

There are three degrees of formality by which an organization at a regular meeting can follow committee rules of debate (See COMMITTEE). The most formal is the COMMITTEE OF THE WHOLE; next is the quasi-committee of the whole (See: COMMITTEE OF THE WHOLE, QUASI-). The least formal procedure for achieving the same purpose is to move that a question or group of related questions be considered informally. As with the other two, the motion to consider informally is simply a variety of the motion to COMMIT.

Debate	The rules for informal consideration are as follows:
	There is no time limit or limit on the frequency with which a member may speak; however, a person who has had the floor once cannot speak again until any who desire to speak but have not done so get their first chance.
Limiting Debate	Unlike the committee and quasi-committee of the whole, it is possible to set a limit on debate during the

period when the motion is being considered informally. In the other two, motions to limit debate must be made before the group goes into the less formal discussion period.

Acceptable
Motions
The motion to consider informally can be applied only to main motions and their amendments. When considering informally, all other motions are subject to ordinary rules of debate.

Voting
Although debate is informal, voting is formal. Once a vote is taken disposing permanently or temporarily of the main motion, the informal discussion comes immediately and automatically to an end.

Reporting
Since the voting is formal, the vote taken while considering informally is the vote of the organization. This is not true in committee or quasi-committee of the whole. Consequently, when informal consideration comes to an end (See VOTING), there is no need for a committee report to be made nor any need for a vote.

CONSTITUTION, BY-LAWS, AND RULES OF ORDER

The constitution and by-laws, along with the rules of order form the basic documents of an organization, describing its purpose, how it is organized, and how it transacts its business. The terms constitution and by-laws are not clearly distinguished. Most organizations today have a single basic document, which they describe either as a constitution or as by-laws. When organizations have two separate documents, the constitution is the more general. The by-laws cover the same points as the constitution, but in more detail, and certain additional material as well. Where organizations are incorporated, the articles of incorporation or charter satisfies the need of a constitution. Articles of incorporation, however, being registered with the state, may require special proceedings to be amended, and must conform with the requirements of state law when adopted (a lawyer should be consulted about incorporation requirements of the various states).

Constitution: A constitution should include the following material:

The name of the organization

Its purpose (this will be repeated in the by-laws in exactly the same words)

General requirements for membership (which in the by-laws will be expanded to cover different classes of membership, dues, etc.)

Officers with the period of office (expanded in the bylaws, where necessary, to cover qualifications for office, duties, method of election, etc.)

Frequency of meetings (details on meetings — e.g., quorum, calling special meetings — may be added in the by-laws)

Procedure for amending the constitution (this section should be complete, as the by-laws will include only rules for the amendment of the by-laws)

As a rule, where organizations have both constitution and by-laws, the constitution will be made more difficult to amend.

By-Laws: In addition to the information noted above — which will all appear in the by-laws where there is no constitution — the by-laws should include the following:

Executive Committee (size, composition, meetings, rights and duties, rules of procedure)

Standing Committees (naming them and, where it is not obvious, specifying their functions and any other details that may be necessary)

Parliamentary Authority (the standard work to be used as a reference and arbiter on procedural matters)

Rules of Order: The need for rules of order is in large part satisfied by the adoption of an authority, as noted above. However, an organization may have special needs and functions that make local rules necessary, and on other matters, an organization may want to specify which of equally acceptable procedures is to be used, e.g., the method of voting to be used in election, the method of giving advance notice of motions requiring notice. These needs may be satisfied within the framework of the by-laws, being mentioned under appropriate headings, or the local rules may form a separate body called rules of order. The amendment of rules of order, if they are separate, is the same as for amendment of the by-laws. The parliamentary authority is usually designated by words such as these: "The rules in . . . (name) . . . are adopted as if they were a part of this document and shall apply in all situations where they are not in conflict with the by-laws or rules of this organization."

Adopting a Constitution or By-Laws: Though a two-thirds vote, with notice, is required to amend constitution or by-laws, only a majority is required for adoption, because until the documents are adopted no vested interests in preserving them have been created. In setting up a new organization, the first meeting appoints a committee to draft a constitution which is reported at an adjourned meeting of the same session. The constitution is presented as any committee report (See: COMMITTEE REPORTS, and ADOPT REPORT CONTAINING RESOLUTIONS OR RECOMMENDATIONS), and is considered by paragraphs (See: CONSIDERATION BY PARAGRAPH). In the case of adopting constitution or by-laws, a motion to consider by paragraphs is not necessary. That is standard procedure.

While for totally new organizations a majority is sufficient to adopt a constitution, it may be desirable in certain situations for the constitution to specify a different method of adoption, including a larger vote. This might be desirable in the case of delegate bodies being formed to promote the interests of a number of pre-existing local groups, as when organizing a national trade association, or when organizing a city-improvement group based on pre-existing neighborhood associations. Here adoption would probably proceed by each member organization subscribing, quite possibly in a meeting of its own organization. It would not be unusual to state that the constitution will not be adopted until two thirds of groups sending delegates to the organizing meeting have subscribed, or until a certain number have subscribed (the number being determined by that required to justify the existence of, and to support and maintain, the larger group).

CONVENTION

This is a non-technical name, normally reserved for meetings of an organization whose sessions are large, infrequent, and formal. A convention may be composed either of members or of DELEGATES (See: ASSEMBLY).

CORRESPONDING SECRETARY   See: SECRETARY

DEBATE

The purpose of debate is to give both sides a chance to present their points of view so that undecided members can vote in an informed manner. In formal meetings, debate is formal. Presentations concern only the subject at hand. Members address the chair, not each other, and refer to persons only in formal terms: "the speaker," "the gentleman," "the previous speaker," and so on. This formality minimizes personal arguments and encourages fair and speedy presentation of all relevant points. If a member speaks improperly he may be brought to order by the chairman or by a member's rising to a point of order. A member must avoid criticizing others personally, though he may condemn a motion or its effects in strong terms; nor should he criticize past actions unless he is working for their rescission. A member who has been brought to order for an indecorum — violation of one of these rules — must request LEAVE TO CONTINUE SPEAKING.

In general, the debate does not take up complex questions in detail. Instead, debate is confined to important principles. It is impractical to expect a group large enough to require parliamentary formality to come to sensible conclusions on complex issues initiated on the floor.

In Committees: When new and complex issues arise, the normal procedure is to refer them to committee. Committee rules encourage the freer discussion necessary to develop a nebulous suggestion into a concrete program. When the committee has studied a proposal, its report provides a basis for sound decisions in formal debate. It is always a good idea to accompany a proposal with a set of suggestions for carrying it out. Concrete proposals, preferably submitted in writing, provide a framework for the debate. It is possible for an assembly to constitute itself as a committee of the whole or to agree to act as a committee and to abide by the looser rules of committee debate (See: COMMITTEE OF THE WHOLE; and COMMITTEE OF THE WHOLE, QUASI-). These rules set no time limits and no strict requirements for sticking exactly to the point. The opportunity to wander often leads to good suggestions. However, since it absorbs the time of the whole organization, a committee of the whole should not be used when a regular or temporary committee can be assigned to the same task (See: COMMITTEE, *Rules*).

Rules: The debate on any question begins when the chair states the question; it continues until the scheduled time limit ends, or interest is exhausted, or debate is cut off by an action of the assembly. The time limits on debate apply to each question. A subsidiary motion is a new question and each member has the same amount of time to discuss the subsidiary question as he has to discuss the main question. On a main motion a member may speak twice for ten minutes each time. If he speaks once to the main motion before an amendment is moved, he has two ten minute periods to speak to an amendment and when the organization returns to the main question, he has one remaining ten minute period on the main motion.

Obviously, keeping time records in a very formal organization could become quite complicated. In most groups the limits are invoked only when someone obviously takes more time than he should. But, if the group is interested, it may let a speaker take more than his time. In a formal organization, this might be compensated for by reducing by a corresponding amount the time available to another speaker on the same side of the question. A speaker may yield his time to another for such a purpose. However, it is the general practice to require speakers to alternate, pro and con. To be fair, if one speaker is going to be given the floor for more than ten minutes, the members on the other side of the question should be consulted so that they may make similar arrangements. Also, the limits of debate may be extended by a two-thirds vote (See: LIMIT OR EXTEND DEBATE).

The right to debate cannot be cut off by the chairman calling the question. The chair must allow a few seconds between saying, "Are you ready for the question?" and proceeding to the vote. Otherwise, a speaker can interrupt the vote and demand to be heard.

Time Limits: While every organization can adopt its own limits, the following are generally accepted as reasonable limits of debate on one question during one day. (The rights are renewed on other questions, or when the same question is considered on another day.)

1. Each speaker is allowed to speak twice for no more than ten minutes at a time.
2. No speaker can use his second opportunity to speak until all interested and eligible speakers have been heard a first time.
3. The maker of the motion may be allowed to make a closing statement after all others have spoken unless he has used his full twenty minutes.

DECORUM IN DEBATE See: DEBATE and LEAVE TO CONTINUE SPEAKING AFTER AN INDECORUM

DELEGATE

A verb and a noun. As a verb, delegate means to give power, authority, or rights to another person. A delegate is the person to whom such rights have been given. In parliamentary law, the power given is that to exercise the rights of a group of members — to run the organization in behalf of those who have delegated their rights.

Normally, delegates are used in large organizations where full membership meetings would be impossible. Local groups are entitled to choose one or more delegates apiece to represent them in a session — usually an annual session — where they conduct the business of the central group.

Your congressmen and senators are the men to whom you delegate your right as a citizen to run your government.

DIRECTOR See: EXECUTIVE SECRETARY

DIVIDE THE QUESTION

	MAIN MOTION	POSTPONE INDEFINITELY	AMEND	COMMIT	POSTPONE TO FIXED TIME	LIMIT OR EXTEND DEBATE	PREVIOUS QUESTION	TABLE	ORDERS OF THE DAY	QUESTIONS OF PRIVILEGE	RECESS	ADJOURN	SET TIME TO ADJOURN TO
SUBJECT MOTION:													
YIELDS TO			●	●	●	●	●	●	●	●	●	●	●
TAKES PRECEDENCE OF		●											
MAY BE APPLIED TO	●		●										

Class: Incidental Motion
Debatable: NO *Vote:* MAJORITY
Amendable: YES *Second needed:* (See below)
Reconsiderable: NO *Can interrupt speaker:* YES

Purpose and Effect: To separate a motion or resolution consisting of several related parts in order to debate and vote on the parts as separate motions. Do not confuse with DIVISION OF THE ASSEMBLY. For a group to entertain a motion to divide, the sections or paragraphs of the resolution must make sense standing by themselves. The division is especially useful when some parts of a motion are more acceptable than others. When the parts of a motion are unrelated, division may be obtained at the request of a single member. The motion and vote are necessary only when the parts are related. This motion may be made whenever the motion to be divided is immediately pending, but it is preferable to make the motion earlier rather than later.

Form: "Mr. Chairman, I move the division of the question in the following manner. . . ." The mover must state explicitly where he thinks the breaks should occur; it is on this point that the motion is subject to amendment. The breaks must separate the motion into self-sustaining units. Thus, a motion to strike and insert (See: AMEND, *Strike Out and Insert Words*) would not be divided because neither part could stand alone. The division should not require the secretary to rewrite the motion but only to do what is necessary to make its clauses stand as sentences. When it is impossible to divide a motion without rewriting, the division may be achieved, in effect, by a series of motions to strike out different parts of the main motion.

Notes:

Motion and Second   The parts of the divided motion need not be moved separately, because the motion to divide applies to all of them, as does its second.

General	The formality of a vote on the question of division is
Consent	often dispensed with on the assumption of general consent. However, if there is objection, there must be a vote.

Amendment If there are different proposals as to the manner of division, they are considered in the order submitted, except when the number of suggested divisions differs. In the latter case, the one dividing the motion into the most parts is considered first.

Subsidiary No subsidiary motions can be applied to the motion to
Motions divide, except an amendment.

DIVISION OF THE ASSEMBLY

1. When applied to a **viva voce** vote anytime after the question has been called.	MAIN MOTION	POSTPONE INDEFINITELY	AMEND	COMMIT	POSTPONE TO FIXED TIME	LIMIT OR EXTEND DEBATE	PREVIOUS QUESTION	TABLE	ORDERS OF THE DAY	QUESTIONS OF PRIVILEGE	RECESS	ADJOURN	SET TIME TO ADJOURN TO
SUBJECT MOTION:													
YIELDS TO									●	●	●	●	●
TAKES PRECEDENCE OF	1	1	1	1	1	1	1	1	1	1	1	1	1

Class: Incidental Motion
Debatable: NO
Amendable: NO
Reconsiderable: NO

Vote: (See *Purpose*)
Second needed: NO
Can interrupt speaker: YES

Purpose and Effect: To clarify the result of a vote taken either by voice (viva voce) or by show of hands. The result may be checked in several ways. Division proper is a request that those for and those against stand in turn. In most instances, any question of the chair's judgment is resolved in this manner. Such a division requires only the request of a single member. A check may be made by standing count, where those standing for the affirmative and then for the negative are actually counted, or the check may be taken by roll-call vote. For both standing count and roll call there must be a majority vote, unless the matter is approved by general consent.

Form: "Mr. Chairman, I call for a division." "Division," or some such. In asking for a count, the mover must specify the form in which the count should be made. It is unnecessary to obtain recognition to call for division.

When the request for a simple division is made, the chair immediately retakes the vote by asking the affirmative to rise and be seen and, after they are seated, that the negative rise.

Notes:

When Entertained	This motion should be entertained at any time, even after the vote has been announced or after another person has obtained the floor.
General Consent	When the count is requested, the chair may obtain general consent or take a vote. If general consent cannot be obtained, a vote must be taken.
Announcing Vote	The chair announces the result of the division or count as he would announce the result of the first vote on a motion.

ELECTIONS

Election may be to office or to membership. In either case, the process is essentially the same. In an election to membership, the recommendation of the membership committee is equivalent to nomination; adoption of the committee report is equivalent to election. In many organizations, the formalities of election to membership are dispensed with, the only qualification for membership being payment of the dues, which is assumed to indicate commitment to the purposes of the organization (See: TRIAL OF MEMBERS).

Nomination: The suggestion of names of candidates for office. The procedure serves two purposes. First, it narrows the field of contenders for office (without preventing members from voting for some who have not been nominated); and second, it gives potential candidates the opportunity to decline before the election procedure has been completed, thus saving time. A nomination may be considered as a MOTION; however, no second is needed. Nominations may be made in three ways. In most organizations a nominating committee is designated for the purpose of proposing a slate of officers. The nominating committee studies the records and reputations of the members and, in advance of the meeting at which the election is to be held, asks of those it chooses whether, if elected, they are willing to serve. The nominating committee's report is not accepted or adopted, for passage of either motion would be equivalent to election of the nominating committee's slate. A second method is to entertain nominations from the floor during the meeting at which the elections are held. Some organizations use this method exclusively. All that employ a nominating committee should allow additional nominations from the floor after the nominating committee report has been received. In electing members to committees, it is possible to specify a third method of nomination, giving the right of nomination exclusively either to the PRESIDING OFFICER or to the chairman of the committee. (See: COMMITTEE, STANDING).

When election is by ballot or roll call (See: VOTING), nominations are not strictly necessary, since each member has the opportunity to name his choice. When the election is by voice, rising, or standing count, nominations are essential.

Voting: Any voting procedure described in the article on VOTING may be employed in elections. A majority is required for election. When the voting is by voice, rising, or standing count, the election follows the procedure for filling in blanks (See: COMMITTEE, STANDING, *Choosing Members and Officers,* and AMEND, Filling Blanks). If no more nominations are made than there are vacancies, the slate as a whole may be elected on one vote; otherwise, there is a separate vote for the filling of each office. When electing by ballot — the most commonly used method — one vote is taken, each member writing on his ballot one candidate for each office to be filled. If for any of the offices no candidate receives a majority, the voting is repeated, but only for the contested offices. Those eligible in the runoff may be limited to the two candidates receiving the highest number of votes the first time.

Effect: Unless specified otherwise in the constitution or by-laws, if the officers elected are present or if they had consented to nomination in advance, elections take effect immediately; if the candidates had not indicated in advance their willingness to serve, the election is effective immediately upon their being notified and accepting. After an election has taken effect, it is too late to RECONSIDER the vote. Where newly elected officers do not take office immediately, it is necessary to specify exactly when the transfer should take place.

END DEBATE   See: PREVIOUS QUESTION

EXECUTIVE SECRETARY

Organizations with paid staffs are becoming more common in professional fields, industries, social service fields, and even among neighborhood improvement groups. The executive secretary is one of many names given to the director of the paid staff, or to the single staff member in smaller organizations. The principal or only staff member may also be called executive vice-president, director, or executive director.

When an organization has an executive secretary, the chairman or president will be principally a PRESIDING OFFICER, though he is likely to have additional ceremonial functions by virtue of his office, and may, in practice, work hand in hand with the executive director, maintaining almost daily contact.

Duties: The specific duties of the executive secretary will vary considerably with the purposes of the organization, and these duties should be defined, in a general way, in the constitution or by-laws.

The executive secretary carries out the orders of the organization, board, or executive committee for which he works, within the limits set out by the constitution or by-laws. Where there is a paid staff, motions are called orders, rather than RESOLUTIONS, when they are orders to the paid staff. The word *order,* in this sense, is not to be confused with general and special orders.

Specific responsibilities may include:

Correspondence   All of the duties that would otherwise be performed by a corresponding secretary (See: SECRETARY).

Action Committee Staff   Following the directions of action committees, just as he follows the orders of the executive committee, serving as its corresponding secretary, making purchases where needed, negotiating hall rentals for special events, conducting membership campaigns, getting out news releases, etc.

Advisory Committee Staff   Serving as the corresponding secretary to advisory committees, preparing first drafts of reports for consideration by the committee, and obtaining information necessary to the committee's deliberations.

Agenda   Helping in the preparation of the agenda for meetings, even though this is the province of the SECRETARY, because the executive, being more intimate with day-to-day events should have the most thorough knowledge of the items of business that must be covered, and of their relative importance.

Policy   Proposing policy and programs to the executive committee; the executive secretary may be an ex officio member or officer of the group to which he reports, though he will normally refrain from voting.

Reports   Preparing the annual report of the executive committee.

Editor   Editing, when there is one, the organization's newsletter.

Serving the Membership   Providing the members of the organization with any services that are expected; these may range from running a job placement service in a professional organization, through processing zoning complaints in a neighborhood group, to providing technical data in an industrial society.

Office: The office of the executive secretary is normally where the executive committee meets, though the executive committee of some national organizations circulates its meetings around the country.

EX OFFICIO MEMBERS OF COMMITTEES

An officer, usually the chairman, is sometimes designated an ex officio (by virtue or because of an office) member of some or all committees. This privileged status gives the designated person all the rights and none of the responsibilities of committee membership. Its purpose is to lend committees the special help of the ex officio member without making him responsible for continual participation in the work of the committee.

EXPULSION   See: TRIAL OF MEMBERS and NON-MEMBERS, EXPULSION OF

EXPUNGE

A motion similar to RESCIND, but used to indicate condemnation where simple rescission indicates only that the organization has changed its mind. Expunge is not used very often. All rules applicable to rescind apply to expunge, except that the motion is made in the form: "I move that... be expunged from the record."

The secretary should cross out the matter expunged by drawing a line around it and writing across the text "Expunged by order of the assembly." Care should be taken, even if the expunging is done during the heat of anger, that the process of expunging does not actually obliterate the record. At a later date someone may want to question whether the text expunged was exactly that which had been ordered expunged.

GENERAL CONSENT

A means of deciding a question without the formality of a vote, thus saving time and work. Instead of asking for a vote, the chair asks if there is any objection. If no one protests, the matter is considered to be decided as suggested by the chair. General consent is used at the discretion of the chairman. Although the chair may seek general consent when the progress of a debate on a main motion indicates little serious opposition, general consent is more commonly used for INCIDENTAL MOTIONS. A vote by general consent may be entered in the minutes of the organization as a unanimous vote or with the notation that the motion was adopted by general consent. Since a single objection can prevent the use of this procedure, the rights of minorities are safe. Generally, the more formal the meeting, the less voting by general consent will be used. On the other hand, in committees, most business is carried on in this manner.

GENERAL ORDERS   See: ORDERS, POSTPONE TO A FIXED TIME, and ORDERS OF THE DAY, CALL FOR

IMMEDIATELY PENDING   See: PENDING

INCIDENTAL MAIN MOTION

An incidental main motion is handled almost exactly as a main motion. The only difference between the two is that objection may not be made to the consideration of an incidental motion.

Among the more common incidental main motions are the following (note that they have no rank among themselves):

Accept a report
Adopt a report
Adjourn, when not privileged
Amend constitution, by-laws, or anything adopted
Ratify action already taken
Repeal or rescind action already taken
Set the time for the next meeting of a session when not privileged

Incidental main motions may bring business before the assembly but they are never used to present new business. Motions to ratify, repeal, or amend actions already taken, are considered in the same manner as old business. The motion to adopt a report paves the way for bringing the report (which may include new subjects) before the assembly (See: MAIN MOTION).

INCIDENTAL MOTION

An incidental motion is one brought up by a member to assure that a pending motion is:

— understood by all present,
— appropriate,
— handled according to the rules,
— voted on fairly.

Here is a list of the more common incidental motions:

Point of order
Appeal a decision of the chair
Suspend the rules
Divide the question
Consider by paragraphs (seriatim)
Object to considering a question

Division of the assembly
Motions related to method of voting and closing and reopening
  polls
Motions concerning nominations
Requests of various sorts arising from pending business

Incidental motions are in order whenever they arise from a question that is or has just been immediately pending and, with one exception, they may be applied to any question. The one exception is the motion objecting to the consideration of a question. You can object to the consideration only of main motions.

The incidental motion may affect the decision on the motion from which it arises, so the incidental motion must be decided first. In that sense, incidental motions may be said to take precedence over all others. However, once an incidental motion is on the floor, it yields to any PRIVILEGED MOTION.

An incidental motion arising from a privileged motion must be considered first. A privileged motion made after an incidental motion is considered first.

Incidental motions should not be confused with SUBSIDIARY MOTIONS, which are proposals to dispose of pending questions in a certain manner — for example, to table, to postpone consideration, and so on. By and large, subsidiary motions apply only to main motions.

Except as noted under the specific motions, incidental motions are undebatable; they cannot have subsidiary motions attached to them; and they cannot be amended.

INDECORUM See: DEBATE, POINT OF ORDER, and LEAVE TO CONTINUE SPEAKING

INSTRUCT A COMMITTEE

1. As an amendment. Instructions made after vote or referral are main motions.	MAIN MOTION	POSTPONE INDEFINITELY	AMEND	COMMIT	POSTPONE TO FIXED TIME	LIMIT OR EXTEND DEBATE	PREVIOUS QUESTION	TABLE	ORDERS OF THE DAY	QUESTIONS OF PRIVILEGE	RECESS	ADJOURN	SET TIME TO ADJOURN TO
SUBJECT MOTION:													
YIELDS TO					●	●	●	●	●	●	●	●	●
TAKES PRECEDENCE OF	●	●	●										
MAY BE APPLIED TO				1									

Class: (See *Purpose*)
Debatable: YES
Amendable: YES　　　　　　　　　*Vote:* MAJORITY
Reconsiderable: YES　　　　　　 *Second needed:* YES
　　　　　　　　　　　　　　　　Can interrupt speaker: NO

Purpose and effect: To give directions or information to a committee concerning some business before the committee, such as notice of when the report is to be made, where relevant information can be found, what the group's position has been on related issues, etc. Instruction can be made as an independent motion at any time while the matter referred is still in committee. In that case, it is a main motion. Instruction can also be incorporated into a motion to refer, either by the maker of the motion or as an amendment. In the latter case, the motion to instruct is a subsidiary motion, simply a variety of amendment.

Form: "Mr. Chairman, I move the —— Committee be instructed to. . . ."
"Mr. Chairman, I move the —— Committee be informed that. . . ."

Notes:

Class   The motion to instruct may be heard even after the vote is taken to commit, and will have priority over all but privileged motions until the chair states the question on the next business. After that, the motion to instruct will be considered a main motion.

LEAVE TO CONTINUE SPEAKING AFTER AN INDECORUM

1. When it applies to a point of order arising out of the subject motion.	MAIN MOTION	POSTPONE INDEFINITELY	AMEND	COMMIT	POSTPONE TO FIXED TIME	LIMIT OR EXTEND DEBATE	PREVIOUS QUESTION	TABLE	ORDERS OF THE DAY	QUESTIONS OF PRIVILEGE	RECESS	ADJOURN	SET TIME TO ADJOURN TO
SUBJECT MOTION:													
YIELDS TO									●	●	●	●	●
TAKES PRECEDENCE OF	1	1	1	1	1	1	1	1	1	1	1	1	1

Class: Incidental Motion
Debatable: NO   *Vote:* GENERAL CONSENT or
Amendable: NO   MAJORITY
Reconsiderable: NO   *Second needed:* NO
                Can interrupt speaker: YES

Purpose and effect: If a speaker's remarks are decided to be indecorous (See: DEBATE), either by the chairman or by the assembly (See: POINT OF ORDER), he may not resume speaking unless he is granted leave to do so. Request for leave to continue speaking is a type of REQUEST. When a point of order is raised concerning a speaker's remarks for purely procedural reasons, it is not necessary for the speaker to request leave to continue speaking.

Form: "Mr. Chairman, I request leave to continue speaking."

Notes:

General   This request may be granted by general consent. If
Consent   there is any objection, then the chair calls the question: "Shall the gentleman be granted leave to continue speaking?"

LIMIT OR EXTEND DEBATE

1. When it leads to a motion. 2. When it is debatable (not privileged).	MAIN MOTION	POSTPONE INDEFINITELY	AMEND	COMMIT	POSTPONE TO FIXED TIME	LIMIT OR EX-TEND DEBATE	PREVIOUS QUESTION	TABLE	ORDERS OF THE DAY	QUESTIONS OF PRIVILEGE	RECESS	ADJOURN	SET TIME TO ADJOURN TO
SUBJECT MOTION:													
YIELDS TO							●	●	●	●	●	●	●
TAKES PRECEDENCE OF													
MAY BE APPLIED TO	●	●	●	●	●						1	1	1

Class: Subsidiary Motion
Debatable: NO   *Vote:* 2/3
Amendable: YES   *Second needed:* YES
Reconsiderable: YES   *Can interrupt speaker:* NO

Purpose and Effect: When an organization operates according to rules that set limits on debate, it is sometimes desirable to provide more time on complex or urgent issues or less time on relatively unimportant questions. A limit or an extension requires a two-thirds vote. The motion may set the time available to an individual speaker, an hour at which all discussion will end, or a maximum duration for debate. Debate is closed by the PREVIOUS QUESTION, suspended by the motion to TABLE, and suppressed entirely by a two-thirds vote on an OBJECTION TO CONSIDERATION OF A QUESTION.

An unqualified motion to limit debate applies to the immediately pending question and any subsidiary or incidental motions made later. The order to extend debate applies only to the immediate question unless specifically qualified. No subsidiary motion other than an amendment may be made to either motion. Once set, time limits may be changed by another motion to limit or extend, which supercedes the earlier one. The latest time limit adopted takes precedence over earlier ones.

282

Form: "Mr. Chairman, I move that the debate on this resolution should end and the question be put to the membership at 11:30 A.M."

"Mr. Chairman, I move that the debate on this amendment end and the question be put to the membership in forty-five minutes."

"Mr. Chairman, I move that in the debate on this motion and on all subsidiary and incidental motions attached to it, each speaker should be limited to one speech of five minutes' length."

Notes:

Commit and Postpone	After time limits have been set, a motion cannot be committed or postponed unless the time limit is reconsidered. (Committing or postponing would have the effect of rescinding the time limits by a simple majority.)
Table	If a motion is tabled and is not taken from the table before a time limit expires, when it is taken up again it is voted upon immediately, without debate. If the time limit has not expired, the balance of the time assigned is still available.
Subsidiary Motions	If the limits are set on the length of speeches or their number rather than the duration of debate, any motions subsidiary to the pending question are in order.
When Applied	Time limits apply only to the session in which they are made and if the question goes over to another session, the normal rules apply.

MAIN MOTION

A main motion introduces a new subject for consideration. Deciding on the disposition of main motions is the principal function of deliberative bodies. All other types of motions are intended to improve main motions, to insure that they are handled fairly, or to keep the organization operating smoothly.

Since original main motions are the principal business of organizations, they must be given *lowest* priority. If main motions had priority over the motion to adjourn, meetings would be endless, and if main motions had priority over amendments, it would be impossible to modify main motions. Further, many other motions serve either to determine how main motions will be disposed (table, send back to committee), or to assure that they are handled properly (point of order, division of assembly). Such motions would be meaningless if they couldn't be brought up while a main motion was under consideration.

Main motions are debatable, amendable, and can be reconsidered.

While a main motion is immediately pending, the chair may consider any motion except another main motion.

If a main motion is tabled or sent to committee, all subsidiary motions go with it, and when a main motion returns to the floor, the subsidiary motions return also and are considered in order.

MAJORITY See: VOTING

MEETING See: SESSION

MINORITY REPORTS

Purpose and Form: When a committee does not reach unanimous agreement, even if there is only a single dissenter, the minority has the right to present a report of its disagreement with the position of the majority. Such a report should conform to the general requirements for any COMMITTEE REPORTS. However, the minority report should refer only to the area of disagreement and not include a repetition of the matters on which there is agreement. In addition to supportive arguments, the report may present either amendments, substitutions, additions or deletions applicable to the committee report. Thus, after its arguments, the minority might state, "The undersigned believe that paragraph 2 of the committee's resolutions should be deleted, that paragraph 3 should be amended by . . . and that paragraph 6 should be replaced by the following paragraph." (A series of amendments such as that would be better divided when and if they are considered by the organization.) Alternatively, the subcommittee report might offer a complete revision of the committee's report, e.g., "For the above reasons the undersigned recommend the adoption of the following resolutions. . . ."

When one or a few members object to one or a few minor points in a committee report, they may sign the report and append a short statement of their exceptions.

Procedure: A minority report is received after the majority report has been heard and the question on it stated by the chair. The chair may call for receipt of the minority report on his own, the decision to receive it being a matter of general consent. If anyone objects to the reading of the report, a majority vote is needed to counter the objection. The receipt of the report is for information, and the report does not come before the assembly as a question unless it is moved from the floor that the minority report be substituted for the majority report, or that the minority's amendments to the majority report be adopted. Either action is a form of amendment to the majority report and is handled as such (See: AMEND and ADOPT COMMITTEE REPORT CONTAINING RECOMMENDATIONS).

MINUTES

The record kept by the secretary of the business transacted at an organization's meetings. Such a record may also be called a journal or, simply, a record. The amount of detail required in the minutes depends on the uses to which they are put and the desires and traditions of the organization. Congress, for instance, keeps a verbatim report, published as *The Congressional Record,* of every word during a congressional session. Most private societies do not need and could not afford such a complete record.

Degrees of Completeness:

(I) There are times when some private organizations will want a complete record. This may be true in the business meetings of annual conventions, and at some meetings of delegate bodies. In such cases, the secretary should be provided the aid of professional court stenographers or of tape recorders from which typists can later reproduce the text.

(II) More commonly the need for a thorough record is satisfied by the recording of every motion made and of a summary of all speeches. It is usual to identify the speakers and the makers of the motions, but not the seconders. When speakers provide advance texts of their remarks, their complete speeches may be included. Motions withdrawn may be excluded as well as secondary motions that failed, though decisions on points of order and appeals should be recorded whatever their outcome. Here again, stenographic help should be provided the secretary.

(III) A simpler method is to do as indicated under II, but without reporting the debate.

(IV) Finally, it is possible to include only main motions that carry, in the form in which they carried, without detailing the process of amendment. However, it is still necessary to keep the exact text of motions disposed of by any subsidiary motion and of any motion to which, though it failed, a motion to RECONSIDER has been applied. Records are necessary because these motions may reappear at a later time. This method suffices for most small organizations. (A sample of minutes prepared on this pattern is shown in the illustration on page 286.)

Voting Records: Wherever a vote is taken by standing count or by ballot, the minutes should record the exact vote. When a vote is taken by roll call, the vote of every member present should be recorded in the minutes. These remarks apply regardless of the degree of completeness adopted as organization policy (See: VOTING and ELECTIONS).

Formal Requirements: Regardless of the degree of completeness otherwise required, the minutes of every meeting should include the information listed in the upper half of the FORM AND CONTENTS OF MINUTES on page 287.

Tone: Minutes should be written in an impersonal tone. The secretary should refrain from any comment on the events of the meeting. Remember that primarily the minutes record what was done; what was said is secondary, even though the minutes be taken verbatim.

Approval: In the regular business meeting, the minutes are read as the first item after the call to order. It is necessary that they be approved as accurate. After the secretary has read the minutes (the chair says, "The secretary will now read the minutes"), the chair then asks if there are any corrections. (For corrections, see below.) He waits for a few seconds; if no one speaks, he says, "The minutes are approved as read." More formally, a vote may be taken on approval of the minutes. Sometimes, in the interest of speeding business, the reading of the minutes is dispensed with for a meeting. If this done, they should be read at the next regular meeting before reading later minutes. When an organization meets only annually, and sometimes if it meets quarterly, the executive committee is empowered to approve the minutes of organization meetings. Of course, the executive committee also approves the minutes of its own meetings. If the minutes have been dispensed with, they may be called up for reading and approval by a member at any time when no business is pending.

Correction: The purpose of reading the minutes is to assure that they are correct. After they are read, the chairman allows time for members to rise to correct them. A dispute must be settled by vote. Correction of the minutes may be made, even though they've been approved, at any time that an error is discovered, regardless of the time that has elapsed, and without a motion to reconsider. A change in approved minutes that is not a correction can only be obtained through the motions to RESCIND or to EXPUNGE.

Committee Reports: Unless the minutes are to be published (see below), committee reports are not included, though the action taken on such reports is recorded. The reports themselves should be kept by the secretary in a separate file (See: SECRETARY).

When Minutes are to be Published: Published minutes should be either in form I or, more commonly, form II. All reports are included exactly as submitted with additions shown in italics and with sections struck enclosed in brackets.

286

EXAMPLE OF MINUTES

1. The regular meeting of the Springfield Civic Association
2. was held April 6, 1961 in the American Legion Hall. The meeting was
3. opened by the Chairman, Mr. Wilde, at 8:35 P.M. The minutes were
4. read by Mr. Murray, the Secretary, and were approved as read. The
5. treasurer reported a balance of $671.87. There were no standing
6. committee reports. Mr. Byrnes reported for the special committee
7. a resolution that was discussed, amended, and then adopted:
8. Resolved, That the Springfield Civic Association go on
9. record as wholeheartedly supporting the bond issue for the
10. replacement of the central fire house.
11. The motion to sponsor a Christmas party, having been set
12. as a general order for this meeting, was taken up, and, after debate
13. and amendment, was adopted in the following form:
14. Resolved, That a committee of three be elected to run a
15. Christmas party at the County Orphanage on December 23,
16. and that the committee be allowed to spend up to $75.00 on
17. food, decorations, and gifts.
18. Messrs. Cole, White, and Middleton were elected to the committee.
19. During the debate on the above, Mr. Watson, who had voted for the
20. fire house motion, moved to have that vote reconsidered. The
21. reconsideration was not called up. Mr. Cole moved to take from the
22. table the motion suggesting meeting in the Presbyterian Church Hall,
23. which had been tabled at the last regular meeting. After a voice
24. vote was taken, Mr. Franco moved that the vote be retaken by standing
25. count, which was adopted by general consent. The motion to take
26. from the table carried, 28 votes for, 24 against. Attached to the
27. motion to table was the following:
28. Move that the subject motion be referred to the Program and
29. Arrangements Committee, with instructions to investigate
30. other possible meeting places and to report on their com-
31. parative merits at the May meeting.
32. The motion to refer was carried in that form.
33. On the motion of Mr. Byrnes, the meeting adjourned at
34. 10:45 P.M.
35.
36. *Ronald Murray*
Secretary

FORM AND CONTENTS OF MINUTES

The boxes in the illustration at left include the formal information that should be in the minutes:

Line 1   *Type of Meeting;* whether it is regular, special, adjourned regular, or adjourned special

Line 1   *Organization Name*

Line 2   *Date of Meeting*

Line 2   *Place of Meeting;* required only when there is not a regular meeting place, or when the place is changed

Line 3   *Person Presiding;* whoever presides (regularly or not)

Line 3   *Time of Opening*

Line 4   *Secretary;* whether or not it is the regular secretary

Line 34   *Time of Closing*

Line 35   *Signature;* chairman may also be required to sign

ADDITIONAL NOTES

Line 3   If the chairman is not present, the minutes should say "In the absence of the Chairman, —— presided."

Line 4   A similar form is used in the absence of the secretary. If the minutes of the previous meeting had been corrected, these minutes would read, "And, as corrected by Mr. Henry to read, . . . were approved."

Line 6   Indicate by whom reports and motions are made; the names of seconders are not included.

Line 12   The secretary should keep a record of all general and special orders. It should be possible to find reference to this order in the minutes of an earlier meeting.

Line 13   Election or appointment of a committee has priority over all but privileged motions immediately after the adoption of the motion creating the committee.

Line 20   The secretary keeps a record of motions to reconsider because these motions can be called up at a later date.

Line 30   The actual count is recorded. Had the vote been taken by roll call, the vote of every member present would be included in the minutes.

Line 35   "Respectfully submitted" is not acceptable.

MODERATOR See: PRESIDING OFFICER

MOTION

A formal proposal made in a meeting that an organization take some action or state a position (See: RESOLUTION). Motions are generally classified in a manner that partially defines their parliamentary status — that is, when they may be made, to what motions they yield, and to what other motions they may be applied. The classification is as follows:

MAIN (or principal) MOTION

INCIDENTAL MAIN MOTION

SUBSIDIARY MOTION

INCIDENTAL MOTION

PRIVILEGED MOTION

Unclassified

NOMINATING COMMITTEE See: ELECTIONS and ADOPT REPORT CONTAINING RECOMMENDATIONS

NOMINATIONS See: ELECTIONS and COMMITTEE, STANDING

NON-MEMBERS, EXPULSION OF

An organization has the right to determine who shall be present at its meetings and has the legal right to order any non-member to leave. A person refusing to leave may be physically ejected. The chair may order that a recalcitrant visitor be thrown out by any available members. The member who does the ejecting, not the chairman, is liable in case of a damage suit by the person ejected. The basis for such a suit would be that more force than was required was used in the ejection. Using too much force is the fault of the person doing the ejecting rather than of the chairman who ordered the expulsion.

OBJECTION TO THE CONSIDERATION OF A QUESTION

1. Motion entertained only before debate has begun on, or any secondary motions have been applied to, the main motion.	MAIN MOTION	POSTPONE INDEFINITELY	AMEND	COMMIT	POSTPONE TO FIXED TIME	LIMIT OR EXTEND DEBATE	PREVIOUS QUESTION	TABLE	ORDERS OF THE DAY	QUESTIONS OF PRIVILEGE	RECESS	ADJOURN	SET TIME TO ADJOURN TO
SUBJECT MOTION:													
YIELDS TO								●	●	●	●	●	●
TAKES PRECEDENCE OF	1												

Class: Incidental Motion
Debatable: NO   *Vote:* 2/3
Amendable: NO   *Second needed:* NO
Reconsiderable: (See below)   *Can interrupt speaker:* YES

Purpose and Effect: To prevent a motion from being considered. The objection is applicable only to original main motions and questions of privilege. It must be made immediately upon introduction of the motion and cannot be applied to incidental main motions or to the reports of committees on subjects referred to them (See: ADOPT REPORT ON MATTERS REFERRED TO COMMITTEE OR COMMITTED). The motion is actually a special point of order, the purpose of which is not to prevent debate but to avoid frivolous or obstructive questions.

Form: "Mr. Chairman I object to consideration of the motion."
The chair says, "Objection has been made to consideration of the motion. Shall the motion be considered?" Thus, an affirmative vote is against the objection and for the motion.

Notes:

When Entertained	Objection to consideration should be entertained only when it refers to original main motions.
Consideration	The chair may put this question at his own initiative.
Chair's Ruling Appealed	If the chair rules on the question without a vote, his decision may be appealed by the assembly.
Reconsider	An affirmative vote — one sustaining the subject motion — cannot be reconsidered. A negative vote — which sustains the objection — is reconsiderable.

OFFICERS

The members of an organization elected to fill constitutionally defined posts of special responsibility. The most common are the PRESIDING OFFICER (chairman, president or moderator), the VICE-CHAIRMAN (or vice-president), the SECRETARY, and the TREASURER. The exact titles, qualifications, and duties of these and any other officials are described in the constitution or by-laws. Officers are normally selected by ELECTION, procedures for which are described in that article. Duties are reported in the articles on each of the officers named (See: EXECUTIVE SECRETARY).

ORDER OF BUSINESS

Every organization should adopt a standard order in which the business of a meeting can be transacted. This standard order serves as the program where a special one is not adopted. When a special program is adopted, it will generally be used as the outline for the program or agenda. An organization may develop its own order of business (which would be set forth in the by-laws), or use that from a standard work on parliamentary rules. The most commonly used order of business is:

1. Opening or call to order.
2. Minutes
3. Reports of:
    a. officers
    b. board or executive committee, (if there is one)
    c. standing committees
4. Reports of special committees (in order of appointment)
5. Special orders
6. Old business and general orders
7. New business

Women's clubs often adopt the order of business in

Fox's Parliamentary Usage:

1. Call to order
2. Minutes
3. Special orders
4. Communication from president
5. Corresponding Secretary's report
6. Treasurer's report
7. Board of directors' report
8. Standing Committee reports
9. Special committee reports
10. Old business
11. Miscellaneous business
12. Program (i.e., talk, entertainment, book review, etc.)
13. Adjournment

Notice that except for the addition of two items, program and miscellaneous business, the two lists above are essentially the same, Fox's list being somewhat the more specific. Fox's list is included to demonstrate how an organization might vary the common order of business to suit its special needs.

Opening: The opening of the meeting may consist simply in the chair's calling the meeting to order. It can also be a ceremony, including the Pledge of Allegiance, a prayer, or whatever an organization wishes.

ORDERS

Program: An organization's orders are its directions to itself to handle certain business at certain times. The program or agenda of a meeting is one form of order. Although an ordinary business meeting of an organization that meets as often as quarterly need not adopt a program, it may sometimes be useful to do so. A program should always be adopted for large organization meetings and meeting of groups that come together infrequently. Where a program is not adopted, the order of business defined or adopted in the by-laws is the program for the meeting. Normally, there will be in the program or standard order of business a time for the consideration of all general orders postponed to that day (See: PROGRAM and ORDER OF BUSINESS).

General and Special Orders: In addition to the program, there are general and special orders. A general order is an item of business postponed to a certain day or time in order that it may be taken up again as soon as the pending business at the time is completed. An item of business is postponed as a general order by a majority vote. A special order is a postponed item of business that must be taken up at exactly the specified time, even when other business is pending. An item of business may be postponed as a special order only by a two-thirds vote, because a special order actually suspends the rules otherwise applicable at the time to which the business is postponed (See: POSTPONE TO A FIXED TIME).

Special Orders,   Though special orders must be taken up at the time
Rules for   specified, even if that requires the interruption of other
                     business, a special order may be made for a certain day
                     without specifying the hour. If the special order refers
                     only to a certain day, it is taken up in the meeting im-
                     mediately after the reports of special committees (See:
                     ORDER OF BUSINESS). When there is a conflict be-
                     tween special orders, the one made first takes preced-
                     ence, even if the later one was made for an earlier
                     time. (If first an item was made a special order for 9:00
                     P.M., and an item was later made a special order for
                     8:30 P.M., the later order will be considered at 8:30,

but if it is not completed by 9:00, the other one will be taken up and the one begun at 8:30 completed only after the completion of the one set for 9:00.) The only interruption allowed to the consideration of a special order at the specified time is a recess or adjournment previously set. The chair automatically calls the meeting recessed or adjourned by announcing "The hour has arrived for. . . ." At this juncture, the chair should entertain any motion for postponement of the adjournment time, which requires a two-thirds vote. Special orders can also be made for a meeting, specifying that a meeting will be devoted to consideration of one specified subject, or a group of specified subjects.

General Orders,   When general orders are postponed only to a certain
Rules for   day, they are considered, in the order in which they were made, under the head of old business, that is, after special orders. When a general order is set for a specified time, it is taken up as soon after that time as any pending business is completed. Consideration of a general order yields to privileged motions, to special orders, and to action on the motion to RECONSIDER.

Orders of the Day: The orders of the day is the sum of the general and special orders deferred to that day and the program adopted for that day or the order of business applicable in the absence of a formally adopted program. To call for the orders of the day is to demand that the organization proceed according to the directions it has given itself (See: ORDERS OF THE DAY, CALL FOR).

Making Orders: To make a special or general order is to postpone to a fixed time (See: POSTPONE TO A FIXED TIME).

ORDERS OF THE DAY, CALL FOR

	MAIN MOTION	POSTPONE INDEFINITELY	AMEND	COMMIT	POSTPONE TO FIXED TIME	LIMIT OR EX-TEND DEBATE	PREVIOUS QUESTION	TABLE	ORDERS OF THE DAY	QUESTIONS OF PRIVILEGE	RECESS	ADJOURN	SET TIME TO ADJOURN TO
SUBJECT MOTION:													
YIELDS TO										●	●	●	●
TAKES PRECEDENCE OF	●	●	●	●	●	●	●	●					

Class: Privileged Motion
Debatable: NO
Amendable: NO
Reconsiderable: NO

Vote: (See below)
Second needed: NO
Can interrupt speaker:
  (See *Purpose*)

Purpose and Effect: A call for the orders of the day is a request for the assembly to return to a time schedule previously determined. The schedule may have been a program accepted at the outset of the meeting, or it may have been set by a general or special order at a previous meeting. The call for the orders of the day, when it refers to the program or to general orders, cannot interrupt pending business; it can interrupt a speaker making a motion at any time before the chair states the question. When there is a special order, the call can interrupt any pending business except another privileged motion. The call for orders of the day can be made by a single member. If the chair thinks the organization may be interested in continuing the discussion out of order, he may ask "Shall we proceed to the orders of the day?" Unless the negative carries by a two-thirds vote, the assembly will return to the schedule, because refusal to follow orders of the day is a suspension of the rules.

Form: "Mr. Chairman, I call for the orders of the day." Note that the motion is never made in reference to any specific order.

Notes:

Precedence   When the call for orders of the day refers to the adopted program or to general orders, the chair should entertain, at any time before the orders are actually taken up, the motion to RECONSIDER or to call up an earlier motion to reconsider. These motions shall not be entertained if the business brought up by the call for orders of the day is a special order.

Effect of *Rejection*	If the assembly, by a two-thirds vote, rejects the call for orders of the day, the call cannot be made again until the pending business has been completed.	
Time Extension	After the call for orders of the day, it is permissible to entertain a motion to extend the debate on the pending question for a set time before returning to orders. This requires a two-thirds vote.	
Avoiding *Orders*	Once the orders have been called and the question stated, it is permissible to lay on the table, commit, or postpone the business brought up by the call, so as to be able to return to the interrupted discussion. However, the orders cannot be disposed of as a group. Each item must be treated individually. The call for orders followed by the motion to table, etc., may be used to clear the floor for continued discussion of a matter which would otherwise be out of order. Such action avoids a two-thirds vote on suspension of the rules.	

PARLIAMENTARY QUESTION (OR INQUIRY)

1. Takes precedence of any motion out of which it arises.	MAIN MOTION	POSTPONE INDEFINITELY	AMEND	COMMIT	POSTPONE TO FIXED TIME	LIMIT OR EXTEND DEBATE	PREVIOUS QUESTION	TABLE	ORDERS OF THE DAY	QUESTIONS OF PRIVILEGE	RECESS	ADJOURN	SET TIME TO ADJOURN TO
SUBJECT MOTION:													
YIELDS TO									●	●	●	●	●
TAKES PRECEDENCE OF	1	1	1	1	1	1	1	1	1	1	1	1	1

Class: Incidental Motion
Debatable: NO
Amendable: NO
Reconsiderable: NO

Vote: NONE
Second needed: NO
Can interrupt speaker: YES

Purpose and Effect: To obtain information on parliamentary rule. The request is usually made when a member wants to find out whether something is permissible. The parliamentary inquiry should not be confused with a POINT OF ORDER. When a member rises to a POINT OF ORDER, he asserts that he knows the rules and that something is wrong. A point of order may come to a vote, an inquiry may not. However, if a member does not agree with the chair's answer to the inquiry, he may go ahead and do what he wants to do and appeal when the chairman rules him out of order. It is unnecessary to obtain the floor to make an inquiry and, when necessary, an inquiry can interrupt a speaker.

Form: "Mr. Chairman, I rise to a point of parliamentary inquiry."

Notes:

Chair's
Responsibility

The chair is not required to answer general questions of parliamentary procedure, except when the questions are relevant to the pending business. The chair may decline to answer a question not immediately relevant.

Deferred
Answer

When the inquiry interrupts a speaker, the chair should try to minimize the interruption while giving an adequate response. To that end the chair may, if the question is relevant but not urgent, defer answering until the interrupted speaker has completed his presentation.

PASS OVER NEXT ORDER OF BUSINESS

	MAIN MOTION	POSTPONE INDEFINITELY	AMEND	COMMIT	POSTPONE TO FIXED TIME	LIMIT OR EXTEND DEBATE	PREVIOUS QUESTION	TABLE	ORDERS OF THE DAY	QUESTIONS OF PRIVILEGE	RECESS	ADJOURN	SET TIME TO ADJOURN TO
SUBJECT MOTION:													
YIELDS TO						●	●	●	●	●	●	●	●
TAKES PRECEDENCE OF	●	●	●	●									

Class: Subsidiary Motion
Debatable: NO
Amendable: NO
Reconsiderable: NO

Vote: GENERAL CONSENT
Second needed: NO
Can interrupt speaker: YES

Purpose and Effect: To bypass a class of business in order to expedite the consideration of an urgent item. When the urgent item is disposed of, the assembly returns to the order of business. This method is used informally. It may be suggested from the floor or by the chair. In either case, it is handled by general consent. If there is any objection, the same purpose may be achieved by a formal motion to suspend the rules. This procedure would not normally be used in a formal organization.

PENDING

A motion is pending when it has been admitted to the floor as a question but has not yet been disposed of either by a vote or by the passage of a subsidiary motion to table, commit, or postpone. Pending status is ended by the vote, whether favorable or unfavorable, or by passage of any of the above subsidiary motions, or by a vote sustaining an OBJECTION TO THE CONSIDERATION OF A QUESTION.

Notice that, though a question is pending, it is not necessarily immediately pending. Thus, a main motion is pending while intervening subsidiary, incidental, or privileged motions are on the floor. In fact, several questions may be pending at one time, but only one is immediately pending. The immediately pending question is the one actually before the house, that is the one in process of being debated, or if undebatable, the one about to be voted on.

PERMISSION TO MODIFY A MOTION See: PERMISSION TO WITHDRAW A MOTION

PERMISSION TO WITHDRAW A MOTION

1. Takes precedence of any motion out of which it arises.	MAIN MOTION	POSTPONE INDEFINITELY	AMEND	COMMIT	POSTPONE TO FIXED TIME	LIMIT OR EXTEND DEBATE	PREVIOUS QUESTION	TABLE	ORDERS OF THE DAY	QUESTIONS OF PRIVILEGE	RECESS	ADJOURN	SET TIME TO ADJOURN TO
SUBJECT MOTION:													
YIELDS TO									●	●	●	●	●
TAKES PRECEDENCE OF	1	1	1	1	1	1	1	1	1	1	1	1	1

Class: Incidental Motion
Debatable: NO
Amendable: NO
Reconsiderable: (See *Notes*)

Vote: GENERAL CONSENT or MAJORITY
Second needed: NO
Can interrupt speaker: NO

Purpose and Effect: To obtain permission for the mover to withdraw his motion from consideration. The request for withdrawal can be made at any time before a vote is taken, but it is easier to withdraw before the chair states the question. If the chair has not stated the question, permission to withdraw (or permission to modify) is granted automatically, whether or not a second has been made. After the question has been stated, the motion is the property of the organization and cannot be withdrawn or modified at the will of the mover. Permission may be granted by general consent, or that failing, by a majority vote.

Form: "Mr. Chairman, I request leave to withdraw (or modify) my motion."

Notes:

*General
Consent*

When the request to withdraw is made after the chair states the question, the chair asks if there is any objection to withdrawal. If there is none, the withdrawal is permitted. If there is objection, the chair states the questions on permission to withdraw.

Reconsider   Only an affirmative vote on this motion is open to reconsideration. If permission to withdraw is not granted, the vote cannot be reconsidered.

Second   It is a mistake to ask the seconder to withdraw his second, because failure to withdraw the second cannot sustain the motion before the house. The common confusion on this point probably arises from the fact that a seconder may withdraw his second if the mover modifies his motion. Then another second is needed to reinstate the motion as modified.

POINT OR QUESTION OF ORDER

1. Takes precedence of any motion from which it arises. 2. Only when the point is stated as a debatable motion.	MAIN MOTION	POSTPONE INDEFINITELY	AMEND	COMMIT	POSTPONE TO FIXED TIME	LIMIT OR EXTEND DEBATE	PREVIOUS QUESTION	TABLE	ORDERS OF THE DAY	QUESTIONS OF PRIVILEGE	RECESS	ADJOURN	SET TIME TO ADJOURN TO
SUBJECT MOTION:													
YIELDS TO									●	●	●	●	●
TAKES PRECEDENCE OF	1	1	1	1	1	1	1	1	1	1	1	1	1
MAY BE APPLIED TO													
MAY HAVE APPLIED TO IT					2	2	2	●					

Class: Incidental Motion
Debatable: NO (See *Purpose*)   *Vote:* MAJORITY
Amendable: NO   *Second needed:* NO
Reconsiderable: NO   *Can interrupt speaker:* YES

Purpose and Effect: To obtain a decision by the chairman or the assembly on a matter of parliamentary rule or propriety, for example, whether an amendment is germane to the motion it is supposed to amend, whether a motion is in order at the time, whether a speaker has spoken appropriately, and so on. Although it is never too late to raise an objection on a question that is against the basic rules of the organization or is illegal, a question of order should usually be made immediately after the alleged violation. Normally, the chair decides on a question of order. However, the chair may put the question in the form of a motion and call for a vote, in which case the motion may be debatable (the rules of APPEAL apply as far as debatability is concerned). Decisions of the chair may be appealed to the assembly.

Form: "Mr. Chairman, I rise to a point of order," or sometimes simply, "Point of order!" When recognized by the chair the speaker states his objection. If the point is an indecorum of a speaker, the person objecting may say, "I call the speaker (or the gentleman) to order." If the chair decides to call a vote on the question rather than decide himself, he puts it in the following form: "All who are of the opinion that the objection is well taken (or, that the motion is appropriate, etc.) . . . ."

Notes:

Decision by Chair	If the chair decides the question, it is undebatable. In deciding, the chair may consult with experienced members or may consult a reference.
Initiated by Chair	The chair has the duty of keeping order. If a person speaks improperly, he may, at his own initiative, say, "I call the gentleman (speaker) to order," just as he would if the impropriety were called to his attention by a point of order raised from the floor. The chair may also rule on other matters, such as the appropriateness of a motion, on his own initiative.
Appealable Priority	Any decision of the chairman may be appealed (See: APPEAL). The question of order takes precedence of whatever matter it pertains to. It yields only to privileged motions.

POSTPONE INDEFINITELY

1. May be applied when these motions have brought a main question to the floor or when they are treated as main motions.	MAIN MOTION	POSTPONE INDEFINITELY	AMEND	COMMIT	POSTPONE TO FIXED TIME	LIMIT OR EX-TEND DEBATE	PREVIOUS QUESTION	TABLE	ORDERS OF THE DAY	QUESTIONS OF PRIVILEGE	RECESS	ADJOURN	SET TIME TO ADJOURN TO
SUBJECT MOTION:													
YIELDS TO			●	●	●	●	●	●	●	●	●	●	●
TAKES PRECEDENCE OF													
MAY BE APPLIED TO	●								1	1	1	1	1
MAY HAVE APPLIED TO IT						●	●						

Class: Subsidiary Motion
Debatable: YES
Amendable: NO
Reconsiderable: See *Notes*

Vote: MAJORITY
Second needed: YES
Can interrupt speaker: NO

Purpose and Effect: Postpone indefinitely is used to reject the main motion to which it is applied. If adopted, the main motion is killed for the SESSION, unless the vote is reconsidered. (Sometimes the motion to TABLE is used for the same purpose, but that is an abuse and should be discouraged. The motion to table gives too great a power to the opponents of the main motion, because table has a higher parliamentary priority and is undebatable, which limits the rights of the main motion's partisans to fully present their views.) The motion to postpone indefinitely opens the main question to debate. Since this subsidiary motion is a new question, one of its effects is to renew the right to debate the main question. A parliamentary tactician might move to postpone indefinitely in some circumstances in order to renew debate where rights have expired. However, he would not do so unless he was reasonably certain that the motion to postpone would fail.

Form: "Mr. Chairman, I move the question be indefinitely postponed."

Notes:

Reconsider   The vote on the motion to postpone indefinitely is open to reconsideration only if it passes.

Renew   This motion cannot be renewed.

Commit   A pending motion to postpone indefinitely cannot be committed when the motion to which it applies is committed. If the motion to commit passes, the effect is to kill the motion to postpone indefinitely.

POSTPONE TO A FIXED TIME

	MAIN MOTION	POSTPONE INDEFINITELY	AMEND	COMMIT	POSTPONE TO FIXED TIME	LIMIT OR EXTEND DEBATE	PREVIOUS QUESTION	TABLE	ORDERS OF THE DAY	QUESTIONS OF PRIVILEGE	RECESS	ADJOURN	SET TIME TO ADJOURN TO
SUBJECT MOTION:													
YIELDS TO						●	●	●	●	●	●	●	●
TAKES PRECEDENCE OF		●	●	●									
MAY BE APPLIED TO	●												
MAY HAVE APPLIED TO IT			●			●	●						

Class: Subsidiary Motion (See *Notes*)
Debatable: YES
Amendable: YES   *Vote:* MAJORITY (See *Purpose*)
Reconsiderable: YES   *Second needed:* YES
                       Can interrupt speaker: NO

Purpose and Effect: To put off discussion of a question to another time. The time may be indicated in one of several ways: a date, a date and hour, the next meeting, after something else has happened, and so on. The postponement may be a general order requiring a majority vote or a special order requiring a two-thirds vote. A general order to postpone is subject to general rules of order. If the time set is three o'clock the next day, the motion will be considered as soon as the business being considered at three o'clock is completed. A special order for three o'clock would mean the postponed question would interrupt anything else in order at three o'clock. The motion may be amended as to the time of postponement or as to status as special or general order. Debate is allowed so long as the discussion refers to the subject motion no more than necessary to determine the propriety of postponement, e.g., it would be proper to point out that postponing a proposal to have a Christmas party until the next meeting would be futile because the next meeting is after Christmas.

Form: "Mr. Chairman, I move that the question be postponed until the next meeting (be made a special order for 2:30 tomorrow) (be postponed until the city budget proposal is available)."

Notes:

Class	The motion to postpone to a fixed time is a main motion if made when no business is pending. When business is pending, it can be applied only to the pending question.
Special or General	When the subject motion to be postponed is not specified as a special order, the effect is to make the motion a general order for the specified time.
Time Limit	Postponement cannot be set for a date later than the next session.
Cannot Refer to Class	It is not permissible to postpone a class of business. The effect can be achieved by suspension of the rules, requiring a two-thirds vote, or by the informal action of passing over.
Tabling Postponement	If the motion to postpone is tabled, it carries with it the motion which was to be postponed.
Reconsider	A motion postponed until a certain time cannot be taken up before that time except by suspension of the rules or by reconsideration of the motion to postpone.
Main Motions Only	The motion to postpone can only apply to main motions.

PRESENT

Call used in a roll call vote to indicate that the member is abstaining (See: VOTING).

PRESIDENT See: PRESIDING OFFICER

PRESIDING OFFICER

The presiding officer is the officer in authority at organizational meetings. He may be given a special title by the organization's constitution, the most common being chairman, president, and moderator. He is given his authority to conduct meetings and maintain order by the organization. His decisions on conduct and procedure at meetings may be overruled only by a majority vote of the assembly, from which his power is derived. The presiding officer may also be an executive officer — he may have responsibility for other matters besides the running of meetings — but such other duties are outside the scope of parliamentary procedure. Additional duties should be defined in the constitution or by-laws.

Enforcement of Rules: The responsibility of the presiding officer is to aid the organization in carrying out its deliberative tasks expeditiously and fairly. To that end, he must exercise reasonable judgment in the enforcement of parliamentary rules. He must be able to sense from the situation when relaxing the rules will speed deliberation and when it will cause confusion and repeated bickering on points of order.

Where relaxation seems in order — in small groups without strongly distinguished factions — he should not await a motion on routine matters, nor should he wait for a second where he expects no significant disagreement; he should use general consent rather than formal voting; he should allow debate much as in a COMMITTEE; and he should not attempt to show off his knowledge of the more specialized rules of procedure.

In large groups, and whenever there is objection arising because of his leniency, the chairman should stick closely to the rules, for he will find that business is handled much more promptly. In any case, he should allow brief remarks, if they will be helpful, even when the pending motion is undebatable.

Decorum and Demeanor of the Presiding Officer: In *Robert's Rules of Order*, the following is said of the chairman: "He should set an example of courtesy, and should never forget that to control others it is necessary to control one's self. A nervous, excited chairman can scarcely fail to cause trouble in a meeting. No rules will take the place of tact and common sense on the part of the chairman."

Speaking to a Question	The chair should restrain, as much as possible, his desire to participate in debate, since his ability to control the assembly depends in large measure on his (apparent) impartiality. When he does speak to a question, he should leave the chair (except to speak in his own defense on an APPEAL, or to comment on the effect of a motion to ADJOURN), and the vice-chairman should take his place, But, in general, the chairman should not avail himself of this privilege. He should especially avoid the temptation to interrupt for the purpose of correcting or expanding upon a speaker's remarks.
Reference to Self	The chairman does not say, "I decide," but "The chair decides," always referring to himself in this impersonal manner.
Standing to Speak	Except in small groups, the presiding officer should stand: when he calls the question, but not when he states it; when he addresses himself to a pending appeal, whether or not it is debatable; and when giving the reasons for his decision on a point of order. In these cases he does not call anyone to replace him in the chair.
Motions Referring to the Chair	Whenever a motion is made that compliments or condemns the chairman, either alone or along with others, the chairman should yield the chair to the vice-president (if he is not also referred to), or to another officer, or even to the maker of the motion when no eligible officer is available (See: VOTING, Voting for Oneself). If the motion concerns only the assignment to some duty, as appointment as convention delegate or as committee member, or concerns the authorization of payment for a disbursement made by the chair, the presiding officer need not leave his position. However, if the motion for payment is actually a motion to RATIFY the chair's action, he should leave his position in favor of another.

Protecting the Assembly from Annoyance: Although the chairman does not have the right to cut off debate, he does have means for controlling members whose intent is to disrupt the meeting or to prevent the majority from proceeding with its intentions. These include the refusal to recognize a speaker seeking the floor and the refusal to entertain a frivolous or obstructive motion. In using these powers, the presiding officer must demonstrate his greatest tact and common sense.

He should take care to ascertain that he is not sacrificing, simply in the name of efficiency, the legitimate desires of members for information, or their legitimate rights to object to certain proceedings. If an appeal is taken on a parliamentary decision, the chairman may interpret a victory for his decision as approval of a policy of refusing to recognize certain members, or a refusal to entertain their frivolous motions. But, these powers should be exercised only when it is clear beyond doubt that the members are simply trying to disrupt business. Patience is a prime virtue in the good chairman. (See: NON-MEMBERS, EXPULSION OF and TRIAL OF MEMBERS.)

Voting: The chairman is entitled to vote when voting is by ballot, but not after the ballots are counted. He is otherwise privileged to vote only when his vote would change the outcome, as by making or breaking a tie. A tie vote does not carry a motion nor does it upset the chair's decision on a point of order (See: VOTING).

Succession: When the chairman must vacate his position during a meeting, he may appoint a temporary chairman for the balance of the meeting, if the vice-chairman or other eligible officer is not present. However, the chairman cannot appoint a substitute in advance, as when he knows he will not be present at a future meeting. If an officer is not available, the organization elects a temporary chairman (chairman pro tem) by majority vote.

When the chairman dies, or for some reason is unable to continue his duties, the vice-chairman takes over the chairmanship. If there is a second vice-chairman, he moves up to the post of first vice-chairman, and so on through any number of vice-chairmen. The post left vacant is that of the lowest vice-chairman, and that is filled by special election. An organization may specify in its constitution any other order of succession.

Other Duties: Other duties of the chairman are listed throughout this Parliamentary Dictionary under the appropriate topics.

PREVIOUS QUESTION

1. When it leads to a motion. 2. When it is debatable (not privileged).	MAIN MOTION	POSTPONE INDEFINITELY	AMEND	COMMIT	POSTPONE TO FIXED TIME	LIMIT OR EX-TEND DEBATE	PREVIOUS QUESTION	TABLE	ORDERS OF THE DAY	QUESTIONS OF PRIVILEGE	RECESS	ADJOURN	SET TIME TO ADJOURN TO
SUBJECT MOTION:													
YIELDS TO								●	●	●	●	●	●
TAKES PRECEDENCE OF													
MAY BE APPLIED TO	●	●	●	●	●	●				1	●	2	●
MAY HAVE APPLIED TO IT													

Class: Subsidiary Motion
Debatable: NO
Amendable: NO (See *Notes*)   *Vote:* 2/3
Reconsiderable: (See *Notes*)   *Second needed:* YES
                                         Can interrupt speaker: NO

Purpose and Effect: To end debate and bring the subject motion to an immediate vote. If the previous question is approved, the subject motion is voted on immediately. If the previous question fails, the assembly resumes debate on the subject motion. The motion may be qualified to apply to any series or part of a series of pending questions so long as the questions are consecutive and begin with the one immediately pending. When the previous question has been approved to apply to a series of motions, they are voted on immediately and in succession, though the vote may be interrupted to *table* any motion not yet voted on. A vote under the previous question may be reconsidered while there are yet other votes to be taken; in that case the motion to reconsider is undebatable and unamendable. (See: RECONSIDER.) If the questions affected by the previous question include ones to commit or postpone the main motion, a vote in favor of commitment or postponement ends the effect of previous question. If commitment or postponement fails, voting on the series of motions proceeds until the main motion has been decided. To table is the only subsidiary motion that takes precedence over the previous question and, as noted under TABLE, if it carries, the previous question sometimes remains alive on the table.

Form: "Mr. Chairman, I move the previous question on the following motion(s) . . . ." If the previous question fails, the chair states, "Since the motion is not favored by two thirds of the assembly, the previous question is lost; the question now is. . . ."

Notes:

Reconsider   The previous question itself cannot be reconsidered once the vote on the subject motion has been taken. An affirmative vote to reconsider the call for the previous question kills it without taking a separate vote on the previous question.

Amend   The effect of amending the previous question can be achieved by following a motion on the previous question with one or more others that apply to a different group of pending items. In the case of such a series of previous questions, they are handled as filling in blanks, the one applying to the largest number of pending motions being voted on first. The first previous question to obtain majority support is adopted (See AMEND, *Filling Blanks*).

Renewal   If the previous question is lost, it may be entertained on the same motion at the same session only after some progress has been made in handling the business.

PRIVILEGE, QUESTION OF

If question of privilege leads to motion, the motion is treated as main motion once it is on the floor.	MAIN MOTION	POSTPONE INDEFINITELY	AMEND	COMMIT	POSTPONE TO FIXED TIME	LIMIT OR EXTEND DEBATE	PREVIOUS QUESTION	TABLE	ORDERS OF THE DAY	QUESTIONS OF PRIVILEGE	RECESS	ADJOURN	SET TIME TO ADJOURN TO
SUBJECT MOTION:													
YIELDS TO											●	●	●
TAKES PRECEDENCE OF	●	●	●	●	●	●	●	●	●				

Class: Privileged Motion (See *Notes*)
Debatable: NO (See *Notes*)   *Vote:* MAJORITY
Amendable: NO (See *Notes*)   *Second needed:* NO
Reconsiderable: NO   *Can interrupt speaker:* YES
                    (See *Notes*)

Purpose and Effect: To call to the attention of the organization an urgent matter related to the rights of the organization or the rights of the member raising the question. Those questions related to the rights of the organization are said to concern the privileges of the assembly. If there is a conflict in obtaining the floor, a question on the privileges of the assembly takes precedence over a question of personal privilege. A question of personal privilege might refer to an assertion about the character of the member, where, if the assertion were true, the member would have to be expelled. Questions affecting the assembly include the following: the comfort of the members; their ability to hear a speech; the conduct of members, employees, officers, the press; punishment for conduct; accuracy of reports; accreditation of delegates; etc. Many questions of privilege can be settled by the chairman, whose decision may be appealed by *two* members; other questions will result in a motion that requires a majority vote. Thus, a member may move, as a question of privilege, that all non-members be asked to leave. A member might also ask that the windows be shut because it is getting cold. Such a question would not be put in the form of a motion.

Form: "Mr. Chairman, I move that all non-members be asked to leave during the discussion of this question."

"Mr. Chairman, as a question of privilege, I request that the windows be closed because it's getting too cold."

Notes:

Class	To raise a question of privilege is a privileged question. However, the question itself may be in the form of a motion. When the question of privilege requires a motion, it is debatable and amendable. The treatment of a motion on a question of privilege is the same as the treatment of a main motion, except that the former has the priority of any question of privilege.
Interrupt	A question of privilege may interrupt a speaker when it is essential that the question be decided immediately. It is up to the chairman to decide the urgency of the question. If he feels a decision can wait until a speaker completes his statement, he allows the speaker to continue and calls up the question of privilege as soon as the speech is completed. If the question is urgent, he directs the speaker to be seated while the question of privilege is being decided and allows the speaker to resume when it is disposed of. A question of privilege cannot interrupt a vote or verification of vote.

PRIVILEGED MOTIONS

Privileged motions do not refer to a pending motion, but are of such importance that they may be entertained while any other motion is pending. Like subsidiary motions, privileged motions have a rank among themselves. In the list below, the first motion has the highest privilege and will be entertained when any below it are pending. A motion lower on the list cannot be entertained when a higher one is before the house:

Set a time for the continuation of the present session (also called "To fix the time to which to adjourn")

Adjourn, when it will not dissolve the organization

Recess

Questions of privilege (not to be confused with privileged questions)

Orders of the day

Since motions to recess and adjourn have a high privilege and are readily renewable (See: RENEW), a minority that objects to considering some particular business can use these motions to harass the efforts of the majority. The rule that privileged motions cannot be debated helps to eliminate abuses. Further, these motions should not be reviewed unless some progress in carrying out the organization's business has been made since the motion was last entertained. The only subsidiary motions that may be applied to privileged motions are those that fix a time, such as for adjournment or for the length of a recess.

PROGRAM

Types: A program for an organizational meeting may be either informal or formal. An informal program is simply a listing, for the aid of the chairman, of the business to come before the organization at that meeting. The formal program includes essentially the same information but it gains a special status by being adopted as the program by the organization.

Informal Program: It is the duty of the secretary to provide the chairman with a list of all the business that must come before the organization. The list should be prepared according to the sequence adopted by the organization (See: ORDER OF BUSINESS). The secretary is the person in the organization who would normally have that information. The minutes of previous meetings indicate to the secretary, who is their keeper, which committees and officers are due to report, what old business there is, and what general and special orders have been made. The secretary also has the organization's correspondence from which new business may arise or be initiated. The chairman may, of course, add to the list from his personal knowledge. This list does not have any legal status. The chair cannot be called to order for failing to follow the order of business prepared by the secretary, unless that failure is also a violation of rules of procedure or of the orders of the day (See: ORDERS and ORDERS OF THE DAY, CALL FOR).

Formal Program: Where organizations meet infrequently or where a great deal of business must be accomplished by a large group, the program notes of the chairman and secretary might be published in advance, and the program be adopted by majority vote immediately after the opening of the meeting. If that is done, all items of business have parliamentary status and the program cannot be varied except by a two-thirds vote. To save the delegates' time, the suspension of the program should not be debated. The program should be followed as closely as possible, and where business is set for consideration at a given hour, the chair should call the question on any business pending so that the group can proceed with the schedule.

Motion to Adopt Program: The motion to adopt the program as proposed by the chairman, program committee, or secretary, is a main motion, subject to all rules applicable to other main motions (See: MAIN MOTION).

PROPERTY OF ORGANIZATIONS

Where organizations own property, their actions affecting disposition of the property can cause legal complications and should be taken only with competent legal assistance. Problems are especially likely to arise where an organization breaks off from another with which it had been affiliated, or where, because of internal factions, an organization divides in two. In either case, title to the property may fall into dispute.

PROXY VOTE See: VOTING

PUNISHMENT OF MEMBERS See: TRIAL OF MEMBERS

PUT THE QUESTION See: CALL THE QUESTION

QUASI-COMMITTEE OF THE WHOLE See: COMMITTEE OF THE WHOLE, QUASI-

QUESTION OF PRIVILEGE See: PRIVILEGE, QUESTION OF

QUORUM

The number of members that must be present at a meeting for the meeting to act validly in the name of the organization. The constitution should define the number required. For a delegate organization meeting in convention, a quorum is generally set as a majority of the accredited delegates in attendance. For most private organizations, the quorum should be no greater than the average number of members that might be expected to appear in all but the worst weather. In committees, including executive committees and boards, a quorum is a majority of the members, unless the constitution states otherwise. The quorum of a COM-

MITTEE OF THE WHOLE is the same as that for the meeting, and if it is noted during the committee of the whole that there is no quorum, the committee rises, reports the lack of a quorum, and the meeting adjourns.

In the Absence of a Quorum: Without a quorum, a meeting may only set a time for the next meeting of the same session, recess, adjourn, or take action toward obtaining a quorum (this last may be done only in legislatures, where it is possible to compel attendance). If, during the course of a meeting, enough members leave so that there is less than a quorum remaining, a member noticing the fact may call it to the attention of the chair, as long as, in doing so, he does not interrupt a speaker. Business transacted before the absence of a quorum is noted may not be later questioned; business transacted in emergency when the absence of a quorum is recognized should be later ratified when a quorum is present (See: RATIFY). When a quorum is not present at the hour appointed for the beginning of a meeting, the chairman should wait for a few minutes before calling the meeting to order.

Note on Some Religious Organizations: When a constitution fails to specify to the contrary, it is taken that a quorum shall consist of a majority of the membership. However, when organization members are automatically enrolled for life, as is the case in some religious societies, it would be impractical to demand that a majority of the membership be present to transact business. In such situations, the need for a quorum is usually considered as satisfied by the number of members who appear.

RATIFY

	MAIN MOTION	POSTPONE INDEFINITELY	AMEND	COMMIT	POSTPONE TO FIXED TIME	LIMIT OR EXTEND DEBATE	PREVIOUS QUESTION	TABLE	ORDERS OF THE DAY	QUESTIONS OF PRIVILEGE	RECESS	ADJOURN	SET TIME TO ADJOURN TO
SUBJECT MOTION:													
YIELDS TO		●	●	●	●	●	●	●	●	●	●	●	●
TAKES PRECEDENCE OF													

Class: Main Motion
Debatable: YES
Amendable: YES (See *Notes*)
Reconsiderable: YES

Vote: MAJORITY
Second needed: YES
Can interrupt speaker: NO

Purpose and Effect: To approve an action taken by a member, officer, or committee in the name of the organization, but without advance approval. Sometimes, in emergency situations, especially when an organization meets infrequently, it is necessary for action to be taken without the approval of the organization. In taking such an action, a member, officer, or committee is taking the chance that the organization may disapprove of the action. For instance, where a member must make a purchase or state a position, he should, at the earliest opportunity, request the organization to ratify his action so that he may be reimbursed, or so that the organization in fact becomes committed to the position stated. In the case of payment, he cannot be reimbursed until the organization ratifies his expenditure (if it is of such size that it cannot be approved by the treasurer).

Form: "Mr. Chairman, I request that . . . be ratified."

"Mr. Chairman, I request that the purchase of . . . be ratified, and that a check on the treasury be drawn to cover the payment."

Notes:

Amendment   This motion may be amended to change it from ratification to censure. Conceivably, an organization might decide to pay only part of a bill submitted, if it was thought that the officer, member, or committee had been overcharged as a result of negligence.

RECESS, TO TAKE A

Treated as main motion if introduced when no business is pending.	MAIN MOTION	POSTPONE INDEFINITELY	AMEND	COMMIT	POSTPONE TO FIXED TIME	LIMIT OR EX-TEND DEBATE	PREVIOUS QUESTION	TABLE	ORDERS OF THE DAY	QUESTIONS OF PRIVILEGE	RECESS	ADJOURN	SET TIME TO ADJOURN TO
SUBJECT MOTION:													
YIELDS TO												●	●
TAKES PRECEDENCE OF	●	●	●	●	●	●	●	●	●	●			

Class: Privileged Motion (Sometimes Main Motion)
Debatable: NO (See *Notes*)   *Vote:* MAJORITY
Amendable: YES (See *Notes*)   *Second needed:* YES
Reconsiderable: NO   *Can interrupt speaker:* NO

Purpose: A recess is actually a combination of the motion to adjourn and the motion to fix a time for continuation of the present meeting (to set the time to which to adjourn). Recess both ends a meeting and sets the time for reconvening. Usually the time period of the recess is relatively short, a few minutes or a few hours, to give the members time to stretch their legs or to eat. However, a recess can be, theoretically at least, for any length of time shorter than the interval between the present and the next regular meeting. The recess does not in any way affect the business of the meeting. When the period of the recess is over, the meeting is called to order and the business taken up exactly where it was left off (See: ADJOURN and SET TIME FOR CONTINUATION OF PRESENT MEETING).

Form: "Mr. Chairman, I move the meeting be recessed until 2:00 P.M." (Or, "for twenty minutes.")

Notes:

Class	The motion to recess may be either a main motion or a privileged motion, depending on when it is made. If there is no business pending, it is a main motion. If the proposal to recess interrupts other business, it is privileged.
Debate	When the motion is privileged, it is undebatable; when it is a main motion, it is debatable, just as any other main motion.
Amendment	The motion to recess may be amended but only as to the period of the recess. No other amendment should be considered germane.
Recess Provided in Program	When a program has been adopted that includes a time for recess, the chair automatically adjourns the meeting at the time specified. To continue the meeting after the time planned for the recess requires a two-thirds vote, as it is a suspension of the rules.

312

RECONSIDER

1. The motion, only. 2. Yea vote, only. 3. Until the committee has taken the matter up. 4. Nay vote, only. 5. Carries subject and adhering motions, too. 6. When debatable.	MAIN MOTION	POSTPONE INDEFINITELY	AMEND	COMMIT	POSTPONE TO FIXED TIME	LIMIT OR EXTEND DEBATE	PREVIOUS QUESTION	TABLE	ORDERS OF THE DAY	QUESTIONS OF PRIVILEGE	RECESS	ADJOURN	SET TIME TO ADJOURN TO
SUBJECT MOTION:													
YIELDS TO													
TAKES PRECEDENCE OF	1	1	1	1	1	1	1	1	1	1	1	1	1
MAY BE APPLIED TO	●	2	●	3	●	●	●	4					●
MAY HAVE APPLIED TO IT					5	6	6	5					

Class: Unclassified Motion
Debatable: (See *Notes*)   *Vote:* MAJORITY
Amendable: NO   *Second needed:* YES
Reconsiderable: NO   *Can interrupt speaker:* YES

Purpose and Effect: The motion to reconsider makes it possible for an organization to review a prior decision when that decision could not be raised again by other means, or within a reasonable length of time, or when it could be raised only in the form of a motion to RESCIND. Reconsideration may be moved (only by a person who voted on the winning side) at any time up to the instant the chairman states that the meeting is adjourned. However, the motion to reconsider is not necessarily acted upon right away. There may be a time lapse between moving reconsideration and deciding it, because reconsideration can be debated and voted on only at a time when the question to which it refers would be in order.

Let us say that a main motion is pending. There had been a motion made to send the main question to committee, which had failed. Subsequently, someone moved to postpone the main motion to a later date. Before that vote was taken, someone else moved the previous question. The motions would be considered in the following order:

1. Previous question
2. Postpone to a fixed time
3. Main motion

If, at this point, a member who had voted against the motion to commit moved to reconsider that vote, the motions would be acted upon in the following order:

1. Previous question
2. Postpone to a fixed time

3. Reconsider the vote to commit (Commit, only if the reconsideration was approved)
4. Main motion

After disposing of the previous question, and if the motion to postpone fails, the chair states the question on the reconsideration. (If the motion to postpone passes, the question of reconsideration is considered in its same relative position when, after the period of postponement, the main question again comes to the floor.) If the reconsideration is approved, the chair immediately states the question on the motion to commit; if the motion to reconsider fails, the chair states the question on the main motion. (Notice that the motion to reconsider was made while that on the previous question was pending, but action was not taken on the reconsideration until the motion to which it applied — in this case the motion to commit — could have been entertained as an original motion.)

Sometimes, after a motion to reconsider is made, it is the chair's duty to state the question on reconsideration as soon as it is in order. Other times, some member must take the initiative to call up the motion to reconsider at a time when it would be in order. (Calling up a motion to reconsider is much like moving to take from the table, except that no vote is needed. If the reconsideration is in order, it can be called up by a single member.)

In the interim between moving to reconsider an original motion and acting upon the reconsideration, the original motion is held in abeyance; nothing ordered by the original motion can be done. This effect terminates, for organizations that meet less than quarterly, at the end of the session during which the reconsideration was moved. In organizations with sessions as often as quarterly, this effect lasts through the session at which the motion to reconsider was made and the subsequent session. Failure to call up the reconsideration during the period of its effect kills the motion to reconsider and reinstates the original motion.

The effect of passing the motion to reconsider is to bring the original motion immediately to the floor. If the reconsideration is called up, either by the chair or by a member, during the same day in which it was moved, everything is just as it was before the original vote was taken; speakers who had already used their speaking right cannot speak again. If reconsideration is not called up until a later day, speaking rights begin anew.

Form and Procedure: The methods for reconsidering questions vary, depending on the question to be reconsidered, in the following ways:

Main Question   When the motion to reconsider applies to a main question, the motion to reconsider can be acted upon only when any main motion would be in order — when there is no pending question. Calling up the motion to reconsider takes precedence over any other main motion, even over general orders, when no business is pending. The responsibility for calling up the motion to reconsider a main motion rests with the members rather than with the chairman. If, when a member wants to call up a motion to reconsider, others are seeking recognition, the member should state that he rises to call up a motion to reconsider, and the chair should give him preference over the others.

Form: "Mr. Chairman, I move reconsideration of the vote to condemn the school-board bond issue." If action on the reconsideration is not immediately in order, the chairman says, "Mr. Peterson has moved reconsideration of the vote on the school-board bond issue. The secretary will note it in the minutes." (No note of the second is necessary, though it should be made.) Had the reconsideration been in order, the chair would have immediately stated the question: "The question is, will the organization reconsider the vote on the school-board bond issue?" The chair would state the question in the same form if the question on reconsideration was called up at a later time. Calling up the motion to reconsider is done in the following manner: "Mr. Chairman, I rise to call up the motion to reconsider the school-board bond issue." As soon as the question on the motion to reconsider has been stated, the member who moved the reconsideration is given the floor. Debate proceeds as noted above (See: *Purpose and Effect*).

Subsidiary Question After Action Has Been Taken on the Main Question — Second-Degree Amendment After Action Has Been Taken on the First-Degree Amendment

If it is desired to reconsider the vote on a subsidiary question after the main question has been decided, it is necessary to reconsider the vote on the main question and on any intervening subsidiary questions except one affecting the limits of debate. Thus, if a member desires to reconsider a motion to commit after an amendment and the main question have been approved, it is necessary to reconsider the vote on all three questions. However, since the intent is only to reconsider the question to commit, that is the only question that may be debated. (The rule is that when several related questions are reconsidered, the only one that may be debated is the one voted on first. That, presumably, is the question the mover is aiming at, but the others must be voted too, in case a reconsideration of the earlier question leads to a reversal that might affect the membership's attitude toward the subsequent questions. However, in the example at hand, if the motion to commit carries, having been lost before, the effect of the motion to reconsider is ended; when the committee reports, debate proceeds on the amendment and the main question, according to the rules applicable when considering a committee report.) The rules stated here apply when reconsidering a second-degree amendment to a first-degree amendment that has already been adopted.

Form: The bringing up of the reconsideration is handled in the same manner as under *Main Motion,* except that the mover must state his motion so that it includes all questions that will have to be reconsidered. In the case above, the member might say, "Mr. Chairman, I move to reconsider the votes on the motion condemning the school-board bond issue, on the amendment to strike *condemn* and insert *commend,* and on the motion to commit." If the effect of the reconsideration motion is not to dispose of the main question, once the first vote is debated and decided, the chair immediately calls the question on the next motion, no debate being allowed.

Subsidiary Question When No Action Has Been Taken on the Main Question
An example of this situation was described under *Purpose and Effect.* Here, when the reconsideration is in order, the chairman should state the question, though if he neglects to do so, the motion may be called up from the floor. The motion to reconsider is in order whenever the motion to which it applies is in order.

Form: See *Main Question, Form.*

Amendments of the Same Degree While Main Question Still Pending
When it is moved to reconsider the adoption of one amendment while another of the same degree is pending, the pending amendment is decided first; then the chair states the question on reconsidering the other.

Form: See *Main Question, Form.*

Amendments to an Immediately Pending Question	If the purpose is to reconsider a first-degree amendment to an immediately pending question, or a second-degree amendment to an immediately pending first-degree amendment, the chair immediately states the question on the motion to reconsider.

Form: See *Main Question, Form.*

Motions That Cannot Be Reconsidered:

Adjourn
Recess
Suspend Rules
Reconsider
Commit, after the committee has taken up the question referred
Table
Take from the table
Suspend order of business
Questions of privilege

Negative Vote Only Can Be Reconsidered on:

Orders of the day
Rescind
Amend constitution, by-laws or rules of order
Adopt constitution, by-laws or rules of order
Election, when person has not declined
Reopen nominations

Affirmative Vote Only Can Be Reconsidered on:

Postpone indefinitely

Notes:

When Motion May Be Made	The motion to reconsider may be made only on the day on which the vote to which it refers was taken, or on the next succeeding business day when a session lasts more than one day. The motion may be called up during the period for which it is effective (See: *Purpose and Effect*).
By Whom Made	The motion to reconsider may be made only by a person who had voted with the winning side.
Debate	The motion to reconsider is undebatable if the question to which it is applied is undebatable. When debatable,

the merits of the motion to which it applies may be freely discussed (See: Subsidiary Question After Action Has Been Taken on the Main Question). Although the effect of the PREVIOUS QUESTION is to cut off debate, a motion voted on as a result of the previous question may sometimes be reopened to debate when reconsidered. If the previous question had been applied to several motions, and the reconsideration is in order before the votes on all the motions to which the previous question applied have been taken, the subject motion cannot be debated. However, if the effect of the previous question had been exhausted, the subject motion can be debated.

Withdraw   The motion to reconsider cannot be withdrawn if it is too late to RENEW the question to which it applies.

Renew   See: RENEW

Vote   Whatever the vote required to pass the motion being reconsidered, only a majority vote is necessary to pass the motion to reconsider.

In Committees   In standing and special committees, a motion to reconsider is in order regardless of the time that has elapsed since the question was voted, and it may be moved by anyone who did not vote with the losing side. A two-thirds vote is required if all members who voted on the winning side are not present, or if advance notice had not been given. In committee of the whole, a vote may not be reconsidered.

RECORDING SECRETARY See: SECRETARY

RENEW A MOTION

To renew a motion is to bring it to the floor again as if it were a new item of business after it had once been considered and disposed of. The purpose of the rules that define when a motion may be renewed is to prevent organizations from being harassed by having the same business brought up repeatedly. There are ways in which many motions can be brought again to the attention of an organization, but they require the organization to approve the review. (See RESCIND, RECONSIDER, and TAKE FROM THE TABLE.) There are, however, circumstances in which it is possible to introduce in the form of new business a proposal already considered. The circumstances under which renewal is permitted depend on the type of motion.

Types: Motions can be divided into four classes as far as their renewability is concerned.

(Class I) A motion in this class may not be renewed at the session at which it was disposed of, whether by defeat, tabling, indefinite postponement, or by a successful objection to its consideration. Organizations having sessions as often as quarterly should not allow renewal either in the session in which the motion was disposed of or in the succeeding session. The motions in this class are:

Original main motions

Amend constitution or by-laws

Ratify

Rescind

Postpone indefinitely (even if the motion to which it was applied is substantially amended)

Amend

Object to consideration of a motion

Reconsider (unless the motion to which it is applied was substantially amended since the earlier motion for reconsideration)

Point of Order (cannot be raised a second time if substantially the same one was defeated earlier, but one that succeeded may be made as often as the same problem is repeated)

Set time for continuation of present session (set time to adjourn to)

(Class II) The one motion in this class cannot be renewed during the same meeting, though it can be renewed at a subsequent meeting on the same day.

SUSPEND RULES

(Class III) Motions in this class may be renewed as soon as the business that led to their being defeated has been completed.

Orders of the day

Take from the table

(Class IV) Motions in this class may be renewed if there has been progress in the debate since their defeat.

Commit

Postpone to a fixed time

Limit or extend debate

Previous question

Table

Recess

Adjourn

The problem for a chairman in handling the question of renewal is to decide whether in fact a question that is similar to an earlier one, but differently phrased, is an essentially new question. Where there might be particular difficulty, guiding rules are set forth under specific motions in this Dictionary. But wherever the chair is convinced that an amendment or original question is the same as an earlier one, he should refuse to entertain it. And when the chair is convinced that motions in Class IV are being repeated solely for the purpose of harassment, he should refuse to entertain them. These decisions are, of course, appealable.

REPEAL   See: RESCIND

REQUEST

During the course of business, there are times when a member wants to request information, parliamentary advice, or permission. The most common requests include:

A parliamentary question or inquiry (not to be confused with a point of order, which asserts that something is amiss)

A request for information on a matter of substance rather than procedure

A request to allow a paper to be read

A request for permission to withdraw or modify a motion

A request to be excused from a duty (for instance, a committee assignment)

Requests are lumped together for parliamentary purposes, though they are of two distinct types. Those for information, whether parliamentary or substantive, are never subject to vote and have little similarity with motions. They are probably classed as motions to give them parliamentary status. (The status of all requests is that of incidental motions.) The other requests are much more like motions, and may be voted on, though they are usually handled by general consent. They are actually motions for the benefit of the person making them. Instead of saying, "I move that I be allowed to modify my motion," the speaker requests permission to modify his motion (See: INCIDENTAL MOTIONS and specific requests by name).

REQUEST FOR INFORMATION

1. Takes precedence of any motion from which it arises.	MAIN MOTION	POSTPONE INDEFINITELY	AMEND	COMMIT	POSTPONE TO FIXED TIME	LIMIT OR EXTEND DEBATE	PREVIOUS QUESTION	TABLE	ORDERS OF THE DAY	QUESTIONS OF PRIVILEGE	RECESS	ADJOURN	SET TIME TO ADJOURN TO
SUBJECT MOTION:													
YIELDS TO									●	●	●	●	●
TAKES PRECEDENCE OF	1	1	1	1	1	1	1	1	1	1	1	1	1

Class: Incidental Motion
Debatable: NO
Amendable: NO
Reconsiderable: NO

Vote: NONE
Second needed: NO
Can interrupt speaker: YES

Purpose and Effect: To obtain, usually from a speaker on the floor, substantive information (procedural information is supplied by the chairman; see: PARLIAMENTARY QUESTION). A member may seek the floor to obtain information by requesting of the chairman permission to question a speaker (hence it is necessary to permit interrupting the speaker). However, even though a question is directed to a speaker, it is addressed to the chairman.

Form: "Mr. Chairman, I rise for information." (Or, "to a point of information.") Or the member may say, "Mr. Chairman, I would like to ask the gentleman a question."

Notes:

Speaker's Rights	The speaker is not obliged to answer a request for information. The chairman asks the speaker, and if he agrees to answer, the time he spends in answering counts against the time he is allowed to speak.
Decorum	Although both questioner and responder address the chair, the chair does not speak during the exchange unless for some reason the two cannot hear each other distinctly.
Chair's Rights	If the question should be asked of the chair rather than the speaker, the chair may decline to answer until the speaker has completed his presentation, unless the question clearly should be answered immediately.

REQUEST TO ALLOW A PAPER TO BE READ

1. Takes precedence of any motion from which it arises.	MAIN MOTION	POSTPONE INDEFINITELY	AMEND	COMMIT	POSTPONE TO FIXED TIME	LIMIT OR EX- TEND DEBATE	PREVIOUS QUESTION	TABLE	ORDERS OF THE DAY	QUESTIONS OF PRIVILEGE	RECESS	ADJOURN	SET TIME TO ADJOURN TO
SUBJECT MOTION:													
YIELDS TO									●	●	●	●	●
TAKES PRECEDENCE OF	1	1	1	1	1	1	1	1	1	1	1	1	1

Class: Incidental Motion
Debatable: NO
Amendable: NO
Reconsiderable: NO

Vote: GENERAL CONSENT or MAJORITY
Second needed: NO
Can interrupt speaker: YES

Purpose and Effect: To read to the assembly a paper submitted by the maker of the request or by someone else — the paper may originate from another member or may be referred to the organization by a non-member. A request for permission to read or have read an article is generally granted if there is no objection. If there is objection, a majority is needed to obtain the reading. However, if the assembly is expected to vote on the paper, any member has the right to have it read upon presentation and, if debate or amendments have intervened, to have it read again before the vote. The chair may also order the second reading.

Form: "Mr. Chairman, I request permission to read a paper entitled. . . ."

"Mr. Chairman, I request that the paper presented by —— be read to the assembly."

"Mr. Chairman, I request that the paper be read as amended."

Notes:

General Consent and Objections
Upon hearing a request to have a paper read concerning which there is to be no vote, the chair asks if there are any objections. Hearing none he permits the reading. If there is objection, he states the question.

Reading during Debate
A member may, without special permission, read a paper or article during the time he is allowed to debate, so long as he does not abuse the privilege by reading instead of debating.

Obstructive Intent
The chairman should keep in mind that the reading of papers can be a great waste of time and that requests

for permission to read papers are sometimes obstructive in intent.

Rereading A member who was absent, even on business, when a reading took place cannot request that a paper be re-read. Rereading is allowed only as noted above under *Purpose and Effect*.

REQUEST TO BE EXCUSED FROM DUTY

1. Takes precedence of any motion from which it arises.	MAIN MOTION	POSTPONE INDEFINITELY	AMEND	COMMIT	POSTPONE TO FIXED TIME	LIMIT OR EXTEND DEBATE	PREVIOUS QUESTION	TABLE	ORDERS OF THE DAY	QUESTIONS OF PRIVILEGE	RECESS	ADJOURN	SET TIME TO ADJOURN TO
SUBJECT MOTION:													
YIELDS TO									●	●	●	●	●
TAKES PRECEDENCE OF	1	1	1	1	1	1	1	1	1	1	1	1	1

Class: Incidental Motion
Debatable: (See *Purpose*)
Amendable: NO
Reconsiderable: NO

Vote: MAJORITY, when vote is needed
Second needed: If a motion is made
Can interrupt speaker: (See *Notes*)

Purpose and Effect: To be relieved of an assignment about to be made or to resign after an assignment has been made and accepted. To decline a nomination or an appointment is undebatable. When positions are filled by appointment the chair should ask each person being considered whether he will accept. If a member nominated or appointed is absent, someone should be delegated to ask him if he is willing to serve. When a post has been accepted and later conditions require resignation, the request to be excused from duty is debatable and is voted on in the form of a resignation to be accepted or rejected by the assembly. It is unwise to refuse a resignation, unless the resignation is clearly a test of confidence.

Form: "Mr. Chairman, I respectfully decline the nomination" (or "the assignment").

"Mr. Chairman, I request the organization to accept my resignation" (or "excuse me from duty"). It is common practice in more formal organizations to put resignations in writing.

Notes:

Stating Question When a resignation is submitted, the chairman should state the question, on his own initiative, if no motion is heard from the floor.

Policy on Resignations   If a member does not immediately decline a nomination or appointment, he is under a moral obligation to serve. Since few organizations are able to bring any other than moral pressure to bear on a member who fails to carry through duties it is inadvisable to refuse a resignation, unless the tendered resignation is clearly a request for the confidence of the membership.

Effect of Resignations   The responsibility of one who tenders a resignation does not end until the resignation is accepted.

When Entertained   That a resignation is a request to be excused from duty and, therefore, an incidental motion, does not entirely determine when the submission of a resignation is in order. Incidental motions are in order only when they are genuinely incidental to another motion.

RESCIND (REPEAL, ANNUL)

1. May be applied to all main questions, including privileged questions when they are brought up as or lead to main questions.	MAIN MOTION	POSTPONE INDEFINITELY	AMEND	COMMIT	POSTPONE TO FIXED TIME	LIMIT OR EXTEND DEBATE	PREVIOUS QUESTION	TABLE	ORDERS OF THE DAY	QUESTIONS OF PRIVILEGE	RECESS	ADJOURN	SET TIME TO ADJOURN TO
SUBJECT MOTION:													
YIELDS TO		●	●	●	●	●	●	●	●	●	●	●	●
TAKES PRECEDENCE OF	1												

Class: Incidental Main Motion
Debatable: YES (See *Notes*)   *Vote:* 2/3 or MAJORITY (See
Amendable: YES   *Purpose*)
Reconsiderable: (See *Notes*)   *Second needed:* YES
                                                    Can interrupt speaker: NO

Purpose and Effect: To cancel an earlier action, decision, or policy statement. The motion to rescind cannot be used where an earlier motion to reconsider can be called up (See: RECONSIDER). The motion to rescind is essentially the same as the motion to AMEND CONSTITUTION OR BY-LAWS. However, while an organization may have special rules on voting and notice for amending its constitution or by-laws, most organizations accept the standard procedure for rescission, i.e., with notice, a two-thirds vote or without notice, a majority of the entire membership (See: AMEND CONSTITUTION OR BY-LAWS). In form, rescission is like an amendment of the type *Strike a Paragraph*

324

as described in the article AMEND, except that the word *rescind* is used instead of *strike*.

Notice of the intention to move to rescind at the next meeting can be given while there is any business on the floor, but not while someone is speaking. Certain actions cannot be rescinded: (1) a decision to act once some action has been taken that cannot be withdrawn; (2) a decision of the nature of an acceptance, or an offer to contract that would be held binding in a court of law; (3) an acceptance of a resignation; (4) an election; (5) an expulsion. An election to office or membership may be counteracted by an expulsion. An expulsion may be counteracted only by normal election procedures.

Form: "Mr. Chairman, I move that . . . be rescinded."

Notes:

Debate The motion to rescind opens to debate the question to which it applies, if that motion is debatable. There is no requirement that debate be limited to the wisdom of rescission; debate may proceed as if the matter proposed for rescission had just been moved.

Reconsider Only a negative vote — a refusal to rescind — can be reconsidered.

RESOLUTION

In parliamentary procedure the term resolution is employed in several ways. Sometimes it is used to mean a main motion, sometimes a part of a main motion, sometimes a certain type of main motion. Because a main motion is often put in the form "Resolved that a certain thing shall be done," motion and resolution are often used interchangeably. However, a motion may consist of several resolutions. In that case, resolution means a single action taken by or proposed to an organization. Finally, resolution sometimes may refer to a motion which states a position, commends, or condemns, that is, a motion that will be followed by no other action. Used in such a manner, a resolution is distinct from a main motion, the latter implying action.

In organizations with a paid staff, the word *resolved* often is replaced with *ordered*. However, resolved is retained in the third sense. "The city council will order the publication of a new ordinance. It will resolve that October 12 is recognized as Springfield Peanut Day."

RESTORE TO MEMBERSHIP OR OFFICE See: RESCIND

RISE See: COMMITTEE OF THE WHOLE

RISING VOTE See: VOTING

ROLL-CALL VOTE See: VOTING

RULES OF ORDER (See: CONSTITUTION, BY-LAWS, AND RULES OF ORDER)

SECOND

This term is used both as a noun and as a verb. As a noun, it means a member who supports, or supports the consideration of, a MOTION made by another. As a verb, it means the offering of that support: "I second the motion," "The motion has been seconded." It is required that all main motions and many others be seconded before they are entertained. The purpose is to prevent motions from being brought to the floor that are of concern to only one person. In some cases, for other than main motions, the chairman may choose not to wait for a second, if he feels there is general support for the motion. The practice for each type of motion is specified under the specific motions (See: PRESIDING OFFICER, *Enforcement of Rules*).

SECONDARY MOTIONS See: SUBSIDIARY MOTIONS and INCIDENTAL MOTIONS

SECRET BALLOT See: VOTING

SECRETARY

Duties: The secretary is the officer of an organization responsible for making and keeping its records. This officer may also be called clerk, scribe, or, where the duties of the office are divided, the name recording secretary is sometimes used. The other duties are performed by a corresponding secretary (the duties listed under *Corresponding Secretary*, below, fall to the secretary if there is only one secretarial position). The records of an organization should be available for examination by members at any reasonable time. COMMITTEES may have their own secretaries. Committee secretaries must make committee records available, but only to committee members. The organizational secretary must also give to any committee such organizational records as are necessary to the committee in fulfilling its function.

Records: The secretary should keep the following records:

Members A complete and up-to-date list of all members, used for mailings and for conducting roll-call votes. If there is a membership committee, the secretary obtains his current information on new members from that committee's report. The person with the responsibility of accepting dues should keep the secretary informed of members who are paid up (this job may be assigned to the secretary, the treasurer, or the chairman of the membership committee).

Constitution, By-Laws, Rules of Order, and Standing Rules
These documents should be kept by the secretary in such form that amendments and additions may be easily inserted while leaving the original intact (a loose-leaf binder is a good idea). When changes are made, the date of adoption should be included and a note should indicate the page in the minutes where the record of adoption appears.

Committees
The secretary should keep a current record of all committees and their members and officers. This record should be brought to every meeting for the aid of the chairman when called upon to appoint new committees (so that he won't burden a few members with too many committee assignments).

Reports
All reports submitted in writing, whether by the officers or by committees (with the exception of financial records) are kept by the secretary. (Some organizations do not bother to keep committee reports unless specifically instructed, as part of a motion to adopt, to do so. In that case, the secretary keeps only those reports which he is instructed to keep.) Committee reports should be signed by the secretary; the date of reception and the action taken should be noted.

Minutes
See MINUTES

Miscellaneous Duties: In addition to record keeping, the secretary has certain other responsibilities:

Call Roll
When a vote is taken by ayes and nays, it is the secretary's responsibility to call out the names and record the responses, which are entered in the minutes (See: VOTING).

Notify
The secretary must notify members of elections or appointment to office when such elections or appointments were made in the members' absence.

Credentials
The secretary must provide delegates with credentials

certifying that the delegates have been duly chosen to represent the organization.

Co-sign
Disbursement
Orders

The secretary, unless the constitution provides otherwise, must co-sign with the chairman any order to the treasurer to disburse money whenever such disbursement is authorized by the organization.

Program

The secretary must provide the chairman with a list of all business to be brought up at a meeting (See: PROGRAM, ORDER OF BUSINESS, and ORDERS).

Chairman
Absent

In the absence of the chairman and vice-chairman, the secretary should call the meeting to order at the appropriate time, and immediately entertain a motion for the election of a temporary chairman (See: PRESIDING OFFICER).

Corresponding Secretary: The duties of the corresponding secretary include the sending of notices to the membership of special (called) meetings, of business where notice is required in writing, and any other notices ordered. The corresponding secretary also receives all mail for the organization and answers it in the manner directed. Responses may be signed, as appropriate, either by the chairman or by the corresponding secretary. Additional duties may be defined by constitution or by-laws.

SESSION

The difference between a session and a meeting is sometimes confusing, because, though a session may consist of several meetings, it may also consist of just one meeting. A session is one meeting or a series of meetings in which one ORDER OF BUSINESS is handled. When a session consists of several meetings, such as in a convention, each meeting takes up the order of business where it was broken off at the close of the previous meeting. When two meetings are separate sessions, in each the order of business is taken up at the beginning. Thus, in each meeting there will be a reading of the minutes, followed by reports of officers, standing committees, special committees, etc. When the meetings are part of the same session, the only repetition that may occur is the reading of the minutes, though even that is often dispensed with so that business may be taken up immediately.

Another distinction between a meeting and a session is the manner in which they adjourn. When a motion to meet again at a later date (ADJOURN TO, SET TIME TO, or SET TIME FOR CONTINUATION OF PRESENT SESSION) is adopted during the course of one meeting, the subsequent meeting will be a continuation of the same meeting and it will be called an adjourned meeting of the same session. When a meeting adjourns without a day having been set for the next meeting (sine die), the next meeting will be the one required by the constitution or by-laws and it will be another session.

It is common usage to speak of organizations meeting quarterly or annually, but it would be more accurate to speak of them having quarterly or annual sessions. The difference between a meeting and a session is important in determining the period for which the motions to TABLE, to POSTPONE INDEFINITELY, and RECONSIDER are effective, and the period in which it is not proper to RENEW A MOTION.

A meeting interrupted by a RECESS shorter than overnight is still considered a single meeting, which means the reading of the minutes would not be in order after the recess.

SET TIME FOR CONTINUATION OF PRESENT SESSION (Set time to adjourn to)

Treated as main motion if introduced when no business is pending.	MAIN MOTION	POSTPONE INDEFINITELY	AMEND	COMMIT	POSTPONE TO FIXED TIME	LIMIT OR EXTEND DEBATE	PREVIOUS QUESTION	TABLE	ORDERS OF THE DAY	QUESTIONS OF PRIVILEGE	RECESS	ADJOURN	SET TIME TO ADJOURN TO
SUBJECT MOTION:													
YIELDS TO													
TAKES PRECEDENCE OF	●	●	●	●	●	●	●	●	●	●	●	●	

Class: Privileged Motion (See *Notes*)
Debatable: NO
Amendable: YES
Reconsiderable: YES
Vote: MAJORITY
Second needed: YES
Can interrupt speaker: NO

Purpose and Effect: To fix the time for a subsequent meeting of the same session. The effect is to make the next meeting a continuation of the present meeting, taking up where the present meeting leaves off. Instead of becoming old business, pending business is considered at the next meeting immediately after the reading of the minutes. The time to which the meeting is adjourned must be earlier than the next regularly scheduled meeting. This motion might be used when the business of an annual meeting cannot be completed at one sitting.

Form: "Mr. Chairman, I move that we adjourn until (or 'meet again at,' or 'adjourn to') 7:30 P.M. Monday."

Notes:

Class   The motion to adjourn to a set time has the highest privilege when it interrupts pending business, but it is only a main motion if there is no business on the floor.

Location Set   When there is no regular meeting place, the motion should include a place where the meeting might be held or instructions to an officer to obtain a suitable meeting place. If arrangements must be made to obtain a meeting place, the chair might suggest the motion, "We adjourn to no later than. . . ." with an officer responsible for locating a place and informing the members when it is available.

When   This motion may be entertained by the chair at any
Entertained   time, even after a vote on adjournment, so long as the vote has not been announced.

SCRIBE See: SECRETARY

SHOW OF HANDS See: VOTING

SINE DIE

Literally, "without day." The expression is used to describe the adjournment of an assembly when no time has been set by the assembly for a subsequent meeting of the same SESSION. Thus, an adjournment *sine die* ends the session.

It is possible to adjourn sine die, even though the constitution sets a date for the following session. Where there is no provision for a subsequent meeting — as in a newly formed organization without a constitution — the effect of an adjournment sine die is the abolition of the assembly. (See: SET TIME FOR CONTINUATION OF PRESENT SESSION.)

SPECIAL MEETING

A meeting called when a regular meeting is not required by the constitution, by-laws, or, in the case of a committee, by its policy or standing rules. The constitution or by-laws normally specify a method for calling a special meeting. As a rule, a special meeting may be called by the presiding officer, but it is usual to allow a set number of members to sign a call if the presiding officer is unable or unwilling to do so. For committees, a call by two members is sufficient to call a meeting.

The number needed to call a special organization meeting will vary with the circumstances of the organization but in any case should be relatively small. A special meeting is sometimes referred to as a called meeting. An adjourned meeting is not a special meeting. A special meeting has its own order of business, and there may be adjourned special meetings in which the order of business of the special meeting is continued (See: SESSION).

SPECIAL ORDERS See: ORDERS, POSTPONE TO A FIXED TIME, and ORDERS OF THE DAY, CALL FOR

STANDING COUNT See: VOTING

STANDING RULES

Standing rules are minor rules concerning operating procedure, such as the time, day of the week or date on which meetings are held, the closing hour for meetings, the place where meetings are held, or the procedure for opening meetings (Pledge to the Flag, prayer, etc.). Standing rules are adopted by a majority vote and may be amended or rescinded by a two-thirds vote, or by a majority vote if there is notice (See: AMEND CONSTITUTION OR BY-LAWS, *Voting, Notice*). Because standing rules are simple to make, amend, and rescind, they should include only those rules which do not affect the rights of the members. Those rules which would affect the rights of members should be included in the by-laws where they are less accessible to change. To propose a standing rule is a main motion. Reference to amending a standing rule may be found under AMEND, where all the information is applicable except that concerning the vote.

STATE THE QUESTION

It is the chairman's duty to keep the organization informed of the business legally before it. He does this by stating the question. This action consists simply in describing, or reading if necessary, the motion before the assembly at any time that there might be a question. No business comes before the assembly until the question is stated. If the chairman intends to entertain a motion, he must state the question after the motion is made. If a motion is made and a secondary motion intervenes, when the intervening business is completed, he must state that the original question is again before the assembly. Stating the question should not be confused with putting or calling the question (See: CALL THE QUESTION).

SUBCOMMITTEES See: COMMITTEE

SUBSIDIARY MOTIONS

Subsidiary motions are motions intended to dispose of other motions in an appropriate manner. They propose that some specific action other than normal debate and vote be taken on the pending main motion. Here is a list of the subsidiary motions in order of precedence. A motion higher on the list may be entertained when a lower one is pending. One lower on the list may not be entertained when a higher one is pending.

Table
Previous question
Limit or extend debate
Postpone to a fixed time
Commit (refer) or recommit
Amend
Postpone indefinitely

Subsidiary motions may be applied to any main motion and to a few others, as noted under the specific motions. For instance, the motion to amend a subsidiary motion can be applied to other subsidiary motions as well as to some incidental and privileged motions. However, the motion to amend is a MAIN MOTION when it applies to the constitution, by-laws, or a motion or resolution already adopted (See: AMEND CONSTITUTION OR BY-LAWS and RESCIND).

The previous question and the motions to limit or to extend debate require a two-thirds vote. The others require only a majority vote. The motions affecting debate and the motion to table are undebatable. The rest are debatable.

SUSPEND ORDER OF BUSINESS   See: SUSPEND RULES

SUSPEND RULES

1. Takes precedence of any motion from which it arises.	MAIN MOTION	POSTPONE INDEFINITELY	AMEND	COMMIT	POSTPONE TO FIXED TIME	LIMIT OR EXTEND DEBATE	PREVIOUS QUESTION	TABLE	ORDERS OF THE DAY	QUESTIONS OF PRIVILEGE	RECESS	ADJOURN	SET TIME TO ADJOURN TO
SUBJECT MOTION:													
YIELDS TO								●		●	●	●	●
TAKES PRECEDENCE OF	1	1	1	1	1	1	1	1	1	1	1	1	1

Class: Incidental Motion (See *Notes*)
Debatable: NO
Amendable: NO
Reconsiderable: NO

Vote: (See *Notes*)
Second needed: YES
Can interrupt speaker: NO

Purpose and Effect: To suspend a procedural rule to allow an otherwise unpermissible action, such as letting a non-member speak, considering a question in improper order, or limiting or extending debate (See: LIMIT OR EXTEND DEBATE). Certain rules may not be suspended, particularly those for the protection of absentees, for example, the rule requiring advance notice of intent to amend the constitution or by-laws, and the rule requiring a majority vote of the entire membership in lieu of notice. If election is by secret ballot, that rule cannot be suspended either.

Form: Since the motion to suspend the rules always has a particular purpose, it is made so as to describe and emphasize its purpose rather than to detail the rules to be ignored. "Mr. Chairman, I move the suspension of the rules that would conflict with . . ." (followed by a description of the purpose intended). When the motion is intended to prevent debate and to adopt a motion immediately, the maker says, "I move suspension of the rules and adoption of the following resolution . . . ." Thus, the suspension and the subject motion are combined and voted on at the same time, eliminating the need for two votes on essentially the same subject.

Notes:

When Entertained (Class)	The motion to suspend the rules may be entertained only if no other business is pending or if the suspension concerns the pending business. If introduced when no business is pending, the motion to suspend the rules is a main motion.
General Consent	Suspension of the rules is often handled by general consent, with a formal vote. The chair asks if there is any objection to suspension, and if none is heard, the suspension is allowed.
Vote	Most suspensions require a two-thirds vote. If the suspension is of a standing rule, rather than of a rule of order or a by-law, a majority is sufficient. Standing rules are those that do not materially affect the rights of the members, including any rule that may be adopted by a simple majority. Any rule adopted by a two-thirds vote requires a two-thirds vote for suspension. Rules that can be adopted by majority with advance notice also require a two-thirds vote to be suspended.

TABLE

	MAIN MOTION	POSTPONE INDEFINITELY	AMEND	COMMIT	POSTPONE TO FIXED TIME	LIMIT OR EXTEND DEBATE	PREVIOUS QUESTION	TABLE	ORDERS OF THE DAY	QUESTIONS OF PRIVILEGE	RECESS	ADJOURN	SET TIME TO ADJOURN TO
SUBJECT MOTION:													
YIELDS TO									●	●	●	●	●
TAKES PRECEDENCE OF	●	●	●	●	●	●	●						

Class: Subsidiary Motion
Debatable: NO   *Vote:* MAJORITY
Amendable: NO   *Second needed:* YES
Reconsiderable: NO   *Can interrupt speaker:* NO

Purpose and Effect: To get on to more urgent business in such a way that the pending question can be returned to later with priority over new business. The motion to table applies, with a few exceptions, exclusively to main motions, but all subsidiary and incidental motions adhering to it are tabled with the main motion. The effect is to hold the tabled motion in the hands of the secretary until it is brought up again by a motion to TAKE FROM THE TABLE. For organizations meeting less than quarterly, this status lasts the length of the session or through the session in which tabled and through the one succeeding in organizations meeting as often as quarterly. When the tabled status ends, the motion can arise again only as new business. When a motion is removed from the table, all incidental and subsidiary motions come with it and are handled as if nothing had happened except that the previous question has effect only during the session it was placed on the table.

Form: "Mr. Chairman, I move to table the motion." "Mr. Chairman, I move to lay the question on the table." It is not necessary to specify which motion, because it applies only to the pending main motion.

Notes:

No Related Questions Considered   While a question is on the table no motion affecting the tabled question can be entertained. The tabled motion must be taken up and amendments or substitutions suggested.

One Question Only   The motion to table applies only to a pending question and not to a class, that is, old business cannot be tabled to proceed with new business. A class of business can be *passed* by general consent, or rules can be suspended by two-thirds vote.

When Qualified If the motion to table is qualified in any way, it is treated as a motion to *postpone,* which is debatable.

Renewal If the motion to table has been lost, it cannot be entertained in reference to the same business at the same session unless some action, such as debate or amendment, has intervened to suggest that the assembly may have completed whatever it wanted to do with the subject motion.

Reconsider When the motion to *reconsider* is tabled, the motion being reconsidered is tabled also.

Caution This motion should not be used to kill an item of business. That purpose should be achieved with the motion to POSTPONE INDEFINITELY.

TAKE FROM THE TABLE

1. Entertained only when no business is pending. Takes precedence of any main motion not yet stated as a question.	MAIN MOTION	POSTPONE INDEFINITELY	AMEND	COMMIT	POSTPONE TO FIXED TIME	LIMIT OR EXTEND DEBATE	PREVIOUS QUESTION	TABLE	ORDERS OF THE DAY	QUESTIONS OF PRIVILEGE	RECESS	ADJOURN	SET TIME TO ADJOURN TO
SUBJECT MOTION:													
YIELDS TO	1	●	●	●	●	●	●	●	●	●	●	●	●
TAKES PRECEDENCE OF													

Class: Unclassified
Debatable: NO
Amendable: NO
Reconsiderable: NO

Vote: MAJORITY
Second needed: YES
Can interrupt speaker: NO

Purpose and Effect: To bring back to the floor for further consideration business temporarily laid aside by the motion to TABLE. When the motion to take from the table passes, the tabled motion and all secondary motions tabled with it come up again exactly as they were when tabled. There is an exception: a pending motion to postpone to a fixed time is killed by the tabling. If a question is taken from the table the same day it was tabled, members may speak for the length of time left them from earlier speeches. But if the question is not taken from the table until a later day, a member's earlier speeches are not counted; the right to speak begins all over again.

Form: "Mr. Chairman, I move that the motion to sponsor a Christmas party be taken from the table." If, when a speaker wants to make this motion, another has risen for recognition, the speaker should say at once that his purpose is to move to take from the table. The chairman should then give him precedence over the other(s) who rose.

Notes:

When Entertained	The motion to take from the table can be entertained only when there is no business pending, and only if some business has intervened since the question was tabled.
Precedence	When no business is pending, the chair should entertain a motion to take from the table in preference to any other main motion. However, if another main motion reaches the point where it is stated by the chair, the motion to take from the table cannot be entertained until the intervening main motion is disposed of. This right to precedence over main motions lasts only through the meeting at which the subject question was tabled, and through the subsequent meeting if the organization meets at least quarterly.

TIE VOTE   See: VOTING

TREASURER

Duties: The treasurer keeps the funds of the organization and all organization income should be deposited with him. From the funds deposited he draws to pay bills submitted to him over the signature of the president and the secretary. (It may be required that any disbursement be voted on by the assembly in small organizations that meet frequently. Otherwise, the executive committee or officers may be allowed to disburse funds for certain purposes and when the bill does not exceed a certain amount. In any case, the treasurer is responsible for making payments that have been duly authorized.)

Reports: The treasurer must keep an accurate record of all income and expenses. He may be required to report the organization's financial status at every regular meeting, if so desired, but he should be required to give a complete report at least annually. No action is taken on the treasurer's report; adoption would show acceptance of the figures. The treasurer's written report is given to the chairman for transmittal to an auditing committee. The treasurer should present all receipts, records, and check stubs when his report is to be audited, as it should be once a year. When the auditing committee reports, the chair calls the question on its adoption. For organizations meeting less often than quarterly, the treasurer should submit his report and data to the auditors in advance of the meeting at which the annual report is due, otherwise, the material is turned over to the chairman at the meeting previous to that at which the auditors are to report.

The report read at a meeting is purely for the information of the membership. Since the members want only a general picture of the financial status, this report should not include dates of transactions or listings of specific transactions, unless they are exceptional. The report should consist of general categories: receipts from dues, contributions, fund-raising activities, disbursements for rent, stationery, utilities, etc.; it should also indicate the balance at the beginning and end of the period reported. The report should be signed by the treasurer and, when audited, countersigned by the members of the auditing committee.

TRIAL OF MEMBERS

Every voluntary organization has the right to exercise some control over its members. A member has the choice of accepting this control or leaving the organization. Of course, if the controls are too arbitrary or too strict, the membership is likely to dwindle.

In practice, the rights of an organization are enforced first of all by threat of expulsion from membership. Lesser penalties include such controls as are allowed by law to maintain order in meetings and reasonable discipline among members. The only limitation — other than legal — on such sanctions is the patience of the member. When sanctions become too unpleasant a member refuses to put up with them. Among sanctions commonly used, short of expulsion, are refusal of the right to the floor for some period after an indecorum, a vote of censure, and fines set by the STANDING RULES for various specific violations. Such sanctions may be successfully imposed in many organizations where the satisfactions or advantages of belonging are strong enough to keep a member from resigning rather than paying a fine for being late.

Sanctions short of expulsion will normally be imposed by the chairman, with the right of appeal to the assembly (See: LEAVE TO CONTINUE SPEAKING AFTER AN INDECORUM and PRESIDING OFFICER, *Protecting the Assembly from Annoyance*).

Expulsion from Membership: This is the final sanction available to an organization and, in fairness to the member concerned, should be carried on by trial. When a charge has been brought against a member, a committee is appointed to investigate and make a recommendation. If the committee recommends expulsion (as a resolution concluding its report), it should also move to SET A TIME FOR CONTINUATION OF THE PRESENT SESSION (at which meeting the trial will take place), and to instruct the secretary to order the accused member to appear at the adjourned session. After a committee recommends prosecution, the accused is deprived of his rights as a member, to be renewed only if he is cleared. If the accused is not present when the investigating committee reports, the clerk should send him a copy of the charges.

At the trial, the accused may be represented by another member as counsel and has the right to answer the charges preferred. Witnesses may be brought by either side (members can be required to testify on pain of expulsion) and they may be cross-examined. The committee first presents its case; the accused has the opportunity to answer and to present his own witnesses; the committee is then allowed to respond to the defendant's answer. When the evidence has been taken and arguments heard, the accused leaves the room and the society debates and decides the question. A two-thirds vote is necessary for expulsion. The vote should be by ballot unless there is GENERAL CONSENT to a public vote.

Secrecy

It is highly desirable, for the legal protection of the society and out of a sense of delicacy, that the trial be held in private session, with no non-members allowed. If the trial were open to the public, the accused might have grounds for a lawsuit. For the same reason, an organization should not make public the reasons for expulsion.

Standing Committees in Professional Organizations

It is quite common among professional societies to have standing committees charged with investigating all complaints against members. Among the goals of such organizations as medical and legal associations is the promotion of good practice and the maintenance of ethical standards. In such societies, expulsion is a very serious affair, for it can radically limit a person's opportunity to earn a living in his chosen field. That being the case, trials should be handled circumspectly. However, as pernicious as defamation of character is, the tendency to ignore or soft-pedal malpractice may be worse. Professional organizations have a semipublic status and a responsibility to the community at large, as well as to their own members.

Evidence   It is not necessary that evidence for eviction from an ordinary organization be as clear cut and indisputable as in a court of law. A person commonly known as a criminal, despite the inability of the police to bring about a conviction, would be expelled by any organization reasonably jealous of its reputation. On the other hand, where expulsion is liable to seriously hurt the member, an organization should come as close to the rules of law in determining guilt as is possible (but see note above).

TWO-THIRDS VOTE   See: VOTING

UNAMENDABLE MOTIONS

The following motions cannot be amended:

Adjourn, except when qualified or when there is no provision for another meeting
Amendment to an amendment
Appeal
Consider out of proper order
Division of the assembly
Fill a blank
Leave to speak after an indecorum
Nomination
Objection to consideration of a question
Orders of the day
Point of order
Postpone indefinitely
Previous question
Reconsider
Requests (any)
Suspend the rules
Table
Take from the table

UNANIMOUS VOTE   See: VOTING

VICE-CHAIRMAN

For parliamentary purposes, the vice-chairman (vice-president) has responsibility only for assuming the duties of the PRESIDING OFFICER in his absence and of succeeding to his office in the event of his vacating it during a term of office. Additional duties may be defined in the constitution or by-laws of an organization. It is not uncommon to have more than one vice-chairman, in which case the offices are usually identified by number — first vice-chairman, second vice-chairman.

VIVA VOCE See: VOTING

VOICE VOTE See: VOTING

VOTING

Purpose: Voting is the method by which an organization expresses its desires on the disposal of a question brought to its attention. For a question to be decided in the name of an organization, it is necessary that some specific number of people vote for or against.

Types: The number of people necessary to carry an issue in behalf of an organization is always more than that needed to defeat it. However, the number required varies with the issue being voted on. Assuming that a QUORUM is present an issue may be carried by:

One more vote than half of all votes cast; this is called a *simple majority,* or just majority.

One more vote than half of all the members present at the meeting where the vote is taken; this is called a *majority of those present.*

One more vote than half of all the members of the organization; this is called a *majority of the membership.*

Two thirds of all those voting; this is called a *two-thirds vote* and is what is meant wherever that term is used without qualification.

Two thirds of all those present; this is called a *two-thirds vote of those present.*

Two thirds of all members; this is called a *two-thirds vote of the membership.*

The vote required for any specific type of question may be defined in the constitution or by-laws or may be taken from standard rules of order adopted in the constitution or by-laws. The types most commonly used are the simple majority, the two-thirds vote, and, less often, a majority of the membership. The two-thirds vote of the entire membership should be required only with considerable circumspection; it is seldom possible to get two-thirds of the membership to a meeting. The vote required for each type of motion is specified under the motion in the glossary.

Plurality: More votes than any contender. When more than two choices are available in a vote, the one receiving the most votes has a plurality. A plurality may well be less than a majority. Since the question of plurality is significant only when there are more than two choices to be voted on, the question of accepting a plurality vote normally applies only in an election where there may be more than two candidates for a given office. All other votes are taken in a "Yes" or "No" form, so that one side or the other will have necessarily a simple majority. Standard procedure does not allow an action to be carried by a simple plurality. When no one of several candidates receives a majority, the two receiving the greatest number of votes have a runoff, that is, a second election in which only two names are on the ballot, and hence, one candidate must receive a majority (unless there is a tie vote). However, a constitution may specify that a plurality vote is sufficient to elect.

Methods: There are several ways for determining how the organization votes on an issue. The vote may be taken by:

Voice
(Viva Voce)

This is the simplest method and the least accurate, but it is satisfactory when there is a clear majority, and is most commonly used because it is simplest and quickest. After stating the question to be voted on (See: CALLING THE QUESTION), the chair says, "All those in favor, say 'Aye.'" After hearing the affirmative he says, "All those opposed say 'No.'" Having heard both, the chair decides whether the required majority or two thirds supported the motion. If he finds that the motion is carried, he says, "The ayes have it. The motion is carried." If he finds the motion did not carry, he says, "The nays have it. The motion failed." The exact wording varies from organization to organizaiton, in fact, from chairman to chairman. When the chair states his decision the question is decided and not before.

Show of
Hands and
Rising Vote

The vote may be taken by requesting the members to raise their right hands or to stand. These methods allow the chair to make his estimate visually, rather than by ear. The only procedural difference between this method and the voice vote is that after the chair has requested the members to make the appropriate sign, he must also direct the members to lower their hands or be seated when he is satisfied with his estimate. Raising the right hand is used as an alternative to standing only in small meetings.

Standing Count	The vote is actually counted by the chairman or secretary while the members stand. The members in favor are asked to rise and remain standing until the vote is counted; then the chairman asks them to be seated when he has completed his count. The same procedure is followed for those against. In announcing the result, the chair states the actual count.
Roll Call (Yeas and Nays)	Each member or delegate is called by name. He answers "Yes" or "No," or, if he does not want to vote, "Present." The secretary or a clerk calls the roll, writing the vote of each member as it is given and repeating it after he has written to make sure that the vote is recorded correctly. When calling the question, the chair says, "As the names are called, those in favor will answer 'Yes,' those opposed 'No.'" When the vote is completed, the clerk or secretary reports the totals to the chairman, who announces the result.
Secret Ballot	The members indicate their vote on a slip of paper by writing "Yes" or "No," or by writing the name of the candidate favored. To insure that the election is handled fairly, it is desirable to have ballots printed and marked in such way that they cannot be duplicated, though this is not necessary. Ballots may be distributed to the members in their chairs and later collected folded; they may be distributed to members, who bring the completed ballot to a box provided for keeping the votes; or the members may obtain their ballots at a desk — where, if desired, their eligibility to vote may also be checked — to be filled out and placed in a ballot box. The counting procedure should be arranged so that at least two people may see each ballot as it is opened and read off. Ballots may be rejected if they are unclear, have too many names, or in any way give evidence of fraud in voting. The count, which should specify those for, those against, blank ballots, and discounted ballots, is turned over to the chairman who announces it to the assembly. In calling for the vote, the chairman should describe how ballots are to be obtained, what it is appropriate to write on them ("Yes," "No," how many names, etc.), and how they are to be returned.
General Consent	See: GENERAL CONSENT

342

Voting
by Mail

It is sometimes desirable, when an organization's membership is large and scattered, to vote on important issues by mail. This method may be used for amendments to the constitution, by-laws, or rules of order, on main motions involving important policy decisions, or on elections. The ballots should be printed with the motion, amendment, or candidates' names and appropriate places for marking. A mail vote cannot be secret, because, unless the ballots are signed, it is impossible to tell if they are voted by members. In returning votes, the envelopes should be marked "ballot" so they will be opened only by the election tellers.

Choosing a Method: The most common method is the voice vote. When the chair is not satisfied with his ability to interpret a voice vote, he may ask the vote be repeated by show of hands, by standing, or by a standing count. Where the vote has been by voice, a member may ask for a DIVISION OF THE ASSEMBLY, either because he doubts the chair's judgment on the voice vote, or in order to see who voted for and who against the question. A member may also move to have a standing count taken if he is not satisfied by the chair's decision. When the suggestion is made from the floor, it requires a second and a majority vote, or permission may be given by general consent.

The roll-call vote is used in delegate bodies where the delegates want their votes recorded so that their constituents may see how they voted on various issues. The secret ballot is used for secrecy rather than for accuracy. It is used where the members might be embarrassed to vote their true feelings publicly. It is common to have election and admission to membership acted upon by ballot, as well as votes of censure or expulsion. The constitution or by-laws must state in what situations this method of voting will be used. Vote by ballot, by roll call, or by mail can also be obtained by a majority vote. Either motion has the same status as DIVISION OF THE ASSEMBLY.

Announcing the Vote: No vote takes effect until it is announced. When the chair announces the vote, he should immediately state the effect of the vote and the question immediately pending after the vote.

Number of Those Voting: When voting is by ballot, the number of those voting is the number submitting valid ballots. Those that are blank and those invalidated don't count. When several issues are decided on a single ballot, it may happen that some members do not vote on all the issues. In that case, the ballot is counted as a blank on issues not voted on, and as a valid ballot on issues voted.

Tie Vote: A tie vote is interpreted as a failure to carry the motion. The chair may vote either to make or break a tie, except when the voting is by ballot. The chair cannot vote on a tie, or on a tie but one, when the vote by secret ballot has already been taken because he would be the only member whose vote was known.

The Voting Rights of Members:

Voting for Oneself

A member may vote for himself or on issues concerning himself, when the question concerns him in his capacity as a member of the organization, e.g., his election to office, his expulsion, or ratification of his actions, though it would not be appropriate to take advantage of this right when the assembly was considering bestowing an honor. However, when the question concerns the member other than in his capacity as a member, he should abstain from voting — for example, if the society is deliberating whether or not to hire him in his professional capacity.

Changing Vote

A member may change his vote — if it is not by secret ballot — at any time up to the announcement of the vote. If he should want to do so later, he must obtain the consent of the organization by general consent or on a motion with the same status as any other undebatable REQUEST.

Compulsion

No member may be compelled to vote, though a member should vote on any issue on which he has an opinion.

Proxy Vote

When a member expects to be absent, he may not give to another his vote, unless the laws of the organization specifically allow proxy voting. As a general rule, it is not desirable to allow proxy voting in a private, nonprofit organization; however, where it is allowed, it should be required that the proxy be given only to another member. Where proxy voting is allowed in corporations, it is used only in elections, not in the transaction of business, which is done by the elected officers and directors. This is good policy as, in the process of deliberation, it keeps all members on an equal footing.

Unanimous Vote

Every member has the right to vote as he pleases and it is not permissible to record a unanimous vote if there is a single vote against. To indicate unanimity of support, it is a common practice that those who voted for the losing candidate change their vote so that the election is made unanimous. This, however, is impossible with a secret ballot. If the voting is by secret ballot, it is impossible to make a decision unanimous that is not, unless by a second secret ballot there is a unanimous vote to make the earlier vote unanimous. The second vote must be secret too, for the same reason the original vote is secret.

VOTING BY YEAS AND NAYS   See: VOTING

Index